CULTURE & CASTLES
HISTOHOTELS
HISTORIC HOTELS of GERMANY

Zu Gast im SCHLOSS

Ein Reise(ver)führer zu Hotels in historischen Häusern und zu einzigartigen Kulturrouten und Naturlandschaften in Deutschland

wtv

Zu Gast im Schloss

Ein Reise(ver)führer zu Hotels in historischen Häusern und zu einzigartigen Kulturrouten und Naturlandschaften in Deutschland

ISBN: 978-3-941830-25-7

Eduard-Rosenthal-Straße 30
99423 Weimar
Tel.: +49 3643 4933910
Fax: +49 3643 4933919
info@verlag-weimar.de
www.verlag-weimar.de

Herausgeber: Culture & Castles | HISTOHOTELS
Autoren: Michael Maaß, Sandra Ignatzy, Rudolf Matthias von Frieling
Umschlag / Layout / Satz: Typelicious Ltd. & Co. KG; Mathias Karge, Berlin
Lektorat: Anne Schünemann, Heikendorf; Sandra Ignatzy, Weimar
Übersetzung: Anne Schünemann, Heikendorf; büro+sprachen SERVICE Erfurt; Juliane Brittain, Maulbronn; Sandra Ignatzy, Weimar

Printed in the EU

CULTURE & CASTLES
HISTOHOTELS
HISTORIC HOTELS of GERMANY

Zu Gast im SCHLOSS

Herausgeber: Culture & Castles | HISTOHOTELS

Ein Reise(ver)führer zu Hotels in historischen Häusern und zu einzigartigen Kulturrouten und Naturlandschaften in Deutschland

wtv

Einleitung / Introduction

CULTURE & CASTLES | HISTOHOTELS

Historische Gebäude sind steingewordene Zeugnisse vergangener Tage und unserer Herkunft. Eine Vielzahl geschichtsträchtiger Bauwerke wird heutzutage von ihren Besitzern als Hotel oder Restaurant genutzt. Dabei wird häufig der touristische Betrieb in eine harmonische Beziehung zu der historischen Hülle der Häuser und der sie umgebenden Aura gesetzt. Ruhe und Geborgenheit, Wahrhaftigkeit, Beständigkeit sowie Verlässlichkeit, verbunden mit einer herzlichen Atmosphäre, sind das, was Gäste in Zeiten der Beliebigkeit suchen und gerne in Anspruch nehmen.

Historic buildings are witnesses to our history and heritage set in stone. Today, many historic buildings are used as hotels or restaurants by their owners. Often they create a harmonic relationship between the touristic function and the buildings' historic frame and the aura that surrounds them. Peace and the feeling of security, authenticity, stability and reliability combined with a warm atmosphere, are what guests are looking for in times of arbitrariness and what they most willingly make use of.

Kulturgüter für die Zukunft bewahren

Je älter ein Mensch ist, desto mehr Geschichten kann er erzählen. Doch was sind siebzig, oder achtzig, im Vergleich zu siebenhundert oder achthundert Jahren? So alt aber sind oft Häuser, die europäische Geschichte miterlebt haben, und diese oft auch beeinflussten. Es

The older people get, the more stories they can tell. But what are a mere seventy or eighty years compared with seven or eight hundred?

Many buildings that have witnessed and shaped European history are indeed that

sind Burgen, Schlösser, Klöster und Herrenhäuser oder Wirtschaftsgebäude ehemaliger Güter, die viel erzählen können - von Kriegen, von Politik, Grausamkeit und Liebe, von Dynastien und Familien, von Menschen, ihrem Glauben und ihrem Denken, von der Arbeit, dem künstlerischen Schaffen, von Erfindungen und gesellschaftlichen Umbrüchen.

In den letzten Jahrzehnten wurden viele solcher, meist denkmalgeschützten Gebäude aufwendig saniert und als Hotel eingerichtet,

old: castles, fortresses, manor houses, monasteries and agricultural buildings of former estates can recount stories of war, politics, barbarity and love, of dynasties and families, of people, their beliefs and their convictions, of work, artistic creation, of inventions and social change.

In recent times, many such heritage-protected buildings have been painstakingly restored and converted into hotels, their doors finally flung open to the public once

Historisches Ambiente - individuelle Gastlichkeit

damit sie wieder in ihrer Ursprünglichkeit der Allgemeinheit zugänglich gemacht werden konnten. Alte Pracht und verschollene Schönheit kamen so wieder an den Tag. Kassettendecken sind vom gräulichen Schleier der Nachlässigkeit gereinigt, Stuckornamente wurden repariert, originale Lampen illuminieren die edle Ausstattung, die Wände sind von Ölsockeln befreit, keine Raufaser beleidigt den Blick, das Silber glänzt und die Kandelaber funkeln. Was wie die Requisitenanweisung für einen Film klingt, ist Wirklichkeit geworden. Viele Gebäude, zuvor Opfer der Zerstörung und des Verfalls, erstrahlen wieder in altem, neuem Glanz.

Und doch ist die Zeit nicht stehengeblieben. Keine ausschließlich museale Konservierung empfängt den Besucher, sondern eine

more, their original magnificence and grandeur restored. Through extensive efforts, their former splendour and lost elegance have been rediscovered, their panelled ceilings liberated from a greyish veil of neglect and their ornamental pieces repaired, with original lighting illuminating restored period features, walls freed of old coats of paint, rough wood grain removed, and the silver and candelabras polished back to a proper shine. What sounds like an order for props for a film has now become reality. Many buildings, former victims of dereliction and destruction, are now shining again in their old magnificence.

And yet time has not stood still. Museum preservation combined with a modern

Historic atmosphere and individual hospitality

aktuelle Interpretation von Pracht und Luxus. So wird in uralten Refektorien erlesene Spitzengastronomie verwirklicht, tiefe Holzbalken aus der Renaissancezeit zieren das klimatisierte und mit allem Komfort ausgestattete Zimmer und ehemalige Palas oder Ballsäle haben sich in moderne Tagungsräume verwandelt. Erforderliche Technik tritt als Helfer zurück. Exzellenter und individueller Service ergänzt die hochherrschaftliche Kulisse, und Komfort wird ein selbstredender Begriff.

Spitzenköche setzen kulinarische Akzente mit frischen und soweit es geht regionalen Produkten, nutzen jahreszeitlich variierende

interpretation of splendour and luxury awaits the visitor. And so, fine cuisine is prepared in age-old refectories, low timber beams of the Renaissance period adorn the air-conditioned, fully furnished luxury rooms, with former staterooms and ballrooms transformed into modern conference rooms. The necessary technology is present, but takes a back seat to the overall ambience. Outstanding personal service complements the lordly ambience, and comfort is a matter of course.

Top chefs create culinary pleasures with fresh and, as far as possible, regional

Angebote und kredenzen terroirverbundene Weine.

Culture & Castles | HISTOHOTELS sind ein Garant für erfolgreiche Tagungen, unvergessliche Hochzeiten und Familienfeien. Da alle Hotels in überaus kulturträchtigen Regionen und Orten liegen, ist auch bei längeren Aufenthalten für ausreichend Abwechslung gesorgt. Unsere Tipps und Themen-Specials verweisen auf die jeweiligen Angebote und Möglichkeiten. Umgeben von geschichtsträchtigen Mauern, geschmackvollem Interieur, historischen Parks und Schlossgärten, bieten die Hotels sehr individuelle Hochzeits- und Fest-Arrange-

products, making use of seasonal changing offers, and serve terroir connected wines.

Culture & Castles | HISTOHOTELS are a guarantee for successful conferences, unforgettable weddings and family gatherings.

Due to the fact that all hotels are situated in culturally significant regions and towns, there is a sufficient variety of activities even for long-time stays. Our recommendations and thematic specials refer to particular services and possibilities. Surrounded by historic walls and tasteful interior,

Reizvolle Natur und kreative Entspannung

ments an. Diese sind so unterschiedlich wie die Häuser selbst und immer einzigartig.
Zahlreiche Fest- und Veranstaltungsräume laden hierbei zum Feiern ein. Viele Hotels verfügen zudem über ein Standesamt, eine Kapelle oder Kirche und natürlich über romantische Hochzeitssuiten. Kutschfahrten werden ebenso angeboten wie ein krönendes Feuerwerk auf dem Höhepunkt des Festes.
Wo einst Ritter, Mönche und Edelleute an schweren Eichentischen beisammen saßen, bieten die historischen Schlösser, Burgen, Klöster und Herrenhäuser auch den idealen Rahmen für anspruchsvolle Tagungen, Seminare und Präsentationen.
Neben einem historischen Ambiente finden die Teilnehmer selbstverständlich auch eine

historic parks and castle gardens, the hotels offer individual wedding and party arrangements. They are as diverse and unique as the buildings themselves.
Numerous banquet and event rooms invite to celebrate. Many hotels have a registry office, a chapel or a church and of course romantic honey moon suites on their grounds. Coach rides and the final firework as the crowning highlight of the celebration are also among the hotels' offers.
Where once knights, monks and noblemen sat together at solid oak tables, historic castles, monasteries and manor houses present the perfect frame for conferences, seminars and presentations today.

moderne Ausstattung und zeitgemäße Technik vor. Kreativität und Produktivität lassen sich durch eine ansprechende und außergewöhnliche Umgebung, erstklassigen Service und ein besonderes Flair beleben und steigern. Nach vollbrachter Arbeit wird für die Gäste der Wohlfühlfaktor groß geschrieben: Die vielfältigen Angebote reichen von Ayurveda bis Thalasso und decken Beauty, Fitness, Massagen und Sport gleichermaßen ab.

Als Gast eines historischen Hotels kann man gelegentlich auch in jahrhundertealten Parks spazieren gehen, wertvolle Bibliotheken besuchen oder einen Streifzug durch die meist idyllisch gelegene Gegend unternehmen. So erlebt man im hohen Norden die Ostsee in ihrer rauen und unnachgiebigen Weite und Melancholie, im Süden hingegen die Gefälligkeit und den Abwechslungsreichtum der hügeligen

Among a historic atmosphere, participants will also find modern equipment and up-to-date technology. Creativity and productivity can be improved by an appealing and extraordinary environment, first-class service and a special flair. After work is done, guests can enjoy the feel-good comforts of the venue: Various offers range from Ayurveda to Thalasso and cover beauty, fitness, massage services and sports.

Guests at a historic hotel can also take a casual stroll in centuries-old parks, visit valuable libraries or explore largely idyllic surroundings. This is how best to experience the rough and obstinate ex-

Landschaft. Ob Segeltörn, Bogenschießen, Floßbauen, Kutschfahrten, zünftige Rittermahle oder Tai Chi im Klostergarten – bei einem Aufenthalt in einem historischen Hotel werden Geschichte, Kultur und Natur in ihrer intensivsten und angenehmsten Art erlebbar. Culture & Castles | HISTOHOTELS laden Sie dazu ein, einen Streifzug durch die Geschichte Deutschlands zu unternehmen und ab und zu auf der Terrasse eines der historischen Anwesen innezuhalten, das einzigartige Ambiente aufzunehmen, die jeweiligen Köstlichkeiten der regionalen Küchen zu genießen und bei einem Glas Wein die Gedanken schweifen zu lassen.

Diese Zeitreise wird Ihnen in ihrer Exklusivität und Erholsamkeit ganz bestimmt unvergessen bleiben.

panse of the Baltic Sea in the far north and the contrasting melancholy of the south, with its cosy appeal and rich diversity of hilly landscapes. Sailing trips, archery, raft building, coach rides, hearty banquets or tai chi in a monastery garden – in a historic hotel, history, culture and nature come intensely alive in the best way possible.

Culture & Castles | HISTOHOTELS invite you to embark on a journey through Germany's history, to rest awhile on the terrace of one of the historic estates presented here, soak up the unique atmosphere, enjoy the local delicacies and share your thoughts over a glass of wine. This exclusive and restorative journey through time will remain with you always.

Schloss Lütgenhof

Gastgeber/host: Katharina Stinnes

Mecklenburg-Vorpommern

Klassizistisches Schloss am Dassower See bei Lübeck, ideales Refugium für Hochzeiten, Familienfeiern, besondere Gesellschaften und Tagungen.

Neo-classical castle at Dassower Lake near Lübeck, ideal location for weddings, family celebrations, special parties and conferences.

Ulmenweg 10
23942 Dassow
Mecklenburg-Vorpommern
Tel: +49 38826 8250
Fax: +49 38826 82522
www.schloss-luetgenhof.de
reservierung@schloss-luetgenhof.de

Hotel ★★★★
Restaurant ★★★★

Am Naturschutzgebiet rund um den Dassower See liegt das klassizistische Schloss Lütgenhof. Die Gestaltung der 23 Zimmer durch die Deutschen Werkstätten Hellerau und das Interieur im modernen Design verbinden sich zu einer warmen, wohnlichen Farbgebung und stehen in angenehmem Kontrast zum klassizistischen Stil des Schlosses. Im Restaurant wird eine innovative Küche geboten, inspiriert von mediterranen und regionalen mecklenburgischen Einflüssen. Das Schloss ist nur einige Wochen im Jahr für Individualtouristen geöffnet und kann ansonsten für Veranstaltungen, Hochzeiten, Tagungen und Events gemietet werden.

The classical Luetgenhof Castle lies on the protected landscape around the Dassow Lake. The modern design and interior of the 23 rooms combined with a warm, homely colour scheme in the style of German studios stand in contrast to the classical style of the castle. The restaurant offers an innovative cuisine, inspired by Mediterranean and regional Mecklenburger influences. The castle is opened only some weeks in the year for individual tourists and can be rented otherwise for events, weddings and conferences.

Angebot/facility

99-145 €

125-195 €

A/S 180-220 €

15-40

Grevesmühlen 16 km

Lübeck 20 km
Hamburg 90 km

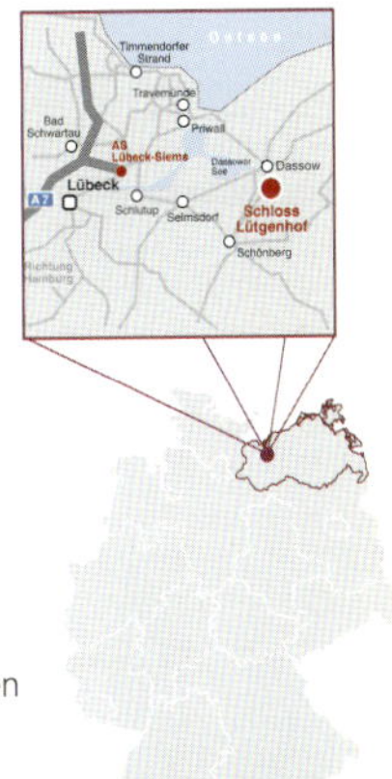

Bereits 1539 wurde Lütgenhof als Lehnsgut eingetragen, doch begannen die Herren von Paepcke erst 1839 mit der Errichtung des Herrenhauses. Im Zuge der Renovierung erfolgten 1890 der Umbau zum klassizistischen Schloss sowie der Anbau des Nordflügels und des Wintergartens. 1945 wurde Familie von Paepcke enteignet. Das Schloss erlebte in den folgenden Jahren sehr unterschiedliche Nutzungen, bis 1992 die komplette Restaurierung begann. Um die Symmetrie der Anlage zu vervollständigen, erfolgte der Anbau des Südflügels mit Schlossterrasse, die heute mediterranes Flair unter uralten Kastanien mit einer Brise Ostseewind versprüht. Als Hotel öffnete Schloss Lütgenhof im April 1999 seine Türen und bietet heute auch einen Wellness-Bereich sowie Ferienwohnungen versteckt im Garten.

Already in 1539 Luetgenhof was registered as a fiefdom, but it was not until 1839 that the Lords of Paepcke began to build the manor house. In 1890, during the course of the renovation, it was converted to a classical castle and the north wing annex and conservatory were built. In 1945 the Paepcke family were expropriated. The castle had many different uses in the following years until the complete restoration began in 1992. In order to complete the symmetry of the annex, the extension of the south wing was built with a castle terrace, which today is bursting with Mediterranean panache under ancient chestnut trees with a Baltic Sea breeze. Luetgenhof Castle opened its doors as a hotel in April 1999 and today also offers a spa as well as holiday apartments hidden in the garden.

In der näheren Umgebung:

Biosphärenreservat Schaalsee (20 km): 30.257 Hektar große, waldreiche Seenlandschaft in Mecklenburg-Vorpommern, mit dem Schaalsee als tiefstem See (72 m) der Norddeutschen Tiefebene; **Naturstrände in Rosenhagen und Barendorf (10 km); Lübeck (25 km):** Heinrich- und Thomas-Mann-Zentrum, Dom als erster monumentaler Backsteinbau an der Ostsee, Lübeck per Kanu entdecken, Hansestadt; **Wismar (47 km):** UNESCO Weltkulturerbe, Hansestadt, Wassertor, mittelalterliche Bürgerhäuser, Wasserkunst auf dem Marktplatz.

In the surrounding area:

Schaalsee Biosphere reservation (12 miles): 75,642 acres of forest-rich landscape of lakes in Mecklenburg-Western Pomerania, with the Schaalsee as the deepest lake (240 feet) of the north German lowlands; **Nature beaches in Rosenhagen und Barendorf (5-6 miles); Lübeck (16 miles):** Heinrich and Thomas Mann centre, cathedral as the first monumental brick building on the Baltic Sea, discover Lübeck by canoe, Hanseatic city; **Wismar (29 miles):** UNESCO world heritage, Hanseatic city, water gate, medieval community centres, Wasserkunst fountain on the market place.

TIPP

Die Gegend rund um Dassow und der Klützer Winkel laden zum Entdecken ein, ob zu Fuß, per Fahrrad oder Auto. Eine Schlössertour im Klützer Winkel von Dassow über Grevesmühlen, einer der ältesten Orte Mecklenburgs, bis nach Lübstorf am Schweriner See bietet sich ebenso an wie eine Radtour durch den Holmer Wald. Der Dassower See lädt als eines der größten Vogelschutzgebiete Deutschlands mit über 300 Entenarten ebenso ein wie eine Stadtführung durch Dassow.

The area around Dassow and the Angle of Kluetzer (Klützer Winkel) invite you to explore by foot, bicycle or car. A tour to the castles located in the Angle of Kluetzer (Klützer Winkel) from Dassow to Grevesmühlen, one of the oldest places in Mecklenburg, and to Lübstorf on the Schweriner Lake is a special experience, as is a bicycle tour through the Holmer Forest. The Dassow Lake, as one of the largest bird protected areas of Germany with over 300 kinds of duck, is just as inviting as a guided tour of Dassow.

Schlosshotel Wendorf

Gastgeber/host: Aikaterini Kasapidi & Johannes Butz

Exklusives Schlosshotel in bezauberndem Park, mit Gourmetrestaurant, Pferdesportarena sowie SPA und Beautycenter.

Exclusive castle hotel in a charming park, with gourmet restaurant, equestrian sports arena and SPA and Beauty Centre.

Hauptstraße 9
19412 Kuhlen-Wendorf
Mecklenburg-Vorpommern
Tel: +49 38486 33660
Fax: +49 38486 336610
www.schlosshotel-wendorf.de
info@schlosshotel-wendorf.de

Hotel ★★★★★
Restaurant ★★★★★

Elegante, ausgesuchte Möbel prägen die großzügigen Salons des Schlosses, von denen es auf eine Gartenterrasse, mit einem herrlichen Blick in den Schlosspark, hinausgeht. Bibliothek, Spielzimmer, Tagesbar und Rauchersalon sowie die wieder aufgebaute Orangerie, die als Frühstücksraum genutzt wird, laden zum Verweilen, Plaudern oder Zeitvertreib ein. Über eine große Holztreppe erreicht man die darüber liegenden Gemächer, eingerichtet mit antiken Möbeln und Bildern, ausgestattet mit exklusiven Marmor-Bädern, die viel Platz bieten und wunderbare Ausblicke in den Schlosspark ermöglichen. Zum Essen lädt das Gourmetrestaurant „Cheval Blanc" in einem Nebengebäude, in dem weitere 12 elegante Suiten eingerichtet sind.

Man spürt die Liebe zum Detail, mit der die neuen Hausherren ihren Besitz zu altem/neuem Glanz aufpoliert haben. Da die Liebe ▸

The spacious lounge rooms in the castle feature elegant, carefully selected furniture and open onto a garden terrace with a splendid view of the castle park. The library, games room, bar and smoking room, as well as the rebuilt orangery, which is now used as a breakfast room, are ideal for relaxing, chatting or just whiling away the time. A large wooden staircase leads to the upper rooms, furnished with antique furniture and paintings, and equipped with luxurious and spacious marble bathrooms offering fabulous views of the castle park. You can enjoy dinner in the gourmet restaurant, the "Cheval Blanc", in an annex to the main building that houses a further 12 elegant suites.

Guests at Wendorf Castle will notice immediately the attention to detail with which the new owners have refurbished and restored their ▸

Angebot/facility

ab 158 €

ab 188 €

A/S 250-790 €

20-40

Schwerin 28 km

Rostock-Laage 55 km

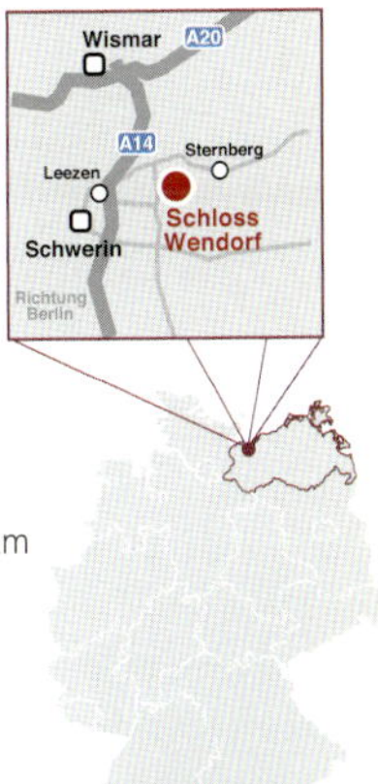

bekanntlich durch den Magen geht, haben sie Simon Schober als Chef de Cuisine und Maria Heimann als Sous Chefin verpflichtet, die auf höchstem Niveau kochen und dabei nur beste, frisch zubereitete Produkte regionaler Erzeuger verwenden. Auf Wunsch der Gäste übrigens auch in den Suiten im Schloss, in denen dazu eigens professionelle Küchen eingerichtet wurden.

Die heutige prächtige Schlossanlage geht auf Pläne des regional bedeutenden Architekten Paul Korff zurück, der Anfang des 20. Jahrhunderts zahlreiche Landgüter und Schlösser aber auch Geschäfts- und Wohnhäuser gestaltete. 1905 wurde Schloss Wendorf und seine Parkanlagen an der Stelle fertig gestellt, wo zuvor von 1220 bis 1895 die alte Ritterburg des Grafengeschlechts derer von Schack gestanden hatte.

property to its former splendour. Since, as we know, the way to someone's heart is through the stomach, they have engaged the services of Simon Schober as chef de cuisine and Maria Heimann as Sous chef, two top-class cooks who only use top-quality, organically grown and freshly prepared produce. On request, meals can also be prepared for guests in the castle suites, which are equipped with their own professional kitchens.

Today's grandiose castle and grounds date back to plans by architect Paul Korff, who designed numerous manor houses and castles of regional significance at the turn of the twentieth century, as well as some business premises and residential homes. Wendorf Castle and its park grounds were completed in 1905 on the site of the ancient fortress of the Counts von Schack, which had stood there between 1220 and 1895.

In der näheren Umgebung:

Golfanlage WINSTONgolf (6 km): wunderschöner, mehrfach prämierter Platz mit insgesamt 45 Löchern, nur 10 min. vom Schlosshotel entfernt. (Limousinen-Service inkl.); **Schwerin (28 km):** in weiten Teilen herausgeputzte ehemalige Residenz- und heutige Landeshauptstadt, Schloss, Museen, Alter Garten, Dom und Marktplatz, historische Schelfstadt, Paulskirche, Freilichtmuseum, Schleifmühle, Planetarium, Spielbank; **Schweriner Seenlandschaft (18 km):** grüne Ufer und versteckte Strände, stille Wälder, bunte Wiesen und kühle Moore, Pfaffenteich, Segeln am Ziegelsee; **Güstrow (47 km):** Gertrudenkapelle, Pfarrkirche St. Martin, Schloss, Städtische Galerie Wollhalle, historisches Wasserkraftwerk.

In the surrounding area:

Golfzentrum Winston Golf (6 miles): beautiful place with 27 holes (further 18 are in the building) and only 10 minutes from the castle hotel; **Schwerin (17 miles):** A former ducal seat and the present-day regional capital, many parts of which have been restored, with castle, museums, the Alter Garten square, cathedral and marketplace, the historic Schelfstadt district, the Paulskirche church, an open-air museum, the Schleifmühle mill, planetarium and casino; **Schwerin lakes (11 miles):** green banks and hidden beaches, colourful meadows, forests and windswept moorlands, Pfaff pond, sailing at the brick lake; **Güstrow (30 miles):** Gertrudenkapelle, St. Martins church, castle, city gallery Wollhalle, historical hydro-electric power plant.

TIPP

Für Pferdeliebhaber ist Schloss Wendorf, umgeben von gepflegten, saftig grünen Koppeln, ein Eldorado. Auf dem Reitgelände werden in regelmäßigen Abständen Trainingskurse mit international bekannten Spitzenreitern und Ausbildern für Dressur und Springen angeboten. Den eigenen Pferden der Gäste stehen großräumige Boxen und fachkundiges Personal zur Verfügung. Ausreiten im wunderschönen Gelände rund um Wendorf ist ein Genuss der Extraklasse. Jagdreiter kommen bis zu zwei mal im Jahr (Frühjahr und Herbst) auf ihre Kosten, wenn die Mecklenburger Meute auf Schloss Wendorf zu Gast ist.

For horse enthusiasts Schloss Wendorf, surrounded by manicured, sappy green paddocks, is a real eldorado. The Equestrian Sports Arena has a modern indoor riding hall (90 x to 180 ft.), in which in a regular base training courses are given by internationally well known top riders and trainers for dressage as well as jumping. For own horses there are roomy boxes available and trained personal will take care. To ride out in the beautiful area around Schloss Wendorf is a pleasure of the extra class. Hunting riders take much pleasure three times in the year, when the Luebeck- or Hamburg-Pack of hounds are guests.

Usedom Palace

Gastgeber/host: Ulrike Erler

Mecklenburg-Vorpommern

Exklusives Strandhotel im traditionellen Seebad Zinnowitz auf der Insel Usedom.

Exclusive beach hotel in the traditional seaside resort Zinnowitz on the island Usedom.

Dünenstraße 8
17454 Ostseebad Zinnowitz
Mecklenburg-Vorpommern
Tel: +49 38377 3960
Fax: +49 38377 39699
www.usedom-palace.de
direktion@usedom-palace.de

Hotel ★★★★★
Restaurant ★★★★★

Nach Restaurierung und Erweiterung um einen großzügigen Wellnessbereich wurde der imposante Usedom Palace im Jahre 2000 an der Strandpromenade des Seebades Zinnowitz wiedereröffnet, ganz in der Tradition von „Schwabes Hotel", welches bereits hundert Jahre zuvor als „erstes Haus am Platze" namhafte Persönlichkeiten aus Politik, Wissenschaft und Kultur als Gäste anzog. Unter ihnen Hans Fallada, Walther Rathenau, Wernher von Braun und die Schriftstellerin Hedwig Courths-Mahler, deren Bücher sich in den Bibliotheksschränken des charmanten Kaminzimmers versammeln und von den Hausgästen bei einem stilechten „Afternoon Tea" gelesen werden können. Gleich nebenan befinden sich die gemütliche Hausbar und das erstklassige Restaurant, in dem es angenehme Pianomusik live zu erleben gibt. Die meisten der 40 geräumigen Zimmer und Suiten gewähren einen direkten Blick aufs Wasser und die weit ins Meer hinausragende Seebrücke.

Das Hotel gehört heute der Germania Fluggesellschaft, deren Eigner das Haus 2000 vor ▸

After restoration and extension of a generous wellness area, the imposing Usedom Palace was reopened in 2.000 right on the beach promenade of the seaside of Zinnowitz. Carrying on the tradition of "Schwabe's Hotel" one hundred years ago as "the first house at the place" which again and again attracted numerous well-known personalities from politics, science and culture as guests. Under those Hans Fallada, Walter Rathenau, Wernher von Braun and the authoress Hedwig Courths-Mahler, whose books can be read in the charming fireplace room, while a authentic „afternoon tea" is served. Directly next door are the cosy house bar and the first-class ▸

Angebot/facility

80-150 €

100-250 €

A/S 200-320 €

20-150

Zinnowitz 1 km

Heringsdorf 30 km

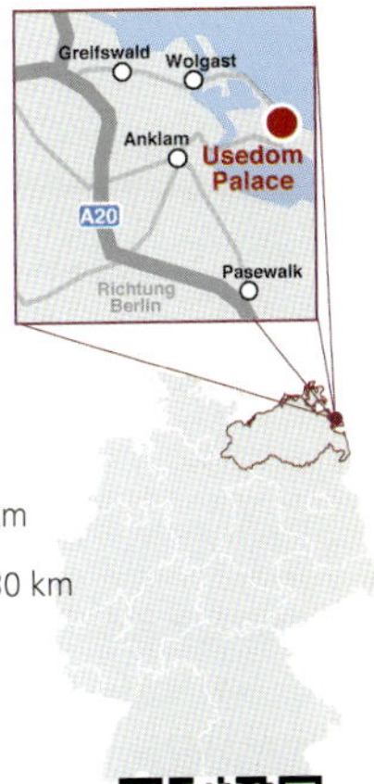

dem vollständigen Verfall bewahrten und mit hohem Aufwand sanierten. Man spürt den Enthusiasmus, mit dem die neuen Hausherren ihren Besitz zu neuem Glanz aufpoliert haben. So kann „Das Palace", wie es von den Einheimischem liebevoll genannt wird, auch wieder mit großen Namen unter seinen Gästen aufwarten. 2009 residierten während der Dreharbeiten zum Film „The Ghostwriter" Roman Polanski, Pierce Brosnan, Kim Cattrall und Ewan McGregor im Usedom-Palace und haben sich dabei sehr wohl gefühlt, wie ihrem Gästebucheintrag zu entnehmen ist.

Im Sommer ist die Insel und das Palace auch leicht mit Air Berlin, OLT und Helvetic zu erreichen, die dann jeden Samstag auf zahlreichen Linien von westdeutschen Großstädten und Wien, Basel, Zürich, Bern aus Heringsdorf auf Usedom anfliegen.

restaurant, in which one can listen to live piano music. Most of the 40 spacious rooms and suits have grant a direct sea view overlooking the seabridge extending into the water.

Today the hotel belongs to the Germania airline. Their owners retained the house in 2000 before they completely declined and reorganized it at high expenditure. One feels the enthusiasm, with which the new heads of the household up-polished their possession to new gloss. So the Palace can offer also again large names among its guests. 2009 during the shootings to the film „The Gost"Roman Polanski, Pierce Brosnan, Kim Catrall and Ewan McGregor resided in the Usedom Palace and thereby felt very well how is to be inferred from their guest book entry. During summertime the island and the Palace can be attained also easily with Air Berlin, OLT and Helvetic.

In der näheren Umgebung:

Lüttenort (5 km): Atelier (Wohn- und Arbeitsstätte mit Skulpturengarten) von Otto Niemeyer-Holstein, das zu den besonderen Anziehungspunkten der Insel zählt; **Benz (17 km):** Holländer Windmühle und Kunst-Kabinett Usedom neben der „Feininger Kirche"; **Wolgast (9 km):** Museum Kaffeemühle, Dampffährschiff „Stralsund", Kapelle St. Gertrud, Philipp Otto Runge Haus; **Bansin (21 km):** Hans-Werner-Richter-Haus: Gedenkstätte für den hier geborenen Schriftsteller; **Golfparadies Balmer See (25 km):** zwei wunderschöne 18-Loch-Golfplätze und ein anspruchsvoller 9-Loch-Übungsplatz.

In the surrounding area:

Lüttenort (3 miles): Studio (apartment and working place with sculpture garden) of Otto Niemeyer-Holstein, which ranks among the special points of attraction of the island; **Benz (11 miles):** Dutchmen windmill and Usedom-Art-Cabinet beside „the Feininger church"; **Wolgast (6 miles):** Museum Kaffeemühle, steam ferry boat „Stralsund", chapel St. Gertrud, Philipp Otto Runge house; **Bansin (13 miles):** Memorial place for the writer Hans Werner Richter, who was born here; **Golfparadies Balmer lake (16 miles):** two beautiful 18-hole-golfcourse and a fastidiously 9-hole exercise area.

TIPP

Usedom ist ideal für Ausflüge mit dem Fahrrad, auch in Kombination mit einer Hin- oder Rückfahrt mit dem Fährschiff. Ein besonderer Ausflug ist eine Tour nach Peenemünde mit anschließender Seefahrt mit dem Versorgungsschiff „Seeadler" zur Ostseeinsel Oie. Dort erwartet die Besucher nach zwei Stunden Seefahrt ein aufregender Nachmittag zwischen Natur pur und den Hinterlassenschaften deutscher Geschichte: Ab 1937 nutzen die Nazis die Insel als Raketenstartplatz für die V2-Raketen. In der DDR-Zeit diente die Insel als NVA-Stützpunkt. Die Überreste der militärischen Anlagen prägen noch immer das Bild der Insel. Nach der Wende wurde der NVA-Stützpunkt aufgegeben, woraufhin die Gebäude der Insel dem Vandalismus ausgeliefert waren.

Usedom is ideal for bicycle trips, also in combination with the ferry boat. A special trip is the route to Peenemuende with a following trip with the supply ship „sea-eagle" to the Baltic island Oie. There the visitors expect after two hours navigation an exciting afternoon between nature purely and the inheritances of German history: Starting from 1937 the Nazis use the island as rocket launching site for the V2 missiles. During the GDR time the island served as NVA base. The remnants of the military plants shape still the picture of the island. After the NVA base was given up, the buildings of the island were delivered to vandalism.

Romantik Hotel Rittergut Bömitz

Gastgeber/host: Nicola und Lorenz Flierl

Mecklenburg-Vorpommern

Vorpommersches Rittergut, umgeben von einer romantischen Landschaft, die schon Caspar David Friedrich zu seinen berühmten Bildern inspirierte.

Manor house surrounded by a romantic landscape which had already inspired Caspar David Friedrich to his famous paintings.

Dorfstraße 14
17390 Bömitz (Rubkow)
Mecklenburg-Vorpommern
Tel: +49 39724 22540
Fax: +49 39724 22541
www.rittergut-boemitz.de
info@rittergut-boemitz.de

Hotel ★★★★
Restaurant ★★★★

Schlichte Eleganz prägt die individuell eingerichteten Zimmer des Gutshauses, von denen man auf die idyllische Gartenterrasse und den sich dahinter anschließenden Park blickt. In ihm befindet sich ein verwunschener Pavillon, der schon vielen Neuvermählten ein intimer Rahmen für das Ja-Wort war. Die Diele empfängt in privater Gutshofatmosphäre. Knarrende Dielen, das Klirren der Gläser an der Bar und das Knistern der Holzscheite im Kamin vermitteln eine heimelige Gemütlichkeit. Zum Essen lädt das Feinschmeckerrestaurant „Jägerstube", welches vor allem saisonale und lokale Produkte aus erstklassigem Anbau verarbeitet.

Das Rittergut Bömitz hat eine wechselvolle Geschichte, die bis ins Jahr 1340 zurückreicht. ▸

Pleasant elegance characterizes the individually decorated rooms of the manor house, out of which one looks of the idyllic garden terrace and the magic park behind.

In it there is an enchanted pavilion, which was already an intimate setting for many newlyweds. The hall is set in private estate atmosphere. Creaking floorboards, the clink of glasses at the bar and the crackle of logs in the fireplace provide a cozy comfort. The Gourmet Restaurant "Hunt Room" invites to dinner and offers mainly fresh, seasonal and local products from first-class production.

The manor house Bömitz has a checkered ▸

Angebot/facility

55-69 €

70-98 €

A/S 95-120 €

70

Anklam 11 km

Flughafen Rostock-Laage 135 km
Heringsdorf auf Usedom 40 km

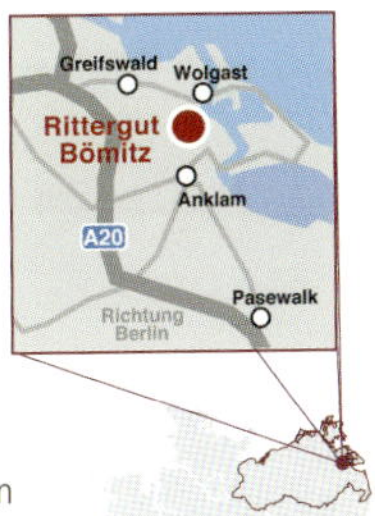

Ende der 1980er Jahre war das Haus in einem solch ruinösen Zustand, dass das Heim geschlossen werden musste. Plünderungen und Verwüstungen richteten danach das Anwesen vollständig zu Grunde. Erst der Erwerb des Anwesens durch die heutigen Besitzer führte zur Sanierung und Neunutzung als Hotel. Mit deren ungeheuerem Engagement erwacht seither in dem alten Gutshof nun Stück für Stück wieder das Flair früherer Tage.

history, dating back to 1340. Since that time it was run in rapid succession of different owners. In the late 1980s the house was in such a ruinous state that the home had to be closed. Looting and devastation then destroyed the property completely. Only the acquisition by the current owners led to the restoration and new use as a hotel. With their immense commitment the charm of earlier days comes alive now piece by piece in the old manor.

In der näheren Umgebung:

Wanderungen und Radtouren direkt ab dem Gutshof; von Kranichen bevölkerte Boddenlandschaft; wildreiche Jagdreviere; **Hansestadt Anklam (11 km):** mittelalterliche Stadt mit Gebäuden der Backsteingotik; Otto-Lilienthal-Museum; **Wolgast (19 km):** ehemalige Herzogstadt als Tor nach Usedom, Stadt von Philipp Otto Runge (1777-1810), Freund und Kollege von Caspar David Friedrich und Ludwig Gotthard Kosegarten (1758-1818); **Hansestadt Greifswald (32 km):** Universitäts- und Hansestadt mit gut erhaltenem historischen Stadtkern.

In the surrounding area:

Walking and cycling directly from the farm; Bodden-landscape, populated by cranes; wildly rich hunting grounds; **Hanseatic City of Anklam (7 miles):** medieval city with buildings of Brick, Otto-Lilienthal-Museum; **Wolgast (12 miles):** Former Duke City as a gateway to Usedom, town of Philipp Otto Runge (1777-1810), Caspar David Friedrich's friend and colleague and Ludwig Gotthard Kosegarten (1758-1818); **Hanseatic City of Greifswald (20 miles):** University and Hanseatic city with well-preserved historic center; Brick Gothic landmarks; port museum; city of Caspar David Friedrich (1774-1840).

TIPP

Einen besonderen Ausflug bietet Karnin am Peenestrom (20 km). Ein kleines vorpommersches Nest wurde in den 30er Jahren des 20. Jahrhunderts weltberühmt, als 1933 die modernste Eisenbahn-Stahlhubbrücke Europas über dem Peenestrom errichtet wurde und so die Fahrzeit von Berlin nach Swinemünde auf wenige Stunden verkürzt wurde. Die Brücke, bis heute als sehenswertes Denkmal deutscher Ingenieurskunst erhalten, löste drehbare Vorgängermodelle ab und ermöglichte Überfahrgeschwindigkeiten von über 100 Stundenkilometern.

A special trip offers Karnin on Peenestrom (13 miles). This small Vorpommern nest was in the 30s of the 20th Century world famous, when in 1933 the most modern rail lifting bridge of Europe was built on the Peene river, and so the travelling time from Berlin to Swinoujscie was reduced to a few hours. The bridge, still preserved as a monument of German engineering, triggered from rotating predecessors and allowed overtravel of over 62 miles per hour.

Die Georgenkirche in Wismar wird heute mit ihren imposanten gotischen Säulenhallen zu Ausstellungszwecken genutzt.
Georgen church in Wismar with its impressive portico in style of Gothic brick architecture is used as venue for exhibitions today.

Kaufmannssinn und hanseatische Baukunst

Merchant trade and Hanseatic architecture

Entlang der Ostseeküste scheint die Zeit still zu stehen. Mittelalterliche Backsteinbauten zeugen von einer Epoche, in der die Hanse das Leben entlang der Ostseeküsten prägte. Bis heute zeichnen Kirchen, Klöster, Stadttore, Rathäuser, Handelskontore und Bürgerhäuser im Stil der Backsteingotik ein harmonisches Bild.

Im 12. und 13. Jahrhundert besiedelten Kaufleute und Kolonisten aus dem Nordwesten Deutschlands slawische Gebiete östlich der Elbe. Die neu gegründeten Städte verbündeten sich bald darauf zur Hanse. Gemeinsam

Along the Baltic coast, time seems to stand still. Medieval brick buildings bear witness to an era in which the Hanseatic League influenced life on the Baltic coast. Up until today churches, cloisters, town gates, guildhalls, trade offices and community centres built in the style of Gothic brick architecture create harmonic cityscapes.

In the 12th and 13th century merchants and colonists from the Northwest of Germany settled Slavic territories in the east of the river Elbe. Soon after, the new-founded cities for-

Idyllischer Hafen vor der Insel Poel.
Idyllic harbour in front of Poel island.

konnten die Hanse-Kaufleute ihre Ziele besser verfolgen. Von Lübeck aus breitete sich nach 1143 der Handel mit den rohstoffreichen Gegenden Nordrusslands rasch aus. Getreide, Felle, Pelze, Holz oder Wachs wurden von dort nach Westeuropa verbracht, mit hochwertigen Weinen und Tuchen kehrten die Kaufleute zurück und trieben damit weiteren Handel bis in den Orient hinein.

Städtebaulich entstand dabei aus Mangel Individualität. Die damals weit verbreiteten Holz- und Fachwerkkonstruktionen waren für Monumentalbauten wie Klöster und Kirchen nicht geeignet. Naturstein war in den norddeutschen Tiefebenen nicht zu finden. Obwohl die Hanse und ihre Städte auf Handel und Transport spezialisiert waren, gestalteten sich die Transporte von Baugestein als schwierig und

med the Hanseatic League, a union which enabled merchants to pursue their economical aims more successfully. Starting in Lübeck, trade with the Northern Russian areas that were rich in raw material soon spread after 1143. Corn, pelts, furs, wood or wax were transported from Northern Russia to Western Europe and the merchants returned with quality wines and cloth which they traded further even as far as the Orient.

In the urban development individuality increased due to the shortage of building materials. At that time wood and truss constructions were commonly used but these architectural designs were unsuitable for monumental buildings such as cloisters and churches. Furthermore natural stone could not be found in the lowlands of Northern Germany. Even though

Die regionale Spezialität Räucherfisch wird vielerorts an urigen Fischerbuden angeboten.
Many rustic fisher huts sell the local speciality smoked fish.

vor allem teuer. Man war also gezwungen, auf das zurückzugreifen, was in Hülle und Fülle vorhanden war und bediente sich dabei eines Verfahrens, welches schon früher angewandt wurde: Das Brennen von festen Formsteinen aus Lehm. Denn im Gegensatz zu Naturstein war tonhaltiger Lehm, der bei Temperaturen von 900° Celsius zu den charakteristisch roten Backsteinziegeln gebrannt wird, im Überschuss vorhanden. Das Ergebnis konnte sich sehen lassen: Die Backsteine zeichneten sich durch ihre außerordentliche Stabilität und eine immer gleiche Form aus, wodurch sie vielseitig einsetzbar waren. Für diese Steine dominierte das sogenannte Klosterformat: 28x15x9 cm bis 30x14x10 cm. Damit wurde eine enorme Optimierung der Bautechniken erreicht. Formsteine und Abschlusssteine konnten in baustellenunabhängigen Ziegeleien, die damals wie Pilze aus dem Boden schossen, vorproduziert und auf verschiedene Weise eingesetzt werden. Im Gegensatz zur Werksteingotik konnte die gesamte Ziegelproduktion in von Baustellen separaten Ziegeleien hergestellt werden. Es entwickelte sich ein gemeinsamer architektonischer Stil der Backsteingotik, der sich besonders in urbanen Gegenden, aber auch in ländlichen Gebieten durchsetzte. Nach einem verheerenden Stadtbrand im Jahre 1276 in Lübeck, war man in der Stadt sogar dazu verpflichtet, Stein als unbrennbares Baumaterial zu verwenden. In kürzester Zeit entstand nicht nur eine Vielzahl imposanter Kirchen und Klöstern sondern auch

the Hanseatic League and its cities were specialised in trade and transport the transport of building stone proved to be expensive and difficult to arrange. Forced to resort to what was easily available, people took on a formerly used method: The burning of solid shaped bricks out of loam. In contrast to natural stone clayey loam, which is burned to the characteristic red bricks at 900°Celsius, was available in excess. The result was worth looking at: The bricks were characterised by their extraordinary stability and since their form never varied, they proved to be extremely useful. These bricks were shaped after the dominating cloister formats: 11x5.9x3.5 inches up to 11.8x5.5x3.9 inches. This was an enormous improvement in optimising architectural tech-

Die Traditionsgaststätte "Alter Schwede" lädt zum stilvollen Speisen in maritimem Ambiente ein.
The traditional restaurant "Alter Schwede" ("The old Swede") invites you to enjoy a classy meal in maritime ambience.

beeindruckende Profanbauten, wie Bürgerhäuser, Lagerhäuser, Werkstätten und Repräsentationsbauten.

Eindrucksvolle Hansestädte wie Stralsund, Lübeck und Wismar mit ihren historischen Stadtkernen und charakteristischen Backsteingiebeln haben mittlerweile UNESCO-Weltkulturerbe-Status.

Lübeck – „Königin der Hanse und Mutter der Backsteingotik" - hat mit seinen sieben, das Stadtbild prägenden Türmen und einer Vielzahl imposanter Backsteinbauten besonders viel zu bieten. Rathaus, Burgkloster, Koberg, ein Viertel aus dem 13. Jahrhundert mit der Jakobskirche, dem Heiligen-Geist-Hospital und die Patrizierhäuser zwischen Petrikirche und Dom, Salzspeicher und natürlich das weltberühmte Holstentor sind alles Zeugen einer damals blühenden Backsteingotik.

Von Lübeck aus kann man auf der Route der europäischen Bachsteingotik in Richtung Osten reisen und unterwegs neben den landschaftlichen Reizen Mecklenburg-Vorpommerns weitere Hanseatische Kleinode der Backstein-Baukunst erleben.

Die alte Hansestadt Wismar ist dabei unbedingt eine Reise wert. Als Schulungsbeispiel für Hansestadtbau nach lübischem Recht, zeigen sich die Grundrisse der Straßen und Bebauungen nahezu unverändert. Die einstige Bedeutsamkeit dieser Stadt lässt sich beim Anblick des St. Georgen-Kirchhofs, der St. Marienkirche und der St. Nikolaikirche rasch erahnen. Der große Hafen ist ein im Mittelalter angelegter historischer und künstlicher Wasserlauf und somit

nology. In contrast to "ordinary" Gothic architecture that required the stones to be cut on the individual construction site, shaped bricks and completion bricks could now be produced in advance in brickworks that were independent of the construction site and that were sprouting up everywhere at that point of time. A joint architectural style of the Gothic brick architecture developed and became especially common in urban areas but also in rural landscapes. After a tremendous fire in Lübeck in the year 1276, people in the city were even obliged to use bricks as this was a fire-proof building material. Within a short time, not only many impressive churches and abbeys were completed but also profane buildings, such as community centres, ware houses, workshops and representative buildings emerged.

Today spectacular Hanseatic cities such as Stralsund, Lübeck and Wismar impress with their historic city centres and characteristic brick gables. By now, they have been declared to World Heritage Sites by UNESCO.

Lübeck –"Queen of the Hanseatic league and mother of Gothic brick architecture" – has especially much to offer. Its cityscape is characterised by seven towers and many impressive brick buildings. The guildhall, castle monastery, Koberg (a city quarter originating from the 13th century housing the Jakobi church), the Heiligen-Geist-Hospital and Partrician houses situated between Petri church and cathedral, the salt store houses and the world-famous Holsten Gate all bear

Zeugnis des damaligen Machtanspruchs der Seestädte. Auf verschiedenen Touren erfährt man von der wechselhaften Geschichte der Stadt.

Die nächste Station ist Neukloster. Im 2. Weltkrieg weitgehend von Zerstörung verschont, verzaubert die idyllisch am Neuklostersee gelegene Kleinstadt ihre Besucher. Besondere Beachtung verdient der Klosterkomplex. Das Propsteigebäude, der Klosterpark und natürlich St. Maria am Sonnenkamp sind wertvolle Zeugnisse einer nordisch-klerikalen Kultur.

Residiert man im nahen Schloss Wendorf, so ist ein Besuch der Städte Schwerin und Güstrow auf jeden Fall Pflicht. Schwerin zeichnet sich durch sein bekanntes Schloss mitten auf einer Insel im Schweriner See und durch

witness to the once flourishing Gothic brick architecture.

Starting from Lübeck you can travel eastwards on the route of the European Gothic brick architecture. On the journey, not only the beautiful landscape of Mecklenburg-Vorpommern will guarantee beautiful views but also the many Hanseatic gems built in Gothic brick architecture are likely to impress.

The old Hanseatic city Wismar is also well worth a visit. The UNESCO world heritage city is a picture book example of Hanseatic urban development according to Luebean law. The ground plans of streets and buildings present themselves almost unaltered. You can gain a notion of the former importance of this city by looking at St. George cemetery, St. Nicolai

Wasserkunst auf dem Marktplatz in Wismar.
Water-Art on the market square in Wismar.

seinen Dom und weitere Kirchen aus. Der Turm des im neugotischen Stil erbauten Domes aus dem 15. Jahrhundert ist mit seinen 117,5 Metern der höchste Mecklenburgs. Im neogotischen Stil erbaut, ist er Beispiel für die Neuinterpretation der Backsteingotik. Eine zweite berühmte Kirche dieser Bauart ist die Schweriner Paulskirche, die 1869 geweiht wurde. Die Hauptstadt Mecklenburg-Vorpommerns hat außerdem auch interessante Museen, ein Staatstheater, den Markt mit dem Rathaus und viele Restaurants und Kneipen zu bieten.

Auch das als Barlachstadt bekannte Güstrow zählt zu den Repräsentanten der Backsteingotik. Zu sehen bekommt man zunächst die Pfarrkirche St. Marien, deren Turm den Weg

church and St. Mary church. The spacious harbour is a historic, artificially created channel dating back to the Middle Ages and thus reveals the former claim to power of the seaside towns. Many tours explain Wismar's colourful and eventful history.

Our next stop is Neukloster. Located in an idyllic setting at the shores of Lake Neukloster and almost untouched by the destruction of World War II, this small town exudes the atmosphere of long gone days and centuries. The cloister compound deserves particular attention. The provost building, the park of the cloister and St. Maria am Sonnenkamp are precious testimonials of a Nordic-clerical culture.

If you happen to reside at Wendorf castle, a visit to Schwerin and Guestrow comes most

Malerisch umschlossen von hohen Bäumen liegt die alte Klosterkirche in Neukloster.
In a picturesque setting enclosed by high trees lies the old monastery church Neukloster.

Ländliche Idylle: das ehemalige Pfarrhaus Neukloster.
Rural idyll: the former vicarage Neukloster.

Die Innenansicht der Klosterkirche Neukloster bietet faszinierende Backsteinarchitektur.
The interiour view of the monastery church Neukloster offers scenery of spectacular Gothic brick architecture.

naturally. Schwerin is mostly renowned for its castle which is situated on an island in the Lake of Schwerin but also for its cathedral and churches. The tower of the cathedral built in the style of Neogothic brick architecture is a picture book example for the new interpretation of Gothic brick architecture. It dates back to the 15th century and with its 128.5 yards height the tower is the highest in Mecklenburg. Another well-known church built in the same style is St. Pauls church. It was consecrated in 1869. Being the capital of Mecklenburg-Vorpommern, Schwerin has a lot to offer including interesting museums, the state museum, the market square with the town hall and a variety of restaurants and bars.

Guestrow, too, renowned as Barlachtown, is representative of Gothic brick architecture. First to look at is St. Mary's church, whose tower guides towards the city itself. In the middle of an ensemble of town buildings, the oldest school of Mecklenburg and the former

Links: Blick auf den Schweriner Dom St. Maria und St. Johannes vom Pfaffenteich aus.
Left: View of the St. Maria and St. Johannes cathedral from Lake Pfaffenteich in Schwerin.
Der Dom in Güstrow mit seinem imposanten Portal stellt ein beeindruckendes Beispiel der Backsteingotik dar.
The cathedral in Güstrow with its impressive main gate is a fascinating example of Gothic brick architecture.

Der Schwebende Engel von Ernst Barlach im Dom von Güstrow.
"The hovering angel" by Ernst Barlach in Güstrow cathedral.

in die Stadt weist. Inmitten eines Ensembles aus Bürgerbauten, der ältesten Schule Mecklenburgs und dem ehemaligen Hofgericht von Wallenstein erhebt sich ein stattlicher Dom, der noch romanische Züge trägt.

In der alten Handels- und Universitätsstadt Rostock bildet die Nachbarschaft jahrhundertealter und jüngerer Gebäude ein harmonisches Bild. Drei gewaltige Backsteinkirchen prägen auch hier die historische Kulisse der Stadt: die 117 Meter hohe Petrikirche, die im 13. Jahrhundert errichtete Nikolaikirche und die monumentale Backsteinbasilika St. Marien. Nahezu unverändert zeigt sich das um 1270 gestiftete Kloster zum Heiligen Kreuz zwischen dem Hauptgebäude der Hochschule und der Stadtmauer, an der noch historische Stadttore

law court of Wallenstein stands the cathedral – an impressive building that still shows Romanesque traces.

In the old trading and university city Rostock you will find century-old buildings next to those of more recent eras forming a picture of perfect harmony. The city`s historic setting is defined by three huge brick churches: The Petri church, which is 128yards high, St. Nikolai church, which was constructed in the 13th century and St. Marien, the monumental brick basilica. Nearly unchanged, the monastery "Kloster zum Heiligen Kreuz", which was donated in 1270, can be found between the main building of the university and the city wall. The pink painted guildhall, the Katharinen monastery and St. Michaelis church with

Das Rathaus in Stralsund gehört zu einer der schönsten Backsteinbauten in Mecklenburg-Vorpommern.
The town hall in Stralsund is one of the most beautiful brick buildings in Mecklenburg- Western Pomerania.

zu bewundern sind. Auch das rosafarbene Rathaus, das Katharinenkloster, die Michaeliskirche mit Wollmagazin und die umliegenden Giebelhäuser sollte man sich nicht entgehen lassen.
Trotz der baukünstlerischen Vielfalt verschiedenster Epochen zeigen sich im nicht weit entfernten Stralsund die mächtigen Kirchen St. Marien, St. Nikolai, St. Jakobi alle im charakteristischen Backsteinrot. Spektakuläre Zeitzeugen des Mittelalters sind hier das Johanniskloster, das Katharinenkloster, der Alte Markt, das erstmals 1271 urkundlich erwähnte Rathaus sowie zahlreiche Bürgerhäuser, von denen das Wulfamhaus das wohl bekannteste Giebelhaus dieser UNESCO-Weltkulturerbe-Stadt ist.

"Wollmagazin" and the surrounding gabled houses are worth a visit.
Despite the architectural variety of many different eras, the impressive churches St. Marien, St. Nikolai and St. Jakobi, which can be found in the nearby city Stralsund, present themselves in a characteristic brick-red. Spectacular witnesses to the Middle Ages are the Johannis monastery, the Katherinen monastery, the Old Marquet Square, the guildhall, which was first mentioned in records in 1271, as well as many community centres, of which the Wulfam House probably is the most popular gabled house of this UNESCO-Word-Heritage city.
Afterwards, a trip to the cities Wolgast, Anklam and Greifswald is very recommendable.

Im Hafen von Wismar bieten Fischerboote ihre fangfrische Ware und Räucherfisch an.
At the harbour in Wismar fisher boats offer their freshly caught goods.

Die Städte Wolgast, Anklam und Greifswald zu besuchen ist anschließend sehr empfehlenswert.

Fährt man auf der B96 Richtung Südwesten erreicht man Greifswald, ein wahres Kleinod der Hanse und eine der schönsten Städte Vorpommerns. Am Greifswalder Bodden gelegen, wurde die alte Universitätsstadt durch die Klosterruine Eldena, die von Caspar David Friedrich in vielen Bildern gemalt wurde, berühmt. Die drei Kirchen St. Nikolai, St. Marien und St. Jakobi prägen hier das Stadtbild. Vom fast 100 Meter hohen Turm des Domes St. Nikolai hat man einen wunderbaren Ausblick über weite Teile des Inlandes und den Bodden bis Rügen. Auch hier sind märchenhafte Zeugnisse der Backsteingotik zu bewundern, die

Driving further down the B96 into South western direction you will come across another true Hanseatic gem: Greifswald, possibly one of the most beautiful cities in Mecklenburg-Vorpommern. The old university town is situated next to the Greifswald Bodden and gained popularity by the ruins of the Cisterciana Eldena monastery, painted by Caspar David Friedrich on several occasions. The three churches St. Nicolai, St. Marien and St. Jakobi dominate its silhouette. From the top of the cathedral tower of St. Nicolai you can enjoy an amazing view inland and over the Bodden as far as the island of Ruegen. Here you will also be able to spot the beautiful monuments of Gothic brick architecture built by wealthy Partricians. Decidedly special is the museum

Die St. Marienkirche in Greifswald, die "Dicke Marie" genannt, wurde im späten 14. Jahrhundert erbaut.
St. Marien church in Greifswald, nicknamed "Big Marie", was built in the late 14th century.

reiche Patrizier einst errichten ließen. Besonders sehenswert ist der Museumshafen, auf dem historische Schiffe ankern.

Am Peenestrom liegt die alte Hansestadt Anklam, in der trotz starker Zerstörungen im 2. Weltkrieg bedeutende Zeugnisse der Backsteingotik zu bestaunen sind: Die Nikolaikirche, das vom Wohlstand der Bürger und von außerordentlicher Wehrhaftigkeit zeugende Steintor aus dem 13. Jahrhundert und die prächtige Marienkirche, die einen großartigen Blick auf Anklam und die Umgebung bietet.

Die Kleinstadt Wolgast liegt nördlich von Anklam ebenfalls direkt am Peenestrom. Sie bezaubert mit ihren engen Gässchen und kleinen Innenhöfen sowie einer Vielzahl von Sehenswürdigkeiten, wie der weithin sichtbaren

harbour, where only historical ships are allowed to dock.

Next to the Peenestrom, you will find the old Hanseatic city Anklam. Even though it was badly destroyed during World War II, the city offers important witnesses to Gothic brick architecture: Nikolai church, the stone gate, erected in the middle of the 13th century presenting a well-fortified and unusually wealthy city and St. Marien church, which offers a splendid view across Anklam and the surrounding area.

North of Anklam and also situated next to the Peenestrom lies Wolgast. The town's small alleyways and courtyards invite to a leisurely stroll revealing many other sights such as St. Petri, a basilica with three naves built in the

Die Marienkirche in Anklam, eine dreischiffige Hallenkirche, stammt aus dem 13. Jahrhundert.
St. Marien church in Anklam is a gothic hall church, dating from the 13th century.

dreischiffigen Basilika St. Petri aus dem 14. Jahrhundert, prachtvollen Grabstätten der in Wolgast residierenden Herzöge der Linie Pommern-Wolgast und der um 1400 entstandene Kapelle St. Gertrud, die in ihrer zwölfeckigen Konzeption dem Heiligen Grabe in Jerusalem ähnelt. Der in der Abendsonne leuchtende rötlich-warme Ton der Backsteine verabschiedet uns von einer Reise entlang der Zeugnisse einer großen norddeutschen Vergangenheit.

14th century containing the graves of the locally residing dukes of Pommern-Wolgast, and St. Gertrud chapel which was built around 1400 and resembles with its 12-corner construction the Holy Grave in Jerusalem. The warm reddish glow of the Gothic brick architecture in the evening sun lingers in the atmosphere as a final goodbye of a journey along the testimonials of a great North German past.

Das Meeresmuseum in Stralsund verbindet historische Backsteinarchitektur mit modernem Design.
The sea museum in Stralsund combines historic brick architecture and modern design.

Landhaus Bärenmühle

Gastgeber/host: Bettina und Christiane Kohl

Hessen

Stilvolles Refugium in der zauberhaften Landschaft des Naturparks Kellerwald.

A stylish retreat nestled in the enchanting landscape of the Kellerwald Nature Park.

Bärenmühle
35110 Frankenau
Hessen
Tel: +49 6455 759040
Fax: +49 6455 7590422
www.baerenmuehle.de
info@baerenmuehle.de

Hotel ★★★★
Restaurant ★★★★

Im liebevoll hergerichteten Mühlengehöft verteilen sich die mehr als ein Dutzend Zimmer, Suiten und Wohnungen auf drei Gebäude: das alte Wohnhaus von 1850, die historische Scheune und das Hugenottenhaus. Alle Räumlichkeiten sind individuell nach Themen und Personen benannt und eingerichtet, die in der Geschichte des Tales und seiner Umgebung eine Rolle gespielt haben. Bezaubernde Antiquitäten, restaurierte Bauernbetten und Biedermeiermöbel, Eichenparkettböden, italienische Kristalllüster und englische Vorhangstoffe prägen den ländlich gediegenen Stil des Hauses. Umsorgt werden die Gäste von den Schwestern Kohl mit Charme, Professionalität und Herzlichkeit. Die Küche begeistert mit kulinarischen Köstlichkeiten und nordhessisch-französischem Esprit sowie frischen Zutaten, die zumeist aus der Region stammen.

Die Bärenmühle ist eine von fünf historischen Mühlen des Lengeltales bei Frankenau im ▸

The more than a dozen rooms, suites and apartments of this lovingly restored mill homestead are split between three buildings: the historic residence built in 1850, the historic barn and the Huguenot building. Each room features a custom theme, and is named in honour of an individual that has played an important role in the history of the valley and the surrounding area. Charming antiques, restored traditional beds and Biedermeier furnishings, oak parquet flooring, Italian crystal chandeliers and English draperies characterise the dignified country style of the buildings. The sisters Bettina and Christiane Kohl look after their guest with charm, professionalism and cordiality. The cuisine will delight visitors with culinary delicacies and French and North-Hessian esprit, with fresh ingredients that are mostly sourced locally. ▸

Angebot/facility

98-128 €

138-202 €

A/S 148-262 €

20-70

Frankenberg 12 km

Paderborn 150 km

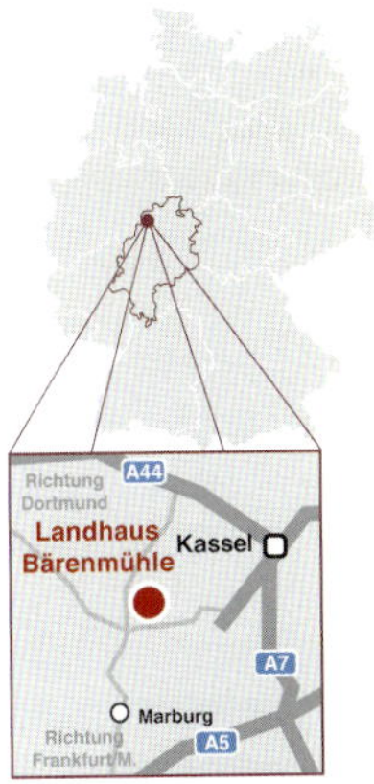

nordhessischen Landkreis Waldeck-Frankenberg. Die Mühlräder der Bärenmühle sind seit längerem abgebaut, die idyllische, naturnahe Lage ist geblieben. In den 50er Jahren des 20. Jahrhunderts kaufte und sanierte der damalige Landrat Heinrich Kohl das Gehöft, in dem seine Frau in den 1960er Jahren eine kleine Pension eröffnete, die sich schnell zu einem Geheimtipp entwickelte. Vom nächsten Ort ist die Bärenmühle etwa einen Kilometer entfernt, ein idealer Ort also, um abseits der Trampelpfade einen erholsamen Urlaub zu machen.

Auf den sattgrünen Wiesen der Bärenmühle weiden die Rinder einer befreundeten Bauernfamilie. Ein Schwimmteich und das gepflegte umliegende Areal stehen den Gästen zur Verfügung, die durch ihren Aufenthalt auch einen Beitrag dazu leisten, diese einmalige Kulturlandschaft zu erhalten. Befreundete Maler bestückten die Räumlichkeiten mit eindrucksvollen Bildern: Frank Suplie aus Berlin, Uwe Paduk aus Hamburg und die ebenfalls in Hamburg lebende Cousine Katharina Kohl.

The Bärenmühle is one of five historic mills in the Lengel Valley near Frankenau in the Waldeck-Frankenberg district of North Hesse. The Bärenmühle millwheels have long since been removed, while the idyllic, natural setting has remained. The farmstead was bought and renovated in the 1950s by the district administrator at that time, Heinrich Kohl. In the 1960s, his wife opened a small guesthouse at the farmstead, which quickly became an insider tip. The Bärenmühle Homestead lies about 0.6 miles from its closest neighbours, making it an ideal location for a relaxing and rejuvenating break, away from the tourist trail.

Cattle belonging to a friendly farmer's family can be seen grazing in the rich green pastures of the Bärenmühle. A swimming pond and well-tended surrounding areas are available to guests, and in staying at the Bärenmühle guests make a viable contribution to maintaining this unique cultural landscape. Painter friends have adorned the rooms with striking visual artwork: Frank Suplie from Berlin, Uwe Paduk from Hamburg and cousin Katharina Kohl, who also lives in Hamburg.

In der näheren Umgebung:

Lengeltal: bezaubernde Kulturlandschaft aus Wiesen, Wald und Feldern, in welche die fünf historischen Mühlen wie bunte Tupfer ins Grün hineingestreut sind; von der Bärenmühle aus gibt es ausgedehnte, idyllische Wanderwege in alle Himmelsrichtungen; **Frankenberg (5 km):** Museum Thonet-Panorama der Stuhlbaukunst; Kreisheimatmuseum im ehemaligen Kloster St. Georgenberg; Liebfrauenkirche, Fachwerkhäuser; **Bad Wildungen (22 km):** malerische Fachwerk-Altstadt, verspielter Jugendstil und prachtvoller Barock, Heilquellen.

In the surrounding area:

Lengel Valley: Enchanting cultural landscape of meadows, forests and patchwork fields, with five historic mills interspersed like dabs of colour on a green canvas. Idyllic hiking trails converge on the Bärenmühle Homestead from all directions; **Frankenberg (3 miles):** Museum Thonet – a panorama of the art of chair-making, museum of local history in the former St. Georgenberg monastery, Liebfrauenchurch, half-timbered houses; **Bad Wildungen (14 miles):** picturesque city centre with half-timbered houses, impressive buildings in Art Nouveau and Baroque style, medicinal springs.

TIPP

An dem noch erhaltenen Teil der äußeren Mauer des Zisterzienserklosters Haina lehnt ein kleines Fachwerkhäuschen. Im 18. Jahrhundert wohnte hier der Schreiner des im Kloster untergebrachten Hospitals. Sein Sohn, Johann Heinrich Wilhelm Tischbein, wurde hier 1751 geboren. Der künstlerisch begabten Bäcker- und Schreiner-Familie Tischbein aus Haina entstammen weitere ca. 40 Künstler, darunter vor allem viele Maler. Das Fachwerkhaus der Tischbeins beherbergt heute ein Museum, in dem man Interessantes über Leben und Werk dieser talentierten Künstlerfamilie erfährt.

A small, half-timbered house rests against the remaining section of the Haina Cistercian monastery's exterior wall. In the 18th century, this building was home to the carpenter of the hospital housed in the monastery. His son, Johann Heinrich Wilhelm Tischbein, was born there in 1751. The artistically gifted Tischbein family of bakers and carpenters from Haina produced some 40 further artists, including many painters in particular. Today, the Tischbeins' half-timbered adobe house is a museum packed full of interesting items recording the life and work of this talented family of artists.

Schloss Waldeck

Gastgeber/host: Volker Deigendesch

Einstige Festung, 200 m über dem Edersee auf einem Felsen erbaut, heute komfortables 5 Sterne Schlosshotel und fabelhafte Gourmet-Adresse.

The Former fortress built on a rock 218 yards above the lake Eder today is a comfortable 5 star Castle Hotel and fabulous gourmet address.

Schloss Waldeck 1
34513 Waldeck
Hessen
Tel.: +49 5623 5890
Fax: +49 5623 589289
www.hotel-schloss-waldeck.de
info@hotel-schloss-waldeck.de

Hotel ★★★★★
Restaurant ★★★★★

Die auf das 11. Jahrhundert zurückgehende Burganlage liegt auf einem felsigen hohen Berg am Ortsrand der Waldecker Kernstadt. Von hier aus genießt man einen grandiosen Blick auf die Landschaft des Nationalparks Kellerwald-Edersee, der zum UNESCO Welterbe zählt. Im Herbst 2009 eröffnete der heutige Gastgeber das neu gestaltete Hotel im Schloss Waldeck. Nach einfühlsamen Veränderungen wurde die anheimelnde Schlossatmosphäre um zeitgemäße Annehmlichkeiten ergänzt. Warme Farben und natürliche Materialien harmonieren mit der kargen Schroffheit der Burg und strahlen Geborgenheit aus. Alle 42 Zimmer gewähren einen unvergesslichen Panoramablick über das Waldecker Land und den Edersee.

The castle built in the 11th century is located on a high rocky mountain on the outskirts of the city Waldeck. From here, you can enjoy a magnificent view of the landscape of the National Park Kellerwald-Edersee, which belongs to the UNESCO World Heritage sites. In fall 2009 the newly designed hotel in the Castle Waldeck was opened by its new owner. Sensitive changes were made and contemporary amenities were added to the cosy atmosphere of the castle. Warm colours and natural materials are in harmony with the sparse roughness of the Castle and radiate a secure feeling. All 42 rooms have an unforgettable panoramic view over the Waldecker land and the lake Eder.

Culinary delights are served in the gourmet restaurant "Alte Turmuhr". Here, Chef Falko So- ▸

Im Gourmetrestaurant „Alte Turmuhr" werden kulinarische Köstlichkeiten serviert. Hier kombiniert Küchenchef Falko Sowinsky Exotisches mit erstklassigen regionalen Produkten zu traumhaft schmeckenden Gerichten. Ein behagliches Kaminzimmer sowie ein Wellness- und Spa-Bereich mit eigenem Garten dienen den Hausgästen zur Entspannung. ▸

Angebot/facility

125-210 €

A/S 145-210 €

2-80

Aldekerk
8 km

Düsseldorf
145 km

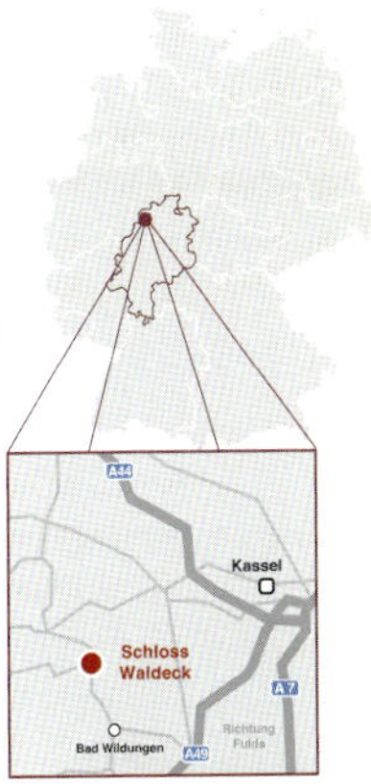

winsky serves wonderfully tasting dishes with a combination of exotics and superb local produces. A cosy fireplace room and wellness and spa area with its own garden are there for the guests to relax.

Waldeck was an ancestral Castle of the earls of Waldeck and seat of Government from the 11th to the 18th century before it found its present

Bevor es die heutige Bestimmung als Schlosshotel fand, war Waldeck vom 11. bis ins 18. Jahrhundert Stammburg der Grafen von Waldeck und Regierungssitz. Mit Erlangung der Fürstenwürde zogen die Grafen um in das neue Schloss Arolsen. Waldeck wurde Landeshauptstadtarchiv, Zeughaus, Landeszuchthaus sowie Fürstliches Hauptforstamt. Heute sind die mächtigen alten Burgmauern zeitgemäß in Szene gesetzt und empfangen den Gast als Hotel mit stilvoller Eleganz.

Bei Burgführungen durch die Verliese, die Gewölbe und den 120 m tiefen Brunnen erlebt man die ereignisreichen Jahrhunderte der Burg. Aus der Zeit des Landeszuchthauses erzählt das Schlosseigene Museum unter dem Titel „Hinter Schloss und Riegel".

occupation as a Castle Hotel. With obtaining the princely dignity, the earls moved into the new Castle Arolsen. Waldeck became city archives, armory, state penitentiary as well as the princely main forestry department. Today the mighty old castle walls are contemporarily set into scene and receive the guests to a hotel with stylish elegance. Through guided Castle tours into the dungeons, the vaults and the 131 yards deep well one can experience the lively past centuries of the Castle. The castle's Museum reports from the time of being a state penitentiary in the exhibition "Behind locked bars".

In der näheren Umgebung:

Schloss Waldeck: Burgmuseum, Führung durch die Verliese, Panorama Terasse; **Nationalpark und Naturpark Kellerwald-Edersee:** Buchennationalpark, Wildpark mit Greifvogelflugshow, Wanderungen mit dem Ranger; **Edersee Staumauer:** einer der größten deutschen Stauseen (202 Mio. m³ Wasser), Radwanderwege (63 km), alle Wassersportarten möglich; **Schloss Arolsen (28 km):** Barocke Residenz mit englischem Garten, Schlossführungen und Museen.

In the surrounding area:

Waldeck Castle: Castle museum, tour of the dungeons, panoramic terraces; **National park and Keller Forest and Eder Lake Nature Park:** Beech national park, game park with raptor show, national park walking tours with the ranger; **Eder Lake/concrete dam:** One of Germany's large reservoirs (202 million m³ of water), cycle paths (39 miles), all watersports available; **Arolsen Castle (17 miles):** New royal residence, Museums, guided tours of the castle.

TIPP

Einen Ausflug wert ist das moderne Heilbäder-Zentrum Bad Wildungen. In der 1200 Jahre alten, heutigen Kurstadt kann man sich in den Heilbädern und Kurparks erholen. Interessierte finden im Kurmuseum nicht nur die Geschichte der Kur- und Badanstalten, sondern auch eine im Keller sprudelnde Quelle. Im Besucherbergwerk Bertsch kann man zu den Bergleuten des Mittelalters hinabsteigen.

The modern therapeutic bath centre in Bad Wildungen is well worth a visit. The present day 1200 year old spa town is a place for relaxation with therapeutic baths and spa gardens. Those interested in paying a visit to the spa museum will not only find the history of the spa homes and baths, but also a gushing well-spring in the cellar. In the Bertsch visitors' mine you can go down to see the miners of the Middle Ages.

Schloss Ludwigseck

Gastgeber/host: Tanja von und zu Gilsa, Thilo von und zu Gilsa

Eine der letzten in Deutschland erbauten Wehrburgen; heute ein einladend charmantes chambres d'hôtes auf einer Basaltkuppe über der Fulda.

One of the last fortified defense castles built in Germany; today an inviting charming chambres d'hôtes on a basalt hilltop near the river Fulda.

36251 Ludwigsau
Hessen
Tel.: +49 6670 205
Fax: +49 6670 1239
www.schloss-ludwigseck.de
casanier@t-online.de

Hotel ★★★★

Schloss Ludwigseck liegt im Herzen Deutschlands auf einer Basaltkuppe unweit des Flusses Fulda. Die ehemalige Wehrburg erhebt sich inmitten der „Riedesel'schen Wälder" in den östlichen Ausläufern des Knüllgebirges. 1419 fertig gestellt, wandelte sich die Nutzung des Hauses im Laufe der Jahrhunderte zum repräsentativen Jagdschloss der Riedesel Freiherrn zu Eisenbach.

Der heutige Schlossherr, Thilo von und zu Gilsa, hat die Passion für die Jagd und die Natur von seinen Ahnen geerbt. Im gut geführten 1600 ha großen Hochwildrevier bietet er den Gästen des Schlosses Ansitzmöglichkeiten und Pirschgänge an. Wer gerne angelt kann einen Tagesschein für den mitten im Wald gelegenen Malchusteich oder den Bachlauf des Rohrbachtales lösen.

Tanja von und zu Gilsa widmet sich vor allem dem Innenleben des historischen Gebäudes. Mit viel Charme und Gespür für Authentizität hat sie für die Gäste fünf Zimmer eingerichtet. In der neuen Schlossküche werden die Gäste liebevoll von der Schlossherrin bewirtet. Durchreisende können nach langen Autofahrten bei einem Abendbrot aus regionalen Produkten ▸

Schloss Ludwigseck in the heart of Germany lies on a basalt hilltop near the river Fulda. Completed in 1419 the former defense castle rises in the midst of the "Riedesel'schen Woods" in the Eastern foothills of the Knüll mountains. Over the centuries the House was transformed into a representative hunting castle of the Riedesel Baron to Eisenbach.

The current Lord of the Castle, Thilo von und zu Gilsa, has inherited the passion for hunting and nature of his ancestors. In the well managed 4000 acres big game area, he offers the guests of the Castle opportunities for stalk or still hunts. For those who like fishing they can buy a day tikket for the Malchusteich situated in middle of the woods or for the stream of the Rohrbach Valley.

Tanja von und zu Gilsa is mainly dedicated to ▸

Angebot/facility

75-95 €

105-120 €

Rotenburg/Fulda 10 km

Frankfurt/Main 150 km

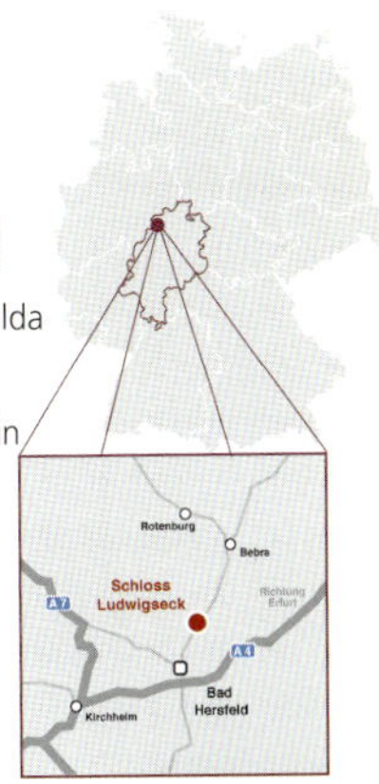

neue Kräfte schöpfen. Für Paare wird das beliebte Romantikarrangement angeboten, das u.a. einen Ausflug in die heimische Wildküche enthält. Kulinarisch neu ist der Royal Tea, der als Nachmittagsbonbon dazugebucht werden kann.

Burggarten, Park und der Gemüsegarten laden zu einer kleinen Erkundungstour direkt um das Schloss herum ein. Wer gerne wandert, kann direkt vom Hoftor aus starten und die wunderschöne hessische Mittelgebirgslandschaft bewundern.

Die Gastgeber geben gerne Auskunft über attraktive Tagesausflüge in die Regionen oder sind bei der Reservierung von Konzertkarten zu den Bad Hersfelder Festspielen behilflich.

interior works of this historic building. With lots of charm and sense of authenticity she has designed five guest rooms. In the new Castle kitchen, guests are lovingly entertained by the chatelaine.

Passers-by can renew their strength after long car drives with a dinner of regional products. The popular Romance package which includes a trip to the local game cuisine is offered for couples. The Royal tea, which can be booked as an afternoon treat is a new culinary highlight. The Castle Gardens, the Park and the vegetable garden invite you to a little exploration tour around the Castle. Walkers can get started directly from the castle gates on, out into the beautiful Hessian low mountain range landscape.

In der näheren Umgebung:

Braach (7 km): monatlicher Bauernmarkt im Sommerhalbjahr; **Rotenburg/Fulda (10 km):** historische Fachwerkstadt mit eigener Kantorei; **Bad Hersfeld (20 km):** hübsche Fachwerkstadt mit Wochenmarkt und attraktiven Einkaufmöglichkeiten, Festspielstadt; **Kassel (56 km):** Schloss Wilhelmshöhe (Sammlung holländischer Meister), Gebrüder-Grimm-Museum, Schloss Wilhelmstal, Stadt der Documenta; **Fulda (65 km):** Sehenswerte Barockstadt mit Dom und einigen interessanten Museen.

In the surrounding area:

Braach (4 miles): monthly farmer's market during the summer season; **Rotenburg/Fulda (6 miles):** historic timber-framed town with its own choir; **Bad Hersfeld (12 miles):** pretty timber-framed town with weekly market and attractive shopping facilities, Festival City; **Kassel (35 miles):** Schloss Wilhelmshöhe (collection of Dutch masters), Brothers-Grimm-Museum, Schloss Wilhelmstal, city of the Documenta; **Fulda (40 miles):** picturesque baroque town with Cathedral and interesting museums.

TIPP

Bad Hersfelder Festspiele 15.Juni bis 05. August

Die Bad Hersfelder Festspiele zeichnen sich durch ihre einmalige Spielstätte in der romanischen Stiftsruine und durch qualitätsvolle Inszenierungen aus. Holk Freytag, Leiter der Bad Hersfelder Festspiele, gestaltet Jahr für Jahr ein anspruchsvolles und vielseitiges Programm. So stehen z. B. neben Shakespeares klassischem Drama King Lear Thomas Manns mystischer Zauberberg und der Musical-Welterfolg Anatevka auf dem Programm. Aktuelle Termine finden sich unter www.bad-hersfelder-festspiele.de. Schloss Ludwigseck bietet einen Shuttle-Service zur Festspielstadt an.

The Bad Hersfelder Festival from15th of June to 5th of August

The Bad Hersfeld festival is characterized by its unique home in the ruins of the romanesque monastery and through the quality productions. A sophisticated and versatile program designed year after year by the head of the festival Holk Freytag. Classical dramas as Shakespeare's King Lear, Thomas Mann's mystical "Zauberberg" and the musical world hit Fiddler on the roof for example are on the program. Current dates can be found under www.bad-hersfelder-festspiele.de. Castle Ludwigseck offers a shuttle service to the festival.

Parkhotel Wasserburg Anholt

Gastgeber/host: Peter und Jörg Brune

Edle Wasserburg nahe Arnheim (Holland) mit größter privater Kunstsammlung des Fürsten zu Salm-Salm und noblem Hotel in der Vorburg.

Noble Wasserburg near Arnheim (Holland), home to the largest private art collection of the Prince of Salm-Salm and stately hotel in the outer bailey.

Klever Straße
46419 Isselburg
Nordrhein-Westfalen
Tel: +49 2874 4590
Fax: +49 2874 4035
www.schloss-anholt.de
info@schloss-anholt.de

Hotel ★★★★★
Restaurant ★★★★★

Die historische Burganlage, die eindrucksvolle Parklandschaft und das unverwechselbare Ambiente machen das Parkhotel Wasserburg Anholt zu einem ganz besonderen Ort der Gastlichkeit. Einzigartig sind das gläserne Restaurant mit kreativer Spitzenküche im Wasserpavillon inmitten des Wassergrabens, die Terrasse über dem Burggraben, das Standesamt sowie die individuell, mit stilvollem Luxus

eingerichteten Zimmer und Salons.
Die Wasserburg Anholt ist von mehreren Barockgärten umgeben und liegt inmitten einer riesigen Gräfte, eingebettet in eine 42 Hektar ▸

The historic site of the castle, the impressive park landscape and the unmistakable ambiance make the Anholt Moated Castle Park Hotel a very special place for hospitality. The glass restaurant with creative state-of-the-art kitchen in a water pavilion in the midst of the moat, the terrace over the castle moat, the registry office as well as the individual, stylishly luxurious furnished room and parlour are all very unique. ▸

Angebot/facility

106-149 €

159-195 €

A/S 225-310 €

50-124

Empel-Rees 5 km

Weeze 40 km
Düsseldorf 90 km

Schließzeiten: So./Mo.
Gourmetrestaurant

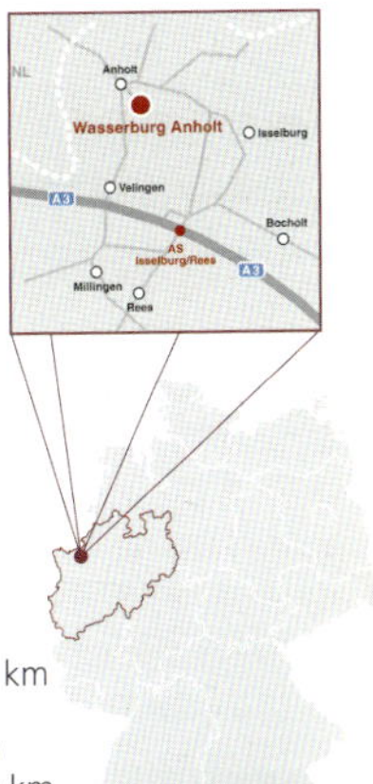

große Parkanlage. Bereits seit 1645 befindet sich Anholt im Besitz der Fürsten zu Salm. Im Zweiten Weltkrieg erlitt die Anlage schwere Zerstörungen, wodurch das dauerhafte Bewohnen nicht mehr möglich war. Im Rahmen des Wiederaufbaus erhielt die Wasserburg eine museale Bestimmung.

Von 1990 bis 2000 führte Fürst Carl Philipp zu Salm-Salm eingehende Wiederherstellungs- und Restaurierungsmaßnahmen historischer Räumlichkeiten sowie zahlreicher bedeutender Kunstgegenstände zur Erschließung und Einrichtung des Museums durch.

Anholt Moated Castle is surrounded by baroque gardens and lies amidst an enormous moat, nestled in 105 acres of parkland. The Princess of Salm have owned Anholt since 1645. In the Second World War the site was almost completely destroyed, to the extent that it was no longer inhabitable. As part of its reconstruction, the moated castle was preserved to become a museum.

Between 1990 and 2000 Prince Carl Philipp of Salm-Salm carried out reconstruction and restoration measures on the historical premises, as well as on numerous important pieces of art for the development and furnishing of the museum.

In der näheren Umgebung:

Golfplatz: 18 Loch; **Anholter Schweiz:** Biotop-Wildpark mit großem Wildgehege und Fasanerie, sog. Nachahmung des Vierwaldstädter Sees; **Isselburg:** Hochseilgarten; **Kleve (29 km):** Kunstsammlungen im Kurhaus; **Schloss Moyland (30 km):** Museum mit Joseph Beuys Archiv (www.moyland.de); **Xanten (30 km):** Archäologischer Park, Kanutouren auf der Issel, Touren mit dem Auto oder Fahrrad durch das Münsterland.

In the surrounding area:

Golf course: 18 holes; **Anholt Switzerland:** Biotope-wildlife Park with big game reserve and pheasantry, which is an imitation of the Vierwaldstädter Lake; **Isselburg:** High rope garden; **Kleve (18 miles):** Art collection in a spa hotel; **Moyland Castle (19 miles):** Museum with Joseph Beuys archive (www.moyland.de); **Xanten (19 miles):** Archaeological Park: Canoeing trips on the River Issel, car drives or bicycle rides through Münster country.

TIPP

Nahe der Wasserburg Anholt erstreckt sich die Anholter Schweiz, ein Biotopwildpark der besonderen Art. Besucher können hier neben zahlreichen seltenen Tier- und Pflanzenarten auch das „Schweizer Häuschen" bestaunen. Das kleine Chalet liegt eingebettet in einen See, welcher als Nachbildung des Vierwaldstätter Sees angelegt wurde. Den Auftrag für diese Imitation erteilte Fürst Leopold zu Salm-Salm im Jahre 1893. Er wollte somit die Erinnerung an seine Hochzeitsreise wahren.

Close to Anholt Moated Castle you will find Anholter Schweiz, a biotope wildlife park of the special kind. Apart from various rare animal and plant species visitors can marvel at the "Schweizer Häuschen". This small chalet lies embedded in a lake that was constructed after the model of the Vierwaldstätter Lake. Prince Leopold zu Salm-Salm gave orders to build this imitation in the year 1893. Thus he wanted to keep the memories of his honeymoon alive.

Schloss Wissen

Gastgeber/host: Raphaël Freiherr von Loë

Nordrhein-Westfalen

550 jähriger Herrensitz derer von Loë mit stilsicher eingerichteten Gästezimmern in der „Boye", in der früher die Angestellten der schlosseigenen Betriebe lebten.

550-year-old Manor house of the von Loë with stylishly furnished guest rooms in the "Boye", where in earlier times the employees of the castle's undertakings lived.

Schlossallee 21
47652 Weeze-Wissen
Nordrhein-Westfalen
Tel.: +49 2837 96190
Fax: +49 2837 961911
www.schloss-wissen.de
culture-castles@schloss-wissen.de

Hotel ★★★★

Über 550 Jahre waren es die Herzöge von Geldern und Kleve, der Große Kurfürst (Friedrich Wilhelm I, 1620-1688), oder die Erzherzöge von Österreich, die als Gäste der Familie (derzeit in der 16. Generation) nach Wissen kamen. Heute sind es Gäste, die Erholung suchen, sich an Kultur und Natur erfreuen, Durch-Reisende oder Teilnehmer privater und gesellschaftlicher Veranstaltungen und Feiern.

Weitab vom Alltag des Geschäftslebens finden Sie in der „Boye" einen ruhigen Ort zur Übernachtung und für Zusammenkünfte. Die „Boye" ist ein kleines Dorf, in dem die Angestellten und Familien der schlosseigenen Betriebe gelebt und gearbeitet haben. Mittelpunkt ist die historische Wassermühle, die ▸

Over 550 years there were the Dukes of Geldern and Cleves, the great elector (Frederick William I, 1620-1688) or the Archdukes of Austria who came and stayed at Wissen as guests of the family (currently in the 16th generation). Today they are guests looking for relaxation; enjoy culture and nature, by-travelers or people taking part in private and social events and celebrations. The "Boye" is a small village, where the employees and families of the Castle's own operations lived and worked. It is a quiet place far away from the daily routine of business which offers accommodation and space for meetings. The Center of the "Boye" is the historic watermill, which today serves the guests as breakfast and meeting room.

Guests have the choice between 17 beautiful and stylishly furnished rooms in various ▸

Angebot/facility

109-140 €

114-145 €

A/S 129-205 €

bis 130

Weeze 3 km

Weeze 7 km
Düsseldorf 70 km

Zuzüglich Frühstück
12,50 €/Person

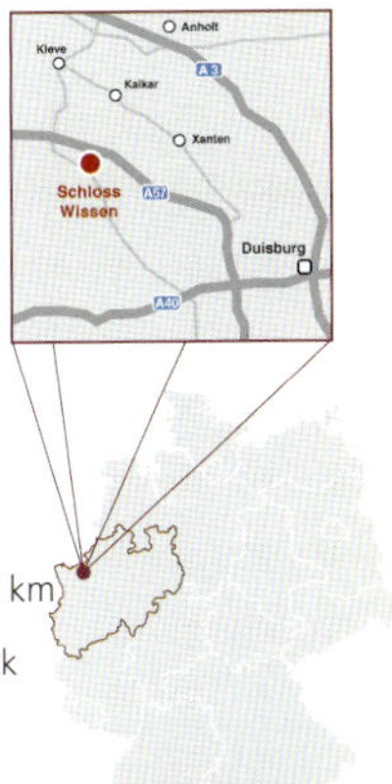

den Gästen heute als Frühstücks- und Veranstaltungsraum dient.
Die Gäste haben die Wahl zwischen 17 schönen und stilsicher eingerichteten Zimmern unterschiedlicher Größe und Ausstattung sowie einer Turmsuite mit einem besonders romantischen Charme. Alle ermöglichen kostenfreie W-LAN Nutzung.
Schloss Wissen verleiht auch Tagungen und Events einen unverwechselbaren und besonders nachhaltigen Charakter. Für die Durchführung von Veranstaltungen stehen drei miteinander verbundene Säle im Schloss selbst sowie kombinierbare Veranstaltungsräume in der historischen Wassermühle zur Verfügung. Deren Lage oberhalb des Mühlenweihers vermittelt ebenso eine besonders stimmungsvolle Atmosphäre wie das erhaltene Fachwerk und die schweren Eichenbalkendecken im Inneren. Die weitläufigen Wiesen, durch das Flüsschen Niers vom dahinterliegenden Wald getrennt, bilden die stimmungsvolle Kulisse für kreative Pausen.

sizes and facilities, as well as a tower suite with a particularly romantic charm. All allow use of free Wi-Fi.
Events and business conferences at Wissen Castle will be a unique and unforgettable experience. There are three interconnected rooms in the castle itself, and combinable conference rooms in the historic water mill available for the organisation of events. Their location above the mill pond gives also a particularly evocative atmosphere, supported by truss that has been preserved such as the heavy oak beams inside. The spacious meadows, separated from the near-by forest by the river Niers, are the atmospheric backdrop for creative breaks.

In der näheren Umgebung:

Wallfahrtsort Kevelaer (4 km): mit über 800.000 Wallfahrern jährlich zählt Kevelaer zu den bedeutendsten Marienwallfahrtsorten Deutschlands; **De Maasduinen (9 km):** im 4.500 ha großen niederländischen Nationalpark genießen die Besucher großartige Landschaften mit vielen besonderen Tieren und Pflanzen; **Xanten (20 km):** Römer-, Dom- und Siegfriedstadt am Niederrhein. Die historische Innenstadt mit dem Dom St. Viktor und die zahlreichen Museen und Freizeitmöglichkeiten überzeugen viele Besucher; **Schloss-Moyland (20 km):** Museum für moderne und zeitgenössische Kunst und ein internationales Forschungszentrum zu Joseph Beuys.

In the surrounding area:

Kevelaer, place of pilgrimage (2.5 miles): one of Germany's most popular places of marian pilgrimage with over 800.000 pilgrims every year; **De Massduinen (6 miles):** in the Dutch national park visitors enjoy great landscapes with a lot of unusual animals and plants on an area of 11250 acres; **Xanten (12 miles):** Roman, Cathedral and Siegfried-town at the Lower Rhine. The historical old town with the cathedral St. Viktor and the numerous museums and free time activities satisfy many visitors; **Moyland Castle (12 miles):** museum for modern and contemporary art and international research centre on Joseph Beuys.

TIPP

Die Kalkarer Mühle gilt mit einem unteren Umfang von fast 35 m, rund ein Meter dicken Wänden und einer Höhe von mehr als 27 m (ohne Flügel) als die größte Mühle am Niederrhein. Die Mühle wird vom Verein Kalkarer Mühle am Hanselaerer Tor e. V. (Mühlenverein) betreut und bewirtschaftet. In der ehemaligen Scheune befindet sich ein Restaurant mit Brauhaus. Von April bis Oktober ist die Mühle am Wochenende nachmittags zu besichtigen, ansonsten nach Absprache. Bei ausreichendem Wind wird die Mühle betrieben.

The mill of Kalkar, almost 38 yards in girth with one yard thick walls and more than 30 yards in height (without wings), is the biggest mill at the Lower Rhine. The mill is managed and maintained by the association "Kalkarer Mühle am Hanselaerer Tor e.V." In the former barn there is a restaurant with a brewhouse. From April to October one can visit the mill at weekend afternoons, otherwise upon consultation. When there is enough wind, the mill operates.

Schlossruine Hertefeld

Gastgeber/host: Graf und Gräfin zu Eulenburg und Hertefeld

Nordrhein-Westfalen

Deutschlands einzige bewohnbare Schlossruine, idyllisch gelegen am Niederrhein, seit mehr als 800 Jahren im Familienbesitz.

Idyllically situated at the Lower Rhine lies Germany's only inhabitable castle ruin which has been owned by the family von Hertefeld for more than 800 years.

Hertefeld 1
47652 Weeze
Nordrhein-Westfalen
Tel: +49 2837 2035
www.hertefeld.de
schloss@hertefeld.de

Hotel ★★★★

Das 1322 erstmals erwähnte Schloss Hertefeld ist eines der ungewöhnlichsten Hotels am Niederrhein. In seiner wechselvollen Geschichte war das historisch bedeutende Rittergut und spätere Barockschloss vielfachem Wandel unterworfen, bis es 1945 durch Kriegswirren bis auf die Grundmauern zerstört wurde. Seit der Renovierung 2004 lässt sich in „Deutschlands einziger bewohnbarer Schlossruine" in originell eingerichteten Räumen vortrefflich feiern, tagen und nächtigen. Im Hauptturm und im Mitteltrakt des Schlosses ist außer dem ▸

Hertefeld Castle, first mentioned in documents in 1322, belongs to the most fascinating hotels at the Lower Rhine. Throughout its eventful history the knights' residence, which later was rebuilt as a Baroque castle, was subject to multiple constructional changes until it was destroyed to the ground during WW II. The owner family von Hertefeld restored the castle in 2004 and made it to "Germany's only inhabitable castle ruin". Today it presents the perfect location for celebrations, meetings or holidays. In the main tower and the middle section the fireplace room and the former groined vault have been created as well as the tower suite, a tribute to the Swedish ancestors of the lord of the castle. In 1906 two guard houses were built on ▸

Angebot/facility

ab 115 €

A/S ab 159 €

15-130

Weeze 1 km
Düsseldorf Hbf.
75 km

Weeze 5 km
Düsseldorf 75 km

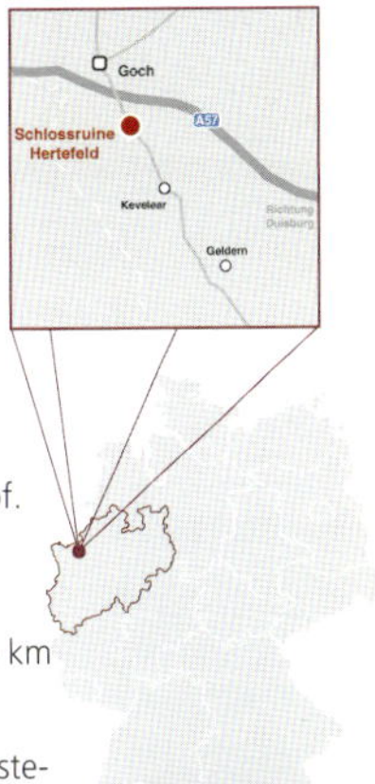

In der "Kangaroo Lodge", einem Gästehaus auf demselben Grundstück, stehen weitere 18 originelle Gästezimmer für bis zu 60 Personen zur Verfügung.

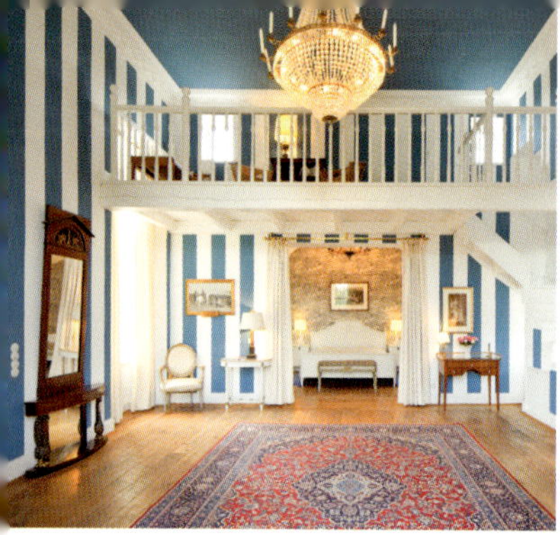

alten Kaminsaal und dem früheren Kreuzgratgewölbe noch eine „Turmsuite" entstanden, eine Reminiszenz an die schwedischen Vorfahren des Hausherrn.

Weitere charmante Gästezimmer haben stets Bezug zur Geschichte des Hauses und seiner Bewohner.

Am nördlichen Parkeingang wurden 1906 durch den Fürsten Philipp zwei Wächterhäuser errichtet, die ab 2005 mit einem Verbindungstrakt versehen und zu einer idyllischen Appartementsuite ausgebaut wurden.

In einem Nebenflügel des ehemaligen Renteigebäudes entstand das sogenannte Sternenzimmer. Es erinnert an einen alten Mercedes Benz 300 S, der hier in den 1950er Jahren untergestellt wurde.

Das ansprechende Denkmalensemble ist ein echtes Kleinod geworden, das sehr authentisch und persönlich geführt wird. Gefrühstückt wird übrigens im wiederhergestellten historischen Kreuzgewölbe, oder auch unter alten Bäumen im rund fünf Hektar großen Schlosspark.

the Northern Park entrance by Duke Philip. Both houses were connected in 2005 to an idyllic apartment suite.

In a side wing of the former Rentei building the Star room was designed. It reminds of a Mercedes Benz 300S which was stored here in the 1950s. The ensemble of heritage listed buildings has become a true gem with authentic and personal service of its hosts. Guests can enjoy breakfast either in the Tower room, in the cross vaults or if the weather permits outdoors in the sun or under trees.

In der näheren Umgebung:

Weeze: Tierpark mit Streichelzoo, Paddeln auf der Niers, Wanderungen, Golfen: auf 13 Plätzen im Umkreis von 40 km; **Kevelaer (6 km):** bedeutendster Wallfahrtsort Nordwesteuropas mit ausgemalter Basilika und einer der größten Orgeln Europas; **Xanten (20 km):** Römischer Archäologiepark „Colonia Ulpia Traiana" mit Sommerfestspielen und neuem Römischen Museum; **Nimwegen/ Nijmegen (50 km):** mit über 2.000 Jahren älteste Stadt der Niederlande.

In the surrounding area:

Weeze: Zoo with Petting Zoo, paddle on the Niers, walks, Golfing on 13 courses within a radius of 40 km; **Kevelaer (4 miles)** the most important pilgrimage North West Europe with a fully painted Basilica and one of the largest organs in Europe; **Xanten (12 miles):** Roman Archaeological Park "Colonia Ulpia Traiana" with summer festival and the new Roman Museum; **Nimwegen/Nijmegen Netherlands (31 miles)**: with over 2,000 years the oldest town of the Netherlands.

TIPP

Ein Erlebnis der besonderen Art bietet eine Fahrt mit einer Grenzland-Draisine. Zwei unterschiedliche Draisinenstrecken bieten Bewegung und Entdeckerspaß auf der grenzüberschreitenden 11 Kilometer langen, alten Eisenbahnstrecke von Kleve über Kranenburg nach Groesbeek (NL), oder auf der 20 Kilometer langen Strecke von Kranenburg nach Kleve und zurück (oder umgekehrt). Draisinen gibt es für 2 - 4 Personen oder Club-Draisinen für 9 bis zu 14 Personen.

A special experience offers a ride on the Frontier railbike. Two different routes provide exercise and fun exploring. One is the 7 miles long cross-border ride on the old railway lines from Cleves via Kranenburg to Groesbeek (NL) and the other is on the 12.5 miles stretch from Kranenburg to Kleve and back (or vice versa.) There are railbikes for 2-4 persons or Club railbikes for 9 up to 14 people.

Burg Boetzelaer

Gastgeber/host: Maximilian Freiherr von Wendt

Nordrhein-Westfalen

Alte Wasserburg mit komfortablen Suiten und herrschaftlichen Gästezimmern, repräsentativen Sälen und Salons.

Old moated castle with comfortable suites and grand guest rooms, representative halls and salons.

Reeser Straße 247
47546 Kalkar-Appeldorn
Nordrhein-Westfalen
Tel.: +49 2824 977990
Fax: +49 2824 9779999
www.burgboetzelaer.de
info@burgboetzelaer.de

Hotel ★★★★

Abseits im Grünen, aber zwischen A3 und A57 sehr gut erreichbar, lädt die Burg mit ihrem historischen Ambiente und einem kleinen angrenzenden Park mit jahrhundertealtem Baumbestand zum Verweilen und Übernachten ein.

In der Haupt- und Vorburg erwarten sieben herrschaftliche Zimmer und drei Suiten die Gäste. Die Zimmer sind zum Teil barrierefrei angelegt und teilweise mit dem Lift erreichbar. Übernachtungsmöglichkeiten bestehen für bis zu 32 Gäste. Gefrühstückt wird im historischen Rittergewölbe der Hauptburg, im Winter am knisternden Kaminfeuer.

Der heute wieder in neuem Glanz erstrahlte Teil der ehemaligen Hauptburg beherbergt fünf Räumlichkeiten verschiedenster Größen, die im Rahmen von Veranstaltungen einzeln oder ▸

Situated in the country and its beautiful green surroundings –but located between the A3 and the A57and thus still easily reachable- the castle captivates its visitors with its historic atmosphere and the small adjacent park with centuries-old trees inviting its guests to stay for a while.

In the main and front buildings of the castle seven grand guest rooms and three suites can be booked. The rooms are partly barrier-free constructed and some of them can be reached by lift. Up to 32 guests can stay over at Boetzelaer Castle. Breakfast is served in the historic ▸

Angebot/facility

110-130 €

109-150 €

A/S 129-220 €

10-120

Rees-Empel 10 km

Weeze 25 km

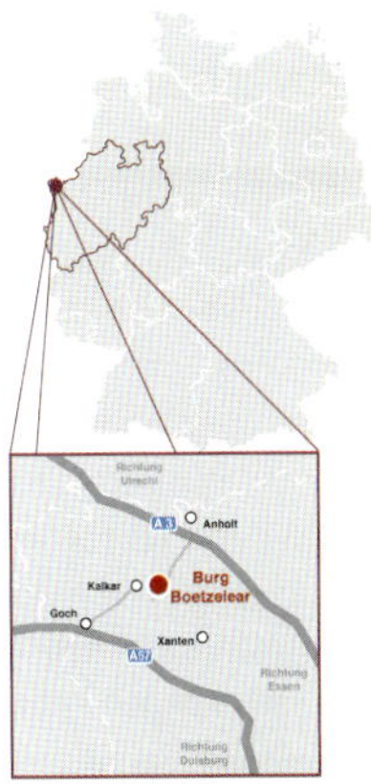

komplett gebucht werden können. Der ehemalige Rittersaal im Erdgeschoss beeindruckt vor allem durch sein Kreuzrippengewölbe aus dem 14. Jahrhundert. Weitere repräsentative Rahmen für Veranstaltungen unterschiedlicher Größe bieten in der ersten Etage der klassizistische Festsaal, ein Kaminsalon, an den die ehemalige Burgkapelle angrenzt, sowie das Herrenzimmer.

In ihrer Glanzzeit im 13. und 14. Jahrhundert war die Burg zu Boetzelaer ein nahezu uneinnehmbares Kastell mit zwei Vorburgen und einem umfangreichen Wassergrabensystem. Dieses wurde verstärkt durch einen siebengeschossigen Bergfried, dessen bloße Existenz die Burg als allodialen Sitz (erbeigen, zinsfrei) eines einflussreichen Geschlechtes charakterisierte. Die Ausmaße der Festung wurden vornehmlich als Machtdemonstration verstanden. Sie hat eine äußerst wechselhafte Bau- und Familiengeschichte und wurde über 500 Jahre von der Familie van den Boetzelaer bewohnt.

knight's vault of the castle's main building, during winter even next to the crackling fireplace.

Today shining in new splendour, the part of the former main building of the castle holds five premises of different sizes that can be booked individually or as a whole for festivities. The former knight's hall on the ground floor impresses especially with its ribbed vaults from the 14th century. More representative locations for events of different sizes offer the classical ballroom, the salon with fireplace – to which the former castle chapel is adjacent – as well as the study.

In its glory days during the 13th and 14th century, Boetzelaer castle was a nearly impregnable fort with two front buildings and an extensive moat system. This was supported by a seven storeys keep, whose mere existence characterised the castle as allodial residence (inherited, interest-free) of a powerful family. The size of the castle was especially understood as a demonstration of power. The castle itself had a very eventful building and family history and was inhabited by the family van den Boetzelaer for over 500 years.

In der näheren Umgebung:

Kalkar (6 km): Städtisches Museum Kalkar mit Sammlung zur Kunst des 20. Jhd., St. Nicolai-Kirche mit wertvollen Kunstschätzen; **Xanten (12 km):** Archäologischer Park Xanten, Römerstadt mit lebensgroßen Rekonstruktionsbauten - Amphitheater und Hafentempel vermitteln einen anschaulichen Eindruck vom Alltag in der römischen Provinz; Römermuseum auf dem Gelände der ehemaligen römischen Metropole Colonia Ulpia Traiana; **Bedburg-Hau (13 km):** „Schloss Moyland", mit weltweit größter Sammlung (4000 Arbeiten) des Künstlers Joseph Beuys, in historischer Parkanlage; **Kleve (20 km):** Museum Kurhaus Kleve, zeitgenössische Kunst und Ewald Mataré-Sammlung;

In the surrounding area:

Kalkar (4 miles): museum Kalkar with a collection of art from the 20th century, St. Nicolai church with valuable art treasures; **Xanten (7.5 miles):** Archaeological park Xanten, Roman town with life-sized reconstructed buildings – amphitheatre, harbour temple give an impressive insight into the everyday life in a Roman Province; Roman museum on the grounds of the former Roman metropolis Colonia Ulpia Traiana; **Bedburg-Hau (8 miles):** "Moyland Castle", with the world's biggest collection (4000 pieces of work) by the artist Joseph Beuys, in historic park; **Kleve (12 miles):** museum Kurhaus Kleve, contemporary art and Ewald Mataré collection

TIPP

Burg Boetzelaer gilt als ein besonders gelungenes Beispiel praktischer Denkmalpflege und als ein Forum zur Präsentation kultureller Angebote der Region: Ausstellungen, Lesungen, Musikabende und Theateraufführungen finden auf Burg Boetzelaer einen angemessenen Rahmen.
Eine Besichtigungstour entführt Sie in eine Welt voller Abenteuer und alter Sitten, gibt Einblick in das höfische Leben vergangener Tage, berichtet von Grausamkeiten und Ritterlichkeit, oder geht der Frage nach der Bedeutung der Frau im Mittelalter nach.

Boetzelaer castle is an especially fascinating example of practical heritage preservation and it constitutes a forum for the presentation of cultural offers from the region: exhibitions, readings, music evenings and theatre performances take place at Boetzelaer castle in an appropriate setting.
A guided tour will take you to a world full of adventures and old customs and will give you insight into to the life at court in past days, reporting from cruelty and chivalry, or will explain the role of women during the Middle Ages.

Schloss Ossenberg

Gastgeber/host: Herzogin Karen von Urach, Herzog Wilhelm Albert von Urach

Nordrhein-Westfalen

Schloss mit prunkvollem Rokokosaal und Bibliothek sowie Gästezimmern in einer gelungenen Mischung aus modernem Design und historischem Gemäuer.

Castle with a magnificent Rococo hall and library as well as with guestrooms designed in a combination of modern style and historic walls.

Schlossstraße 81
47495 Rheinberg
Nordrhein-Westfalen
Tel.: +49 2843 160395
www.schloss-ossenberg.de
info@schloss-ossenberg.de

Hotel ★★★★

Schloss Ossenberg blickt auf eine lange und wechselvolle Geschichte zurück. Der ursprüngliche Rittersitz wurde 1176 erstmals urkundlich erwähnt. 1721 wurde die ursprüngliche Burganlage durch die heutigen Gebäude im Stil des Rokoko ersetzt. Schon immer war Schloss Ossenberg regelmäßiges Ziel für Besucher und interessante Übernachtungsgäste. Im Jahre 1811 stattete Kaiserin Marie Louise, Gemahlin Napoleons I, dem Haus einen Besuch ab. Für den heutigen Gast bietet der großzügige Park mitten in der ländlich geprägten niederrheinischen Landschaft mit Feldern, Alleen und Deichen die Gelegenheit, die Gegend mit dem Fahrrad oder zu Fuß zu erkunden.

Gemeinsam mit ihrem Ehemann machte Herzogin Karen von Urach im Jahre 2004 den Nordtrakt des Schlosses für Übernachtungsgäste zugänglich. Hierbei entstanden drei ▸

Ossenberg Castle bears witness to a long and eventful history. The original knights' residence was first mentioned in documents in 1176. In 1721 the original castle buildings were replaced by the present buildings in style of the Rococo period. Ossenberg castle has always been a popular tourist destination and accommodation to interesting guests. Empress Marie Louise, wife to Napoleon I, came here for a visit in 1811.

For today's guests the extensive park situated amidst the rural landscape of the lower Rhine with its fields, alleys and dikes, presents the perfect opportunity to explore the surrounding area by bike or foot.

Together with her husband, duchess Karen von Urach, opened the northern part of the castle for guests in 2004 and thus created three ▸

Angebot/facility

105 €

140 €

A/S 170 €

bis 199

Rheinberg: 2 km

Weeze 35 km
Düsseldorf 49 km

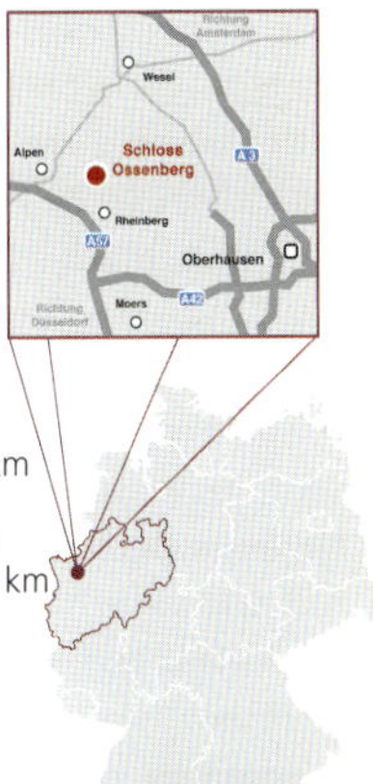

exklusiv ausgestattete Doppelzimmer, eine Suite, ein gemütliches Kaminzimmer als Aufenthaltsraum sowie ein Wintergarten in historischer Bauweise, der als Frühstücks-Pavillon genutzt wird. Für die Gäste ist es im Frühjahr ein besonderer Genuss, wenn sie - nur durch eine Glaswand getrennt - im Wintergarten beim Frühstück Rehe beobachten können, die sich zu dieser Jahreszeit ganz nah an das Schloss herantrauen.

Die Remise des Schlosses bietet Platz für bis zu 200 Personen. Ob Hochzeit, Geburtstag, Familienfeier oder Firmenjubiläum: die weit geöffneten Tore ermöglichen einen bezaubernden Blick in die niederrheinische Landschaft. Ein Empfang im Park, mit herrlichen alten Bäumen, gibt jeder Veranstaltung einen herrschaftlich ländlichen Rahmen.

exclusively designed double rooms, a suite, a cosy fireplace room that serves as guest lounge as well as a historic conservatory which is used as breakfast pavilion. It will be a special pleasure for the hotel guests to enjoy their breakfast in the conservatory during spring time when they can watch – separated only by a thin glass wall- deer that dare to come especially close to the castle during this time of the year.

The former coach house of the castle offers accommodation to up to 200 people. Whether you are looking for the perfect venue for your wedding, birthday, family celebration or your company's anniversary: The widely opened gates will ensure a magnificent view of the landscape around the lower Rhine. A reception in the park with its beautiful old trees will provide a grand rural framework to every event.

In der näheren Umgebung:

Orsoy (12 km): Spaziergang auf den Wällen mit Blick auf die Niederrheinische Landschaft. Gemütliche Gaststätten und Cafés. **Wesel (15 km):** Preußenmuseum in der Zitadelle; anschaulicher Überblick zur Preußischen Geschichte und der Preußischen Herrschaft im Rheinland. **Xanten (17 km):** Archäologischer Park und Römermuseum, Xantener Nord- und Südsee zum Baden und Segeln.

In the surrounding area:

Orsoy (7.5 miles): Walks on the walls with view of the landscape around the lower Rhine; cosy inns and cafés.

Wesel (9 miles): Prussian museum in the citadel; good overview of Prussian history and the Prussian rule in Rhineland

Xanten (10 miles): Archaeological Park and Roman museum, Xanten northern and southern lake to go swimming and sailing

TIPP

Die ehemalige Zoll- und Festungsstadt Rheinberg mit ihrem historischen Flair in der Innenstadt erhielt schon 1233 die Stadt- und Befestigungsrechte durch den Kölner Erzbischof. Viele historische Gebäude mit ihrer Geschichte schmücken die Stadt Rheinberg. Im Herzen der Stadt liegt das Stammhaus der Familie Underberg. Rund um den Marktplatz entdecken Sie Bürgerhäuser aus dem 16. und 17. Jahrhundert. Lernen Sie die Sehenswürdigkeiten von Rheinberg bei einer geführten Tour kennen.

The former centre of duty and fortress town Rheinberg with its historic flair in the city centre received its town charter and the right to built fortifications already in 1233 by the Cologne archbishop. Even today many historic buildings create the unique, fascinating atmosphere of Rheinberg. In the heart of the town the main house of the Underberg family is situated. All around the market square you will find town houses from the 16th and 17th century. A guided tour will give you a detailed overview of the city's sights.

Schloss Leyenburg

Gastgeber/host: Inez van Tienhoven

Nordrhein-Westfalen

Vorbildlich restauriertes Rokokoschloss mit sehr persönlich geführtem Hotel und Beauty Day SPA, in bezauberndem Landschaftsgarten am Niederrhein.

Exemplary restored Rococo Castle and very personally managed hotel with a Beauty Day SPA, surrounded by a charming English landscape garden.

47509 Rheurdt
Nordrhein-Westfalen
Tel.: +49 2845 949921
Fax: +49 2845 949929
www.hotel-leyenburg.de
schloss@leyenburg.com

Hotel ★★★★

Inmitten der wundervollen Niederrheinischen Landschaft, umgeben von einem nach englischem Vorbild angelegten Schlosspark mit See und Wald, liegt Hotel & Spa Schloss Leyenburg. Das mit viel Liebe aufwändig restaurierte Schloss wurde 2004 mit dem Rheinischen Denkmalpreis ausgezeichnet. In der Gastronomie werden kleine hausgemachte Leckereien angeboten. Sei es der selbstgebackene Kuchen am Nachmittag, die Englische Teatime oder eine herzhafte Brotzeit am Abend. Die zehn Zimmer, in den Kategorien Classic und Deluxe, sind nach Blumen benannt und individuell eingerichtet. Stimmige Farben, handgearbeitete oder antike Möbel und auserlesene Stoffe vermitteln eine besondere Atmosphäre. Die edlen Deluxe-Zimmer bieten den Gästen mit ihren gemütlichen Sitzecken ausreichend Raum für gemütliche Stunden und die Muße zum Abschalten. Die Lounge mit Kamin oder die am Abend stimmungsvoll beleuchtete Terrasse laden dazu ein, bei einem Glas Wein den Abend zu genießen. Das Leyenburger Frühstück begeistert mit hausgemachten Marmeladen, ▸

In the middle of the beautiful lower Rhine countryside Leyenburg Castle Hotel & Spa is situated surrounded by an English landscape garden with a Lake and a private forest. The lavishly restored Castle was awarded the Rheinischen Denkmalpreis in 2004 for outstanding restauration. The kitchen offers small goodies, whether it is the homemade cakes for teatime or a hearty snack in the evening.

The ten rooms in the classic and deluxe categories are named after flowers and individually furnished. Consistent colours, hand-made or antique furniture and exquisite fabrics convey a special atmosphere. The noble Deluxe rooms provide guests with a cosy sitting areas and sufficient space for cosy hours and time to relax. The lounge with a fireplace or the, at night illumi- ▸

Angebot/facility

125-210 €

A/S 145-210 €

2-80

Aldekerk
8 km

Düsseldorf
34 km

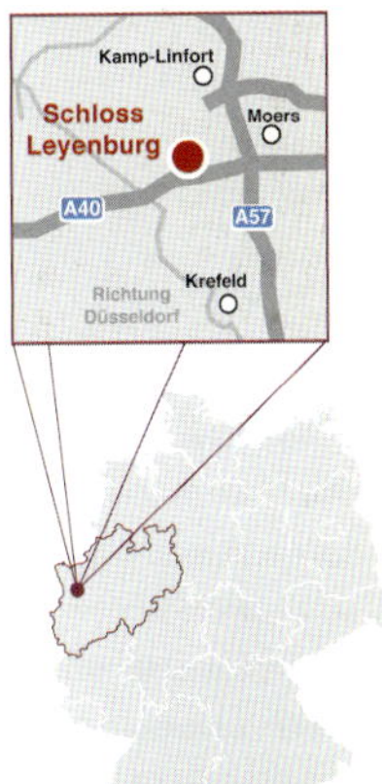

frischem Obst und köstlichen Produkten der Region. Das 2012 neu eröffnete Beauty Day Spa steht Hotel- und Tagesgästen zur Verfügung. Ob ganz für sich allein oder mit den Ihnen vertrauten Menschen: Hier finden Sie für ein paar Stunden den wohltuenden Raum zu nachhaltiger Entspannung.

Der Schlosspark steht ausschließlich den Gastgebern und ihren Gästen zur Verfügung. Die umliegenden Wälder oder der nahegelegene Oermter Berg laden zu Ausflügen in die Natur ein. Zu Fuß oder wenn Sie möchten auch mit dem Rad.

nated, terrace invite to enjoy the evening with a glass of wine.

Breakfast at the Leyenburg excites with homemade jams, fresh fruit and delicious regional products. The 2012 newly opened beauty day spa is available to hotel and day guests. Whether for you alone or with your family and friends: enjoy the soothing space for a few hours to find sustainable relaxation. The Park is exclusively reserved for for the hosts and their guests. The surrounding forests and the nearby Oermter mountain invite to excursions into the nature - walking or if wanted also by bike.

In der näheren Umgebung:

Wasserschloss Bloemersheim (1 km): eines der ältesten historischen Gebäude am Niederrhein; **Kloster Kamp (8 km):** 875 Jahre Geschichte und Tradition, Terrassengarten erinnert an französische Schlossgärten, Kräutergarten; **Duisburg- Landschaftspark Nord (20 km):** Ankerpunkt der „Europäischen Route Industriekultur.", Industriekultur, Natur und faszinierendes Lichtspektakel in weltweit einmaliger Parklandschaft; **Arcen (38 km):** Schlosspark mit Pflanzenhaus, Tiergehegen sowie spektakulären Minigolfplätzen

In the surrounding area:

Water castle Bloemersheim (0.6 miles): one of the oldest historic buildings at the Lower Rhine; **Kamp Abbey (5 miles):** 875 years of history and tradition, terraced gardens remind of French castle gardens, herb garden; **Duisburg-Landschaftspark Nord (12 miles):** anchor point of the "European Route of Industrial Heritage", Industrial Heritage, nature and fascinating light show in worldwide unique park landscape; **Arcen (24 miles):** Castle gardens with greenhouse, vivarium, and spectacular miniature golf courts

TIPP

Eingerahmt vom ausladenden Park und dem See wird das Verweilen auf Schloss Leyenburg zum naturverbundenen Vergnügen. Die weitläufige Schlossanlage mit dem barocken Rosengarten lädt ebenso wie die niederrheinische Landschaft zu ausgedehnten Spaziergängen und Radtouren ein. Der nahegelegene Golfplatz (6,5 km) bietet ausreichende Gelegenheit für sportliche Entspannung.

The extensive park and the adjacent lake will make your stay at Leyenburg Castle an experience close to nature. The large grounds of the castle with the Baroque Rose Garden and the landscape along the lower Rhine invite visitors to take long strolls or to go on cycle tours in the beautiful surroundings. The nearby golf court (4 miles) offers the possibility to relax and exercise.

Kunstsinn und Mäzenatentum

Appreciation of art and Patronage

Die Kunstsammlung Nordrhein-Westfalens am Grabbeplatz in Düsseldorf beeindruckt bereits mit ihrer imposanten Gebäudefassade.
The art collection North Rhine-Westphalia at the Grappeplatz in Düsseldorf fascinates already with its impressive façade.

großartige Kunstsammlungen am Niederrhein

Magnificent art collections on the Lower Rhine

Entlang der holländischen Grenze bis zum Ruhrgebiet gibt es zahlreiche über die Jahrhunderte gewachsene Kunstsammlungen, die von reichem Mäzenatentum und großbürgerlichem Kunstsinn zeugen.

In Düsseldorf haben sich zehn kleine Museen zu einem Projekt namens „Crossart" zusammengeschlossen. Den Schwerpunkt bildet hier die zeitgenössische Kunst, inspiriert von der Natur.

Auf Wasserburg Anholt ist die vermeintlich größte private Bildersammlung Nordrhein-Westfalens zu bewundern. Sie umfasst mehr als 700

Along the Dutch border down to the Ruhr district, one can find various art collections that have been extended over the centuries. They prove the wealthy Patronage and the appreciation of art among the upper middle-class.

In Duesseldorf ten smaller museums have formed the cooperation "Crossart". They have specialized on classic Modernism and contemporary art inapired by nature.

Anholt Moated Castle holds the biggest, historically grown private collection in North

Van de Velde Flügel des Skulpturenraumes im Kröller-Müller Museum.
Van de Velde wing of the sculpture room at Kröller-Müller museum.

Arbeiten europäischer Maler des 17. Jahrhunderts wie Rembrandt, Dolci, van Goyen, Rosa, ter Borch, Bruyn und Holbein. Auch Ausstellungen von wertvollen Kunstwerken aus Porzellan sowie Möbelstücke aus Barock und Renaissance können besichtigt werden.

Im Het Nationale Park De Hoge Veluwe, im nahen Holland, erwartet das Kröller-Müller-Museum mit seiner umfangreichen Werksammlung von van Gogh, Picasso, Léger, Mondrian und vielen anderen Künstlern der klassischen Moderne die Besucher.

Zum Museum gehört einer der größten Skulpturengärten der Welt. Er zeigt auf einer Fläche von 25 ha eine Vielzahl an Skulpturen namhafter Künstler des 20. Jahrhunderts.

Im Schloss Moyland wartet die ehemalige Privatsammlung der Brüder Franz Joseph und Hans

Rhine-Westphalia with over 700 impressive works by Dutch painters from the 17th century such as Rembrandt, Dolci, van Goyen, Rosa, ter Borch, Bruyn, and Holbein. Moreover, exhibitions with valuable art works made of porcelain or fascinating furniture from the Baroque and Renaissance era can be visited.

In the Het Nationale Park De Hoge Veluwe, which is located in nearby Holland, the Kröller-Müller museum offers visitors a unique collection of works by van Gogh, Picasso, Léger, Mondrian and many other artists of the classic Modernism. In its 62.5 acres sculpture garden, which belongs to the biggest of the world, the museum offers a wide range of sculptures created by various renowned artists of the 20th century.

Schloss Moyland beherbergt die weltweit größte Joseph-Beuys-Sammlung.
Moyland Castle hosts the world's greatest collection of works by Joseph Beuys.

van der Grinten, mit Ausstellungsstücken aus dem 19. und 20. Jahrhundert und dem weltweit größten Bestand an Arbeiten von Joseph Beuys auf. Ebenfalls hier untergebracht ist das Joseph Beuys Archiv, das auch als internationale Forschungseinrichtung dient und die weltweit größte Beuys-Sammlung beherbergt.

In den Kunstmuseen Haus Lange und Haus Esters in Krefeld mit einer Sammlung von über 14.000 Exponaten aus der frühen Neuzeit bis zur Gegenwartskunst kommen alle Kunstgeschmäcker auf ihre Kosten, wobei der Fokus auf Kunstschöpfungen ab 1945 liegt. Zu sehen sind nicht nur Werke der Malerei sondern auch Skulpturen, Neue Medien, Grafiken und Fotografien. Eine Vielzahl namhafter Meisterwerke, darunter von Beuys, Tingueley, Graham und Warhol sind hier zu sehen.

Xanten gilt als die Römer-, Dom- und Siegfriedstadt am Niederrhein. Besonders sehenswert ist

Another formerly private collection can be found in Moyland castle. The collection was set up by the two brothers Franz Joseph and Hans van der Grinten and includes exhibits from the 19th and 20th century as well as the world's greatest stock of works by Joseph Beuys. Furthermore, the Joseph Beuys archive is situated at the castle. It also serves as an international research institution and contains the world's greatest Beuys collection.

Xanten at the Lower Rhine is also known as Roman and Cathedral town or the town of Siegfried. Its Archaeological Park is especially worth a visit. The park is located on the grounds of the Roman city Colonia Ulpia Traiana and exhibits various reconstructed buildings from Roman times.

In Duisburg you can become witness to the impressive revival of the city centre's old harbour:

Symbol römischer Macht und Kultur: Die Stadtmauer im Archäologischen Park Xanten.
Symbol of Roman power and culture: The town wall at the Archaeological Park Xanten.

der archäologische Park auf dem Gelände der Römerstadt Colonia Ulpia Traiana mit zahlreichen rekonstruierten Bauten aus der Römerzeit. Die beeindruckende Wiederbelebung eines alten Innenstadthafens ist in Duisburg zu erleben: der Land Art Künstler Dani Karavan legte einen Stadtpark – den „Garten der Erinnerung" - an, der in puncto Innovation und Einfallsreichtum seinesgleichen sucht: Der Bildhauer arbeitete Überbleibsel der alten Bebauung wie Lagerhallen geschickt mit ein und zeigte so facettenreiche Möglichkeiten für die Verwendung der alten Gebäude auf. Über Projekte zeitgenössischer Kunst können Besucher sich im Haus Trinks (ebenfalls im Innenhafen gelegen) informieren. Sehenswert sind außerdem die erste bewegliche Hängebrücke der Welt, das Museum Küppersmühle

The Land Art artist Dani Karavan created a city park - the "garden of memory" - that impresses in terms of innovation and ingenuity: The artist integrated old remains of the former buildings as for instance store halls into his designs and thus shows the multiple possibilities of using the old buildings. At the House Trinks which is situated at the inner harbour of Duisburg visitors will find a range of projects on contemporary art. The world's first mobile suspension bridge and the museum Küppers mill, which includes exhibits by important post-war artists from the collection of the entrepreneur Hans Grothe are well worth a visit. Moreover the museum of the Wilhelm Lehmbruck Foundation, which is renowned across bor-

Die erste bewegliche Hängebrücke der Welt im Duisburger Innenhafen wurde von Jörg Schlaich entworfen.
The world's first mobile suspension bridge designed by Jörg Schlaich is situated at the harbour of Duisburg.

mit Exponaten bedeutender Nachkriegskünstler aus der Sammlung des Unternehmers Hans Grothe und das über die Grenzen hinweg bekannte Museum der Stiftung Wilhelm Lehmbruck, das über eine exzeptionelle Sammlung internationaler Kunstwerke verfügt. Dem deutschen Expressionismus und dem Werk des Bildhauers Wilhelm Lehmbruck (1881-1919) wird eine besondere Aufmerksamkeit gewidmet. Die umfangreiche Sammlung umfasst Skulpturen, Plastiken, Gemälde, Pastelle, Zeichnungen und Druckgrafiken des Bildhauers der Klassischen Moderne. Liebhabern deutscher Malerei des späten 19. und 20. Jahrhunderts wird eine große Sammlung von Exponaten geboten, darunter von dem Brücke-Künstler Ernst Ludwig Kirchner oder Karl Schmidt-Rottluff, Erich Heckel, Otto

ders, offers a wide ranging collection of international art. The Foundation's focus is set on paintings from German Expressionism as well as on works by sculptor Wilhelm Lehmbruck (1881-1919). The collection holds sculptures, drawings, paintings, pastel drawings and prints by Lehmbruck from classic Modernism. Furthermore, the museum exhibits a collection of German paintings from the late 19th and 20th century, such as paintings by the bridge-artists Ernst Ludwig Kirchner, Karl Schmidt-Rottluff, Erich Heckel, Otto Mueller and Max Pechstein as well as many other paintings by artists such as Feininger from Expressionism, Cubism, Surrealism or Bauhaus art. The museum is situated in the city centre of Duis-

Grün angestrahlt leuchtet "Das Krokodil", ein ehemaliger Kran, im Landschaftspark Duisburg-Nord.
The "crocodile", a former tower crane, glows as it is illuminated with green floodlights in the country park Duisburg-Nord.

Zollverein

Mueller und Max Pechstein. Auch Meisterwerke bedeutender Künstler wie Feininger aus dem Expressionismus, Kubismus, Surrealismus und der Bauhaus-Kunst sind im Museum zu sehen. Das Museum liegt im Stadtzentrum Duisburgs, umgeben vom Immanuel-Kant-Park, der als öffentlicher Skulpturengarten mit über 40 Freiluftskulpturen angelegt ist. Hier ist ein weiteres Meisterwerk eines deutschen Künstlers zu begutachten: Der Düsseldorfer Künstler Hans-Peter Feldmann schuf eine aus Epoxidharz mit kräftigen Farben bemalte Nachbildung der berühmten David-Skulptur von Michelangelo. Das eindrucksvolle Kunstwerk, das in grellem Rosa und Gelb schon von weitem farbenfroh leuchtet, ist mit einer Höhe von 9 m ein wahrer Blickfang, der einen Besuch des Immanuel-Kant-Parks zu einem Muss macht.

Auch Essen ist für Kunstinteressierte eine Reise wert. Hier erwartet das Deutsche Plakat Museum seine Gäste. Eine Sammlung mit über 340.000 Exponaten illustriert die Geschichte des Plakats. Im Museum Folkwang gibt es eine umfangreiche Sammlung deutscher und französischer Malerei sowie Skulpturen aus dem 19. und 20. Jahrhundert, u. a. sind Werke von Caspar David Friedrich, Corot, Monet, Manet, van Gogh, Matisse, Pollock, Rothko und Baselitz zu bewundern. Das Museum gilt als eines der renommiertesten Kunstmuseen in Deutschland. Doch nicht nur die Ausstellungen tragen zur Besonderheit dieses Museums bei. Das Gebäude wurde von David Chipperfield Architects, der von der Stadt Essen als Sieger des internationalen

burg, surrounded by Immanuel-Kant Park, which is a public sculpture garden and holds over 40 open air sculptures and another work of a German artist that is worth seeing: The artist Hans-Peter Feldmann from Duesseldorf created a copy of the famous David syulpture by Michelangelo. Feldmann's 9.8 yards high sculpture is made of epoxy resin and painted in strong colours – the bright pink and yellow will catch your eye already from afar and make your visit of Immanuel-Kant Park an unforgettable experience.

Essen is another hotspot for art lovers and well worth a visit. The city`s German Poster Museum holds a collection of over 340.000 exhibits and illustrates the history of the poster. The Folkwang Museum offers an extensive collection of German and French paintings as well as of sculptures from the 19th and 20th century by artists such as Caspar David Friedrich, Corot, Monet, Manet, van Gogh, Matisse, Pollock, Rothko and Baselitz. The museum belongs to the most renowned art museums of Germany. But it is not only its exhibitions that make this museum a special tourist attraction: The building itself was designed by David Chipperfield Architects who was chosen as winner of the international architecture competition by the town Essen. The fascinating design of the museum has created a building with an open, transparent character by use of enormous windows and backyards. Moreover Essen offers the

Das UNESCO Weltkulturerbe und Industriedenkmal Zeche Zollverein in Essen ist einer der Ankerpunkte der Europäischen Route der Industriekultur.
The UNESCO world heritage and industry memorial Zeche (colliery) Zollverein in Essen is one of the central points of the European route of industrial culture.

Architekturwettbewerbs gekürt wurde, entworfen und erhält durch große Fenster und Hinterhöfe die Transparenz des Museums. Zudem gibt es eine öffentlich zugängliche Bibliothek, die Literatur zur Kunst des 20. und 21. Jahrhunderts anbietet. Auch die Villa Hügel, das ehemalige Wohnhaus der Industriellen-Familie Krupp am Baldeneisee, ist als Gebäude ebenso sehenswert, wie die dort bereits seit 1953 stattfindenden Ausstellungen von internationalem Rang.

Ein besonderes Kleinod ist das Weltkulturerbe Zeche Zollverein. Die zur Europäischen Route der Industriekultur zählende Schachtanlage ist ein UNESCO Welterbe von internationaler Bedeutung. Im alten Kesselhaus auf dem Gelände von

possibility to visit a library that holds literature and art from the 20th and 21st century.

The Villa Huegel, too, is well worth seeing as it was the former home of the industrialist family Krupp at the Essener Lake Baldenei and hosts an internationally renowned exhibition since 1953.

A special gem is the world heritage site Zeche Zollverein. The mine that belongs to the European route of industrial culture is a UNSESO world heritage site of international importance. The red dot design museum is located here and a unique exhibition on industrial design in the old halls of the coking

Der Kunstpalast in Düsseldorf lockt zahlreiche Besucher mit seiner Skulptur- und Gemäldesammlung.
The Art Palace in Düsseldorf impresses its visitors with a collection of sculptures and paintings.

Schacht XII finden Besucher hier das red dot design museum. In den Hallen und Anlagen der Zeche bieten Führungen zur Bergbaugeschichte den Rahmen für bleibende Erlebnisse.

Eine herausragende Sammlung von atemberaubenden Arbeiten des 20. und 21. Jahrhunderts von Künstlern wie Picasso, Matisse, Pollock oder Kandinsky gibt es in der Kunstsammlung Nordrhein-Westfalen in Düsseldorf zu bewundern. Neben diesen Schmuckstücken der Kunst reicht der Bestand der umfassenden Sammlung von Werken des Expressionismus über solche der Klassischen Moderne bis hin zum Fauvismus. Auch Exponate des Surrealismus von Miró, Magritte und Dalí sowie Gemälde von Dopo de

plant will delight its visitors. Furthermore, guided tours on the history of the mining industry are offered.

The art collection North Rhine- Westphalia, situated in Duesseldorf, holds a range of highlights for its visitor such as an impressive collection of fascinating works by artists from the 20th and 21st century such as Picasso, Matisse, Pollock or Kandinsky. Apart from these exhibits that have become true icons of art, one will find many other outstanding works ranging from German Expressionism, classic Modernism to Fauvism. Moreover, visitors can marvel at exhibits from Surrealis by Miró, Magritte and Dali as

Abstrakte Skulpturen findet man im Garten des städtischen Museums Abteiberg, Mönchengladbach.
Abstract sculptures are presented in the garden of the city Museum Abteiberg, Mönchengladbach.

Chirico, einem der wohl wichtigsten Vertreter der Pittura Metafisica, hat die Sammlung vorzuweisen, die sogar mit 80 Werken Beuys, darunter Vitrinen, Installationen und Zeichnungen aufwarten kann. Mit seinen drei Standorten ist die Kunstsammlung in der ganzen Stadt verteilt. Die bereits seit einem halben Jahrhundert bestehende Sammlung punktet mit einer außerordentlich guten Qualität seiner Ausstellungsstücke und wird von vielen Deutschen als Lieblingsgalerie gehandelt.

Ein weiteres Museum, das ebenfalls eine hervorragende Kunstsammlung des 20. und 21. Jahrhunderts vorzuweisen hat, ist das Städtische Museum Abteiberg in Mönchengladbach. Der Fokus liegt hier auf Arbeiten der Bildenden Kunst des 20. und 21. Jahrhunderts. Es präsentiert u.a. Kunstwerke des Expressionismus, Dadaismus, Konstruktivismus, Pop Art sowie des Nouveau Réalisme und abstrakter Kunst. Werke von Künstlern wie Andy Warhol, Gerhard Richter, Martin Oehlen, Ulrich Rückriem, Sigmar Polke, Heinz Mack, Gregor Schneider u.v.a. sind hier in einem Bau zu bewundern, der selbst ein eigenes Meisterwerk darstellt.

Die Sammlung des Museums im Kunstpalast in Düsseldorf umfasst Skulpturen und Gemälde vom Mittelalter bis zur Gegenwart. Daneben sind Spezialsammlungen zu Kunstgewerbe, Kunsthandwerk und Design, Graphik sowie eine bedeutende Glassammlung zu sehen. Die drei Schwerpunkte der Gemäldesammlung des Museums sind die Moderne und Alte Malerei sowie die Malerei des 19. Jahrhunderts, wobei man hier der Düsseldorfer Malerschule besondere

well as at paintings by Dopo de Chirico, one of the most important representatives of Pitture Metafisica. The collection also contains 80 works by Beuys, including cabinets, installations and drawings. Kept at three different locations in Duesseldorf, the art collection, which exists for 50 years, is spread over the whole of Duesseldorf and impresses its visitors with the extraordinary quality of its exhibits. Thus it is regarded as the Germans' favourite art gallery.

The city Museum Abteiberg in Mönchengladbach has exhibitions on visual arts from the 20th and 21st century. Presented are, e.g. art works from Expressionism, Dadaism, Constructivism, Pop Art as well as from Nouveau Réalisme and abstract art. In a building that already is a masterpiece by itself visitors can admire works by Andy Warhol, Gerhard Richter, Martin Oehlen, Ulrich Rückriem, Sigmar Polke, Heinz Mack, Gregor Schneider and many more.

The collection of the Art Palace in Düsseldorf holds sculptures and paintings from the Middle Ages up until today. Furthermore, the museum offers a variety of special collections on arts and crafts, design, graphics and an important glass collection. The focus of the paint collection is set on Modernism and Old Paintings, as well as paintings from the 19th century, the latter specialised on the Duesseldorfer School of Painting. The art of the 20th century and contemporary art are combined in the modern department. Among paintings, it also

Aufmerksamkeit widmet. Die Kunst des 20. Jahrhunderts und die zeitgenössische Kunst sind in der modernen Abteilung zusammengefasst. Neben Gemälden werden hier auch Skulpturen und die Objektkunst Neue Medien gesammelt. Der Kunstpalast befindet sich im Gebiet des heutigen Rheinparks Golzheim parallel zum Rhein.

Neben einer vielseitigen und facettenreichen Museumslandschaft mit bedeutenden Kunstsammlungen bietet die Gegend am Niederrhein und das dem Strukturwandel unterworfene westliche Ruhrgebiet natürlich auch zahlreiche Möglichkeiten genussvoller Einkehr, zum kurzweiligen Einkauf sowie mit Musicals, Theatern und Konzertbühnen zur Unterhaltung oder zur sportlichen Betätigung.

contains sculptures and object art New Media. The Art Palace is located in today's Rhine Park Golzheim parallel to the river Rhine.

The area along the Lower Rhine and the western Ruhr district, which is influenced by structural change, does not only offer a diverse museum landscape with important art collections. Visitors will also find a variety of culinary restaurants, shops and also many theatres, musicals and concert halls for entertainment or sports.

Das "Galeriebild um 1640" ist nur eines von über 700 imposanten Werken, die auf Wasserburg Anholt ausgestellt werden.
The "Gallery painting around 1640" belongs to a total of over 700 impressive works that are exhibited at Anholt Moated Castle.

Burghotel Schnellenberg

Gastgeber/host: Stephan und Thomas Bilsing

Nordrhein-Westfalen

Gepflegte Burganlage im Besitz der Familie von Fürstenberg über den grünen Hügeln des Sauerlandes.

Well-tended castle and grounds in the possession of the von Fürstenberg family, gently nestled in the green hills of the Sauerland region.

Schnellenberg 1
57439 Attendorn
Nordrhein-Westfalen
Tel: +49 2722 6940
Fax: +49 2722 694169
www.burg-schnellenberg.de
info@burg-schnellenberg.de

Hotel ★★★★
Restaurant ★★★★

Komfortable, stilvoll eingerichtete Zimmer heißen die Gäste auf Burg Schnellenberg willkommen. Das elegante Restaurant im Gobelinsaal, der rustikale Rittersaal mit Kamin sowie die Bar im Wappenkeller mit der Terrasse im Innenhof und Blick auf Attendorn bieten eine vielseitige Küche und einen gut sortierten Weinkeller. Die wunderschöne Renaissancekapelle aus dem 16. Jahrhundert und ein Standesamt ermöglichen Hochzeiten, Taufen und Festlichkeiten jeder Art.

Über den grünen Hügeln des Sauerlands thront die im Jahre 1222 erstmals urkundlich erwähnte Burg Schnellenberg. Die hoch aufragenden Wachtürme, das mächtige steinerne Torgewölbe, die schweren eisenbeschlagenen Türen und die Schatzkammer mit mittelalterlichen ▸

Comfortable, stylishly furnished rooms welcome the guests to Schnellenberg Castle. The elegant restaurant in the Gobelin Hall, the rustic Knights Hall with fireplace, as well as the bar in the coat of arms cellar with the terrace in the inner courtyard and view over Attendorn, all offer a versatile cuisine and a wellassorted wine cellar. The beautiful Renaissance Chapel from the 16th century with the registry office enable weddings, baptisms and festivities of every kind to take place here.

The Schnellenberg Castle, mentioned in records for the first time in 1222, reigns over the green hills of the Sauerland region. The past is still to be seen represented today by the high rising watch towers, the powerful stone archways, the heavy iron-fitted doors and the treasure chamber with medieval objects of interest. In 1594 the ▸

Angebot/facility

95-165 €

125-220 €

A/S 220 €

1-120

Attendorn 5 km

Dortmund 70 km
Köln 90 km

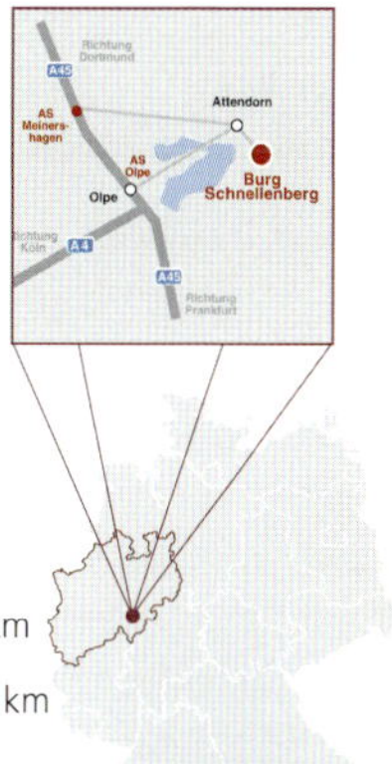

Sehenswürdigkeiten lassen noch heute die Vergangenheit erkennen. 1594 ging die Burg mit allem Grundbesitz an Caspar von Fürstenberg über und ist seitdem im Besitz der Familie. Hier findet der Besucher Gastlichkeit mit jahrhundertealter Tradition vor und wird bereits am oberen Torweg mit dem in grauen Sandstein gemeißelten Spruch „Foris non maneat peregrinus. Ostium meum pateat viatori! ("Draußen nicht bleibe der Fremdling") begrüßt.

castle with its whole estate became the property of Caspar of Fuerstenberg and has since then been owned by the family. Here the visitor can find hospitality with centuries old of tradition and is greeted at the upper gateway by the following dictum chiselled in grey sandstone: "Foris non maneat peregrinus. Ostium meum pateat viatori! Stranger do not stay outside. My door is open to the traveller!"

In der näheren Umgebung:

Attendorn (3 km): Hansestadt mit Rathaus aus dem 14. Jahrhundert, Sauerländer Dom mit mehr als 900 Jahren Geschichte, Südsauerlandmuseum, Atta-Tropfsteinhöhle; **Biggesee (6 km):** Westfalens größte Talsperre, Wassersport, Ausflugsfahrt mit der Weißen Flotte; **Elspe (18 km):** Karl-May-Festspiele (www.elspe.de); **Kirchhundem (25 km):** Panoramapark am Rothaarsteig: 80.000 qm großer Freizeitpark.

In the surrounding area:

Attendorn (2 miles): Hanseatic town with town hall dating from the 14th century, Sauerland Cathedral with more than 900 years of history, South Sauerland Museum, Atta stalactite cave; **Bigge Lake (4 miles):** Westphalia's largest dam, water sports, trip on the 'Weiße Flotte' boat; **Elspe (11 miles):** Karl May festivals (www.elspe.de); **Kirchhundem (15 miles):** nice Panorama park at the Rothaarsteig: 95680 sq yards recreational park.

TIPP

Wer seine Hochzeit auf einer Burg feiern möchte, findet auf Burg Schnellenberg dafür die besten Voraussetzungen: vom Standesamt im Kreuzgewölbe der Schatzkammer, über die Sonnenterrasse vor dem Wappenkeller bis zu den stilvollen Turm-, Jagd- oder Fürstenbergzimmern, einem einzigartigen Ambiente und komfortablen Übernachtungsmöglichkeiten. Ein besonderes Highlight für kirchliche Trauungen ist die private Renaissance-Kapelle des Caspar von Fürstenberg aus dem Jahr 1600 mit ihrer einzigartigen, vollständig im Originalzustand erhaltenen Innenausstattung im Stile des Manierismus.

If you would like to celebrate your wedding in a castle Burg Schnellenberg offers you the best conditions: A registry office in the cross vault of the treasure Chamber, the sun terrace in front of the coat of arms cellar, the stylish Tower-, hunting- or Fürstenberg rooms, all offer a unique atmosphere and comfortable accommodation. A special highlight for church weddings is the private Renaissance Chapel of Caspar von Fürstenberg, built in 1600, with its unique fully preserved interior in the Mannerism style.

Haus Brückhausen

Gastgeber/hosts: Freifrau Franziska von Twickel, Freiherr Franz von Twickel

Malerisches Herrenhaus, eingerahmt von einer Gräfte, inmitten der münsterländischen Parklandschaft.

Picturesque manor house surrounded by a moat, situated in the centre of the "Münsterland" parkland.

Holling 6
48351 Everswinkel-Alverskirchen
Nordrhein-Westfalen
Tel.: +49 2582 277
twickel-brueckhausen@t-online.de

Hotel ★★★★

Unweit von Alverskirchen liegt Haus Brückhausen, über Jahrhunderte hinweg ein einflussreicher Herrensitz der Region. Im Rahmen mehrerer Umbauten - Anfang des 17. und Anfang des 18. Jahrhunderts - entstand das heute noch erhaltene mehrgeschossige Herrenhaus aus Backstein. Besonderes Prunkstück ist der große Saal mit seiner Balkenstuckdecke von 1620.
1363 wurde Haus Brückhausen erstmals urkundlich in einem Kaufvertrag erwähnt. Anfang des 17. Jahrhunderts benötigte der damalige Besitzer, Freiherr Caspar von Höfflinger, einen seiner Stellung als Landrentmeister angemessenen Wohnsitz und baute das Haus zum repräsentativen Herrensitz aus mit einer Gräfte um Haus und Wirtschaftshof. Charakteristisch sind die hohen Giebel mit Firststufen, die an ▸

Not far from Alverskirchen House Brückhausen is situated - for many centuries an important manor estate of the region. In the course of many reconstructions between the 17th and 18th century the present manor house, which is multistoried and made of brick, evolved. An especially precious part of the building is the great hall with its beamed stucco ceiling from 1620.
In 1363 house Brückhausen was first mentioned in written documents in form of a bill of sale. In the early 17th century Baron Caspar von Höfflinger, who then owned the manor, needed a residence that was appropriate for his position as a state bursar and reconstructed the estate so that it became a representative manor house with a moat surrounding the house and the stables. Characteristic are its high gables with roof ridge steps that are decorated with semi-circled ▸

Angebot/facility

110-130 €

Münster 18 km
Hamm 25 km

Münster / Osnabrück 40 km
Dortmund 45 km
Düsseldorf 100 km

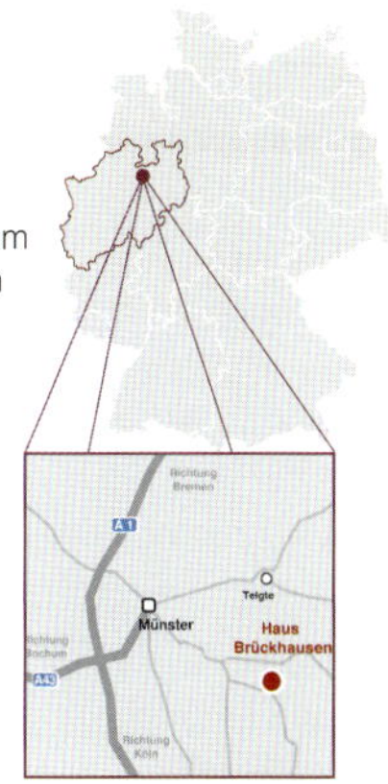

der Nordseite mit Halbkreisaufsätzen und an der Südseite mit Dreieckaufsätzen verziert sind. Die Sandsteinlaibungen der Fenster geben dem Haus in Kombination mit dem roten Backstein das typische Bild eines westfälischen Herrenhauses.

Heute wird Brückhausen von Franz Freiherr von Twickel und seiner Familie bewohnt und landwirtschaftlich bewirtschaftet. 2008 wurden großzügige Gästezimmer ausgebaut.

Hausgäste erhalten ein reichhaltiges Frühstück mit Spezialitäten aus der Region am Kamin oder im Garten. Nach einem Ausflug erwartet sie ein Tee oder Kaffee, bevor der Tag bei einem Glas Wein am offenen Feuer ausklingen kann. Neben den Gästezimmern stehen den Gästen das Kamin- und das Musikzimmer zur Verfügung. Im Haus Brückhausen fühlt man sich ganz wie zu Hause!

Die zentrale Lage in der münsterländischen Parklandschaft bietet vielfältige Möglichkeiten für kulturell interessante Ausflüge.

top parts on the northern side of the building and with triangle top parts on the southern side. The sandstone embrasure of the windows combined with the red bricks of the manor house compose the typical image of a Westphalian mansion.

Today, Brückhausen manor is inhabited by Baron Franz von Twickel and his family who also use the land for agricultural purposes. In 2008 spacious guestrooms were constructed.

Guests of the manor house will be served a rich breakfast including local specialities next to the fireplace or outside in the garden. Having returned from a trip, you may enjoy a cup of tea or coffee before the evening comes to its end with a glass of wine next to the open fire place. Apart from the guestrooms, visitors can also enjoy the manor's magnificent atmosphere in the fireplace room and the music room. At House Brückhausen you will feel at home immediately!

The manor's central location in the parkland of the "Münsterland" region offers various possibilities to go on culturally interesting trips.

In der näheren Umgebung:

Münster (15 km): Stadt des Westfälischen Friedens (im Rathaus wurde 1647 der Dreißigjährige Krieg beendet), Dom, Picasso-Museum, Westf.-Landesmuseum, Lambertikirche mit Wiedertäuferkäfigen; Studentenflair mit urigen Kneipen und buntem Straßentreiben; **Warendorf (15 km):** Bundesgestüt, Bundeschampionate Reiten, Hengstparaden; **Schloss Nordkirchen (40 km):** Barockes Wasserschloss (westfälisches Versailles).

In the surrounding area:

Münster (9 miles): city of the Westphalian Peace (in the town hall the Thirty Years War was ended in 1647), cathedral, Picasso museum, Westphalian State museum, Lamberti church with rechristen cages ("Wiedertäuferkäfige"), student atmosphere with rustic pubs and vibrant street flair; **Warendorf (9 miles):** federal stud, federal riding championships, stallion parades; **Schloss Neukirchen (25 miles):** Baroque moated Neukirchen Castle (Westphalian Versailles).

TIPP

Haus Rüschhaus

Das Wohnhaus und die Schreibstube Annette von Droste-Hülshoffs wurde in der Zeit von 1745 bis 1748 nach Entwürfen von Johann Conrad Schlaun als Sommersitz gebaut. Ihm gelang eine Synthese aus einem westfälischem Bauernhof und einem anspruchsvollem Landsitz in französischem Stil. Annette von Droste-Hülshoff zog 1826 zusammen mit ihrer Mutter und ihrer Schwester Jenny ein und schrieb ihre berühmten Balladen und Vers-Epen sowie „Die Judenbuche".

Das seit 1936 existierende Rüschhaus-Museum kann nur im Rahmen einer Führung besichtigt werden. An Montagen bleibt das Museum komplett geschlossen. Der französische Barockgarten ist jedoch jederzeit für Besucher öffentlich zugänglich.

House Rüschhaus

The former home and study of Annette von Droste-Hülshoff was built from 1745 until 1748 after the drafts by Johann Conrad Schlaun as a summer residence. Schlaun succeeded in creating a synthesis between a Westphalian farm house and a noble country residence in French style. In 1826, Annette von Droste-Hülshoff moved into the house together with her mother and sister Jenny. Here, she wrote her famous ballads and epic poems such as "Die Jugendbuche".

The Rüschhaus museum, existing since 1936, is only open to public during guided tours except on Monday where the whole museum is closed. The French Baroque garden can be visited at any time.

Burghotel auf Schönburg

Gastgeber/host: Barbara und Wolfgang Hüttl

Rheinland-Pfalz

Ehemals bedeutende mittelalterliche Burganlage des Schönburger Adelsgeschlechts, heute romantisches Burghotel mit Blick über den Rhein.

Once an important medieval castle complex belonging to the House of Schoenburg today it is a romantic castle hotel with magnificent views over the river Rhine.

55430 Oberwesel
Rheinland-Pfalz
Tel: +49 6744 93930
Fax: +49 6744 1613
www.hotel-schoenburg.com
huettl@hotel-schoenburg.com

Hotel ★★★★★
Restaurant ★★★★★

Hoch oben auf einem Felsen, mit Blick über den Rhein, befindet sich dieses romantische Hotel in der 1.000-jährigen Schönburg. Geschichte und zeitgemäßer Komfort gehen hier eine harmonische Verbindung ein. Zauberhafte Zimmer mit Himmelbetten, stilvollen Bädern und liebevollen Details laden den Gast zum genussvollen Verweilen ein. Feinschmeckermenüs werden vom Servicepersonal

entweder im gemütlichen Restaurant oder auf der Rheinterrasse serviert.

Erstmalig erwähnt wurde die Burg 1149, wobei jedoch davon auszugehen ist, dass der Bau wesentlich früher entstand. Im 14. Jahrhundert lebten auf der Ganerbenburg gleichzeitig etwa 250 Nachkommen aus dem ▸

High up on a rock formation this romantic hotel is housed in 1.000 year old Schoenburg Castle with a view over the river Rhine. Here history and modern comfort are combined in harmonious connection. Enchanting rooms with four poster beds, stylish bathrooms and loving detail invite the guests to a highly enjoyable stay. Gourmet menus are served either in the cosy restaurant or on the Rhine terrace.

The castle was first mentioned in 1149, however it is to be assumed that the building was established a good deal earlier. At one point ▸

Angebot/facility

120-170 €

220-340 €

A/S 330-360 €

Mitte Januar bis Mitte März

Oberwesel 2 km

Frankfurt/ Main 80 km

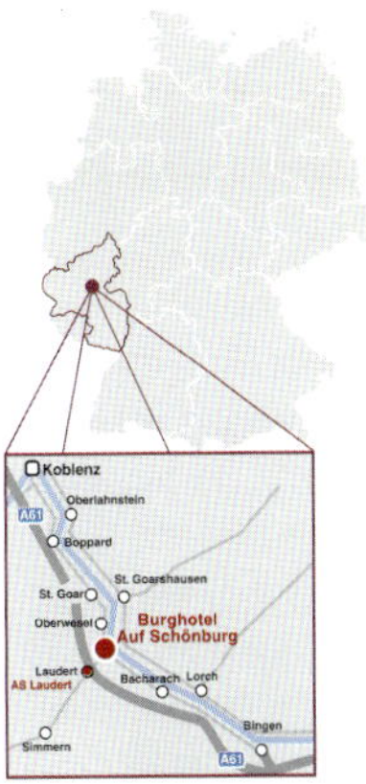

Geschlecht der Schönburger, da alle Burggrafensöhne erbberechtigt waren. Der letzte Schönburger erwarb als französischer General im 17. Jahrhundert viel Ruhm, bevor die Burg 1689 von den Truppen Ludwigs XIV. niedergebrannt wurde. Ab 1885 restaurierte der Bankier Rhinelander, ein einflussreicher Deutsch-Amerikaner, große Teile der Burg. Seit 1957 besitzt Familie Hüttl das Anwesen. Seitdem wurden die Restaurierungen kontinuierlich fortgesetzt und ein Burghotel geschaffen.

during the 14th century about 250 descendants from the House of Schoenburg lived in Ganerben Castle, since all the sons of the burgrave were entitled to inherit. The last of the Schoenburgs acquired much fame as a French general in the 17th century, before the castle was burned down in 1689 by the troops of Ludwig XIV. In 1885 the influential German American banker Rhinelander, restored large parts of the castle. Since 1957 the Huettl family has owned the estate. Since then the restorations were continued and a castle hotel was established.

In der näheren Umgebung:

Oberwesel: mittelalterliche Stadt inklusive Wehrtürmen, Stadtmauern; im Kulturhaus wechselnde Kunstausstellungen und Veranstaltungen; **Bacharach (5km):** mittelalterliches Städtchen; **Loreley (5km)**: sagenumwobener Felsen mit der Geschichte vom schönen Mädchen, das durch seinen betörenden Gesang und seine fesselnde Schönheit die Schiffer in den Tod trieb (Besucherzentrum).

In the surrounding area:

Oberwesel: medieval town with defence towers, town walls; in the cultural centre there are changing art exhibitions and events; **Bacharach (3 miles)**: small medieval town; **Loreley (3 miles)**: legendary rock with the story of the beautiful girl, who with her enticing singing and her binding beauty led the skippers to their death (Visitor centre).

TIPP

Mit dem 2012 eröffneten hauseigenen Burggarten, den nur die Hausgäste exklusiv mit ihrem Zimmerschlüssel für sich erschließen können, gewinnt das Entspannen auf Schönburg noch eine erweiterte Dimension. In mehrjähriger Arbeit entstand rund um den Burgberg ein einmaliger Landschaftsgarten mit Fischteich, Baumhaus und Weingarten sowie weiteren Attraktionen. Eine Park-Bibliothek lädt – Rheinblick eingeschlossen - zum Schmökern ein. Ein gläsernes Gartenhaus bietet auch bei bedeckter Wetterlage Schutz und Ausblick auf das historische Oberwesel; die überdachte Billard-Terrasse verheißt ein Frischluftmatch mit Landschaftsfaktor 1A.

The Schönburg Castle garden, which was opened in 2012, is exclusively reserved for guests. They can enter the garden via the use of their hotel room key and will encounter a new dimension of relaxation at Schönburg Castle here. Throughout several years of work a unique landscape garden with fish pond, tree house and vineyard as well as many other attractions have been constructed around the Castle hill. A park library invites you to browse through books while enjoying a beautiful view of the river Rhine. A summer house made of glass provides protection during cloudy weather and offers a view of the historic Oberwesel; at the roofed Billard-terrace you can enjoy an open-air match in fascinating surroundings.

Romantischer Rheinblick von der Burg Sooneck auf das gegenüberliegende Örtchen Lorch.
Romantic view of the river Rhine from Sooneck Castle to the little town Lorch on the other side of the river.

Romantik am Mittelrhein

Romanticism on the Middle Rhine

Mittelalterliche Burgen und herrschaftliche Schlösser, historische Fachwerkstädtchen, Weinberge an steilen Hängen, dazwischen schroffe Felsen und verschlungene Pfade: die romantische Landschaft entlang des Rheins verzaubert seit Jahrhunderten Besucher und Durchreisende.

Schon seit langer Zeit hat das Mittelrheintal eine große Bedeutung als Verkehrsweg zwischen dem Norden Europas und der Mittelmeerregion. Bereits seit zwei Jahrtausenden nutzen Reisende wie Händler oder Pilger das enge Rheintal als schnelle Route, um von Frankfurt oder Mainz Köln zu erreichen. Anfangs konnte man sich für die urwüchsige, gefahrvolle

Medieval castles and grand mansions, historic towns with timber-framed houses, vineyards on steep hills and between them rough rocks and entwined trails: the romantic landscape along the river Rhine has been fascinating its visitors and travellers for centuries and still captivates them today.

For a long time, the Middle Rhine valley has been one of the most important traffic routes for the cultural exchange between the Mediterranean and Northern Europe. For one bimillenary, travellers such as merchants, business men and pilgrims take the short route through the narrow Rhine valley to get from Frankfurt or Mainz to Cologne. However, in

Auf Raddampfer Goethe lässt sich die malerische Landschaft auch vom Wasser aus genießen.
On the paddle steamer Goethe you can enjoy the picturesque landscape from the water.

Landschaft mit ihren scharfen Felsenriffen allerdings nur wenig begeistern, erschien sie doch als wild und zerklüftet, mit scharfen Felsen und tückischen Untiefen im Flussbett, die nach einer guten Portion Glück verlangten, um heil umschifft zu werden. Doch zu Beginn des 19. Jahrhunderts, in der Epoche der Romantik, entwickelte sich ein neues Bild von der Natur, das den bis dahin gültigen Schönheitsidealen widersprach. Das Mittelrheintal entwickelte sich von einer Durchreisestation auf der damals typischen Bildungsreise nach Italien zum touristischen Hauptziel.

Die beginnende Industrialisierung mit ihren Begleiterscheinungen wie Verstädterung, Landflucht, der Wechsel der Selbstversorgungs- zur

the beginning people were not too passionate about the panorama of the untouched, dangerous landscape. The scenery appeared rather wild and abandoned, with its sharp rocks and treacherous shoals in the riverbed, which took a good bit of luck to be avoided. But in the early 19th century, in the era of Romanticism, a new image of nature evolved that was equivalent to the current ideal of beauty at that time. The valley, previously just a stop for bypassing travellers on their then common educational journeys to Italy, developed into a touristic main destination.

The beginnings of Industrialisation with its side effects such as urbanisation, emigration to the cities and the change from self-supply

Blick auf Kaub mit der als Zollwache errichteten Pfalzgrafenburg rechts im Bild.
View of Kaub with Pfalzgrafenburg Castle (on the right), which was constructed to control the duty on the river.

Fremdversorgungsgesellschaft usw. bewegte zu Beginn des 19. Jahrhunderts vor allem Schriftsteller und Künstler zur Hinwendung zu Natur und Vergangenheit.

Das Jahr 1802, in dem der Philosoph und Schriftsteller Friedrich Schlegel auf dem Weg nach Frankreich das Rheintal durchquerte, kann als das Geburtsjahr der Rheinromantik betrachtet werden. Schlegel lobte das Rheintal mit seinen Ruinen und Burgen für seine Wildheit und sein raues Erscheinungsbild. Damit sprach er ein Landschaftsideal aus, das sich von der vorherrschenden Ästhetik absetzte.

Während man im Zeitalter des Barocks noch nach süßer Idylle suchte, genossen die Romantiker lieber eine reine Natur und historische

to external-supply society gave the impulse for many writers and artists to shift their attention towards nature and past in the early 19th century.

In 1802, the philosopher and writer Friedrich Schlegel passed through the Rhine valley on his way to France. This date remains in our memory as the year of birth of the Rhine romanticism in Germany. Schlegel praised the wilderness and roughness of the Rhine valley with its many castles and ruins, thus he described a new ideal of landscape aesthetics that differed strongly from the dominating ideal.

The Romanticists preferred to enjoy pure nature combined with historic castle ruins that silently reported of the Middle Ages, an era

Historischer Kupferstich der Pfalzgrafenburg aus Halenza's Rheinischem Album, gezeichnet und gestochen von F. Foltz.
Historic copper engraving of Pfalzgrafenburg Castle from Halenza's Rhine album, drawn and engraved by F. Foltz.

Burgruinen, die ihnen vom faszinierenden Mittelalter, nach dem sie sich so sehnten, kündeten. Galten zuvor die klar strukturierten Barockgärten als Maß aller Naturschönheit, so machte sich mit der neuen Generation von Dichtern und Denkern eine Tendenz zur Unberührtheit bemerkbar.

Selbstverständlich hat auch der junge Goethe das Rheintal besucht. Mit seinen Reiseberichten aus den 1770er und 1780er Jahren gilt er neben Friedrich Hölderlin und Heinrich von Kleist als Vorläufer der Rheinromantik. Die Dichterin Adelheid von Stolterfoth schrieb eine Vielzahl von Gedichten, die den Rhein thematisch aufgriffen. Germaine de Staël veröffentlichte ihre Reiseberichte über das Mittelrheintal als eine der ersten in Frankreich.

Für Wieland (1733-1813) diente ein Ausflug an den Rhein, den er neben Italien und Griechenland als eine der großen Bildungslandschaften Europas sah, vor allem der Bildung.

Die Romantik am Rhein beeinflusste auch die bildende Kunst und die Musiker dieser Zeit. Der englische Maler William Turner, den die Einzigartigkeit des Mittelrheins und seiner atemberaubenden Landschaft bei einer Durchreise fesselte, brachte als einer der ersten den dramatischen Gesichtspunkt des Rheins zu Papier. Besonders in England fielen das neue Naturverständnis und der verklärte Blick in die Vergangenheit auf fruchtbaren Boden. Durch Napoleons Kontinentalsperre war man hier lange Zeit gehindert zu reisen, weshalb man nun die gewonnene Freiheit umso

which the Romanticists were fascinated by. Before, clearly structured baroque gardens were the measure of the true beauty of nature but with the new generation of poets and thinkers a new tendency of admiring the untouched and original arose.

Goethe, too, visited these cities in his younger years. He wrote several travel reports in the 1770s and 1780s and therefore is counted to the precursors of the Rhine Romanticism among Friedrich Hoelderlin and Heinrich von Kleist. The German poet Adelheid von Stolterfoth composed numerous pieces of Rhine poetry. Germaine de Staël was one of the first writers who published her travel reports on the Rhine in France.

Referring to Wieland (1733-1813) a journey to the river Rhine especially served one's education as he regarded the landscape along the river among Greece and Italy as one of Europe's important education landscapes. Rhine romanticism also influenced the applied arts and musicians at that point of time. The English painter William Turner, who was fascinated by the uniqueness of the Middle Rhine and its breath-taking landscape on his journey through the valley, was one of the first to put down the dramatic aspect of the river Rhine on paper.

In England, the new understanding of nature and the transfigured view of the past was particularly well received. Because of Napoleon's Continental Blockade people were not able to travel for a long time. Now, the English

Charmantes Altstadtflair versprüht eine der ältesten deutschen Weinstuben: "Altes Haus" in Bacherach.
One of the oldest German wine taverns fascinates with its charming historic flair: the "Altes Haus" ("Old House") in Bacherach.

1368
Altes Haus

mehr auskostete. Der englische Dichter und Maler Lord Byron verschaffte dem Mittelrheintal mit der Verserzählung „Childe Harold's Pilgrimage" von 1818 in England enorme Popularität, in der er die Region in den höchsten Tönen lobte. Damit spornte er viele seiner Landsleute zu einem Besuch in der wilden Rheingegend an. Die gruseligen Gothic novels, zu denen die raue Landschaft des Rheintals perfekt passte, erfreuten sich immer größter Beliebtheit. Mit dem Start des regelmäßigen Dampfschiffverkehrs 1827 gab es in der Rheinregion einen regelrechten Touristenboom. Die aufkommende Euphorie lockte weitere Künstler an, wie die englische Mary Shelley, die ihren weltberühmten Schauerroman „Frankenstein" anhand ihrer Eindrücke,

enjoyed their newly won freedom even more. The English poet and painter Lord Byron helped the Middle Rhine valley gain popularity in England with the publication of his verse composition "Childe Harold`s Pilgrimage" (1818), which praised the valley in glowing terms. This encouraged many of his fellow countrymen to visit the wild Rhine area. The rough landscape of the Rhine valley perfectly matched the scary Gothic novels, which gained more and more popularity.

With the beginning of the use of steam ships in 1827, a touristic boom arose. The growing euphoria attracted more artists, such as English writer Mary Shelley, who composed her world famous scary novel "Frankenstein" based on the impressions she gained during her

Eine wahre Oase: der Pergolagarten auf Schloss Stolzenfels, erbaut von König Wilhelm dem IV..
A true oasis: the Pergola garden at Stolzenberg Castle, built by Wilhelm IV..

die sie während ihrer Reise durch das Rheintal gesammelt hatte, verfasste. Victor Hugo war so begeistert von dem Fluss und seiner Landschaft, dass er ihn sieben Mal besuchte und einen ausführlichen Reisebericht „Le Rhin. Lettres à un ami" in Form von subjektiv geprägten Briefen an einen fiktiven Freund schrieb.
Selbst die Hohenzollern ließ diese hinreißende, geheimnisvolle Landschaft am Mittelrhein nicht kalt. Der preußische Kronprinz Friedrich war dem Rheintal sogar so verfallen, dass er hier die Wiedererrichtung mehrerer Burgen durch bekannte Baumeister veranlasste.
Der Rhein ist bekannt für seine Sagen und Legenden, von denen die der Loreley wohl die bekannteste ist. Die Legende berichtet von einer bildschönen Frau mit güldenem Haar, die

journey through the Rhine valley. Victor Hugo, too, was so fascinated by the river and its surrounding landscape that he visited the area not less than seven times and wrote a detailed travel report, "Le Rhin. Lettres à un ami", which consisted of subjectively influenced letters to a fictional friend. Even the Hohenzollern were not unimpressed by the mysterious landscape along the Middle Rhine. The Prussian crown prince Friedrich was so captivated by the Rhine valley that he initiated the reconstruction of several castles by popular architects.
The river Rhine is renowned for the many legends related to it, the best known of which is the story of the Loreley. According to the legend, Loreley was a beautiful woman with

Aussichtspunkt Maria Ruh mit Blick auf Sankt Goarshausen mit Stadtturm und Burg Katz.
Viewpoint Maria Ruh with view of Sankt Goarshausen with city tower and Katz Castle.

golden hair who mourned the death of her lover and finally drowned herself in the river. Brentano took up the saga of the Loreley several times in his works, e.g. in his "Rheinmärchen", the first time in 1810. Later the image of the mystic character Loreley changed: The innocent beauty became a dangerous mermaid who charmed the sailors that were on their route along the Rhine with her angelic singing and beauty. The sailors were so bewitched by her appearance and voice that their ships were smashed into pieces on the rough cliffs of the riverside.

On 27th June 2002, the cultural landscape of the upper Middle Rhine valley was added to the list of the World-Heritage-sites by UNSECO. The World-Heritage area spreads between Bingen/Rüdesheim to Koblenz. Today, the Rhine valley is still characterised by its mystic wilderness and offers an impressive variety of important cultural treasures as well as a unique, extraordinary landscape making it a very special and inviting travel destination.

sich aus Kummer um ihren Geliebten in den Fluss stürzt. Brentano griff das Thema der Loreley ab 1810 mehrmals in seinen Werken auf, darunter in seinem Rheinmärchen. Später mutierte die Gestalt der Loreley zu einer gefährlichen Nixe, die Schiffer mithilfe ihrer Schönheit und ihres engelsgleichen Gesangs so nah an sich heranlockte, dass ihre Schiffe an den scharfen Felsen des Rheinufers zerschellten.

Die Kulturlandschaft des oberen Mittelrheintals wurde am 27. Juni 2002 in die Liste des Weltkulturerbes der UNESCO aufgenommen. Das Weltkulturerbegebiet erstreckt sich von Bingen/Rüdesheim bis nach Koblenz. Das Rheintal verfügt über einen beachtlichen Reichtum an bedeutenden Kulturschätzen und über eine einzigartige, außergewöhnliche Landschaft, die es zu einem Reiseziel ersten Ranges macht.

Typisch für die Zeit der Romantik: der Salon, in dem diskutiert und musiziert wurde.
Characteristic for the era of Romanticism: the salon where people debated and played music.

CULTURE & CASTLES
HISTOHOTELS
HISTORIC HOTELS of GERMANY

Zu Gast am RHEIN

Sehenswürdigkeiten

Städte ABC

Tipps & Informationen

Tagestouren

Wanderungen

Ein Reise(ver)führer zu historischen Stätten und Sehenswürdigkeiten des romantischen Mittelrheintales zwischen Bingen und Koblenz

wtv

Märchenhotel

Gastgeber/host: Familie Krebs

Rheinland-Pfalz

Älteste deutsche Weinstube, heute ein märchenhaftes Hotel im Ortskern des Moselstädtchens Bernkastel-Kues, mit einem Feinschmeckerrestaurant.

Oldest german tavern, today a magical hotel in the centre of the old Moselle town Bernkastel-Kues, with gourmet restaurant.

Kallenfelsstr. 25-27
54470 Bernkastel-Kues
Rheinland-Pfalz
Tel: +49 6531 96550
Fax: +49 6531 1432
www.maerchenhotel.com
info@maerchenhotel.com

Hotel ★★★★
Restaurant ★★★★

Mitten im verwinkelten Ortskern des Mosel-Städtchens Bernkastel-Kues trifft man auf die „Älteste Weinstube", ein märchenhaft schönes, mittelalterliches Fachwerkhaus, das seit Generationen der Gastgeber-Familie Krebs gehört. Seit Stefan Krebs, eines der jungen Kochtalente der Region, die Regie übernommen hat, kann man märchenhaft wie Dornröschen oder König Drosselbart schlafen und von den Tellern aus der sterneverdächtigen Küche wie der Moselprinz essen, ein herzlicher und kompetenter Service eingeschlossen. Der Grundstein des Fachwerkhauses, einer der schönsten der Region, verweist auf das Baujahr 1678. Von Anfang an als Weingut im Besitz der Familie Krebs, wurden zunächst ▸

Tucked away amongst the winding lanes in the heart of the old town in Bernkastel-Kues, Mosel region, you will find the 'Älteste Weinstube' ('the oldest tavern'), a dazzlingly beautiful, medieval half-timbered building which has belonged to the hosts, the Krebs family, for generations. Since Stefan Krebs, one of the region's rising culinary talents, took over the running of the hotel, guests have been able to sleep a magical slumber like that of Sleeping Beauty or the fabled King Drosselbart, and dine like the Moselle prince on exquisite cuisine; welcoming and professional service included.

The foundation stone of the half-timbered building, one of the most beautiful in the region, gives the year of construction as 1678. Run as ▸

Angebot/facility

90-139 €

A/S 139-179 €

Mo Rest. (Nov.-Apr.)

Bernkastel-Kues 2 km

Trier 20 km
Frankfurt/Hahn 35 km

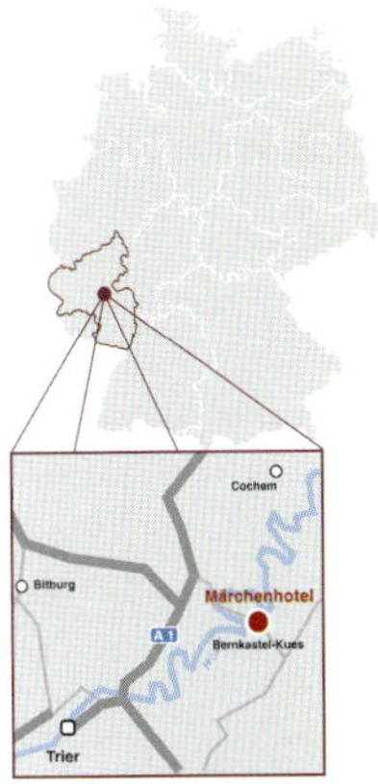

eine Weinstube und eine Metzgerei eingerichtet, zu denen sich im 18. Jahrhundert einige Fremdenzimmer hinzugesellten. Seit 2000 wurden aus 15 kleinen zunächst 10 große Zimmer und Suiten, die die Gäste in eine jeweils andere Märchenwelt entführen. Das verspielt romantische Dornröschenzimmer weckt Prinzessinnengefühle und das freche Max und Moritz-Zimmer sorgt bereits beim Betreten für gute Laune. Das ganze verwinkelte Fachwerkhaus erzählt Geschichten aus seiner über 300-jährigen Tradition und bietet gleichzeitig einen angenehmen, zeitgemäßen Komfort. Seit 2009 gibt es fünf weitere Themensuiten und ein separates Rotkäppchen-Häuschen.

a vineyard by the Krebs family from the very beginning, first a tavern and a butcher's shop were set up, and in the eighteenth century some guestrooms were added. From 2000 onwards, 15 small rooms have been turned into ten large rooms and suites, where guests are whisked away to a fairytale world. The Robin Hood Room, decorated in green, tells epic tales of heroic adventure, the daintily romantic Sleeping Beauty Room stirs feelings of royal grandeur, and the cheeky Max and Moritz Room puts you in a good mood as soon as you step inside. Every beam of this labyrinthine, half-timbered edifice breathes its history, spanning more than 300 years – while simultaneously offering all the comforts of the modern day.

In der näheren Umgebung:

Bernkastel-Kues: mittelalterlicher Marktplatz mit Giebelfachwerkhäusern aus dem 17. Jahrhundert, Burgruine Landshut, ehemalige Sommerresidenz der Trierer Erzbischöfe, Cusanus' Geburtshaus und Cusanus Hospital mit Bibliothek des Universalgelehrten Nikolaus von Kues, Craacher Tor und Weinmuseum; **Zisterzienserkloster Machern (8 km):** Puppen- und Ikonen-Museum, Klosterbrauerei; **Traben-Trarbach (18,5 km):** Jugendstilbauten von Bruno Möhring.

In the surrounding area:

Bernkastel-Kues: medieval market square with gabled half-timbered buildings dating from the seventeenth century, ruins of Landshut Castle, former summer residence of the archbishops of Trier, birthplace of Nikolaus Cusanus and St. Nikolaus Hospital with library of the great philosopher Nikolaus von Kues, Craacher Gate and wine museum; **Machern Cistercian Cloister (5 miles):** doll and icon museum, cloister brewery; **Traben-Trarbach (11.5 miles):** buildings in the Jugendstil (German Art Nouveau) by Bruno Möhring.

TIPP

Beginnend in Trier lohnt es sich, die Spuren der Römer entlang der „Römischen Weinstraße“ zu verfolgen. Interessante Stationen sind: Longuich mit der römischen „Villa Urbana“, einer prachtvoll restaurierten Tempelanlage; Mehring mit der rekonstruierten römischen „Villa Rustica“; Pölich, historisch „pulchra villa“ (schönes Landhaus), mit einer römischen Wasserleitung und Detzem mit der Nachbildung jenes 10. Meilensteins der Römerstraße Trier-Mainz, nach dem Detzem eigentlich benannt ist: „Ad Decimum Lapidem“.

Starting in Trier, follow in the footsteps of the Romans along the 'Roman wine route'. Points of interest along the route include Longuich, with the Roman Villa Urbana, a beautifully restored temple complex; Mehring, with its reconstructed Roman Villa Rustica; Pölich, a historical 'pulchra villa' (a pretty country house) with a Roman aqueduct; and Detzem, with a replica of the tenth milestone on the Roman road which ran from Trier to Mainz, for which Detzem is named – 'Ad Decimum Lapidem'.

Ein wieder errichteter römischer Wachturm steht an der Ausoniusstraße bei Dill und Niedersohren im Hunsrück.
A re-erected Roman watchtower stands along the Ausonius road near Dill and Niedersohren in the Hunsrück.

Auf den Spuren der Römer entlang der Mosel

In the footsteps of the Romans along the river Moselle

Entlang der paradiesischen Mosel kann man in den ältesten Städten Deutschlands die Geschichte von mehr als 2000 Jahren hautnah miterleben.

Am Col de Bussang in Frankreich entspringt die Mosel noch als dünnes Rinnsal. Durch den Zufluss zahlreicher Nebenflüsse entwickelt sich der Fluss jedoch zu einem stattlichen Strom. Nach fast 300 Kilometern trifft sie im Dreiländereck auf Deutschland und Luxemburg, wo sie eine, auch historisch bedeutsame, natürliche Grenze bildet. Ihren Namen erhielt die Mosel bereits von den Kelten, die 500 Jahre vor Christus hier siedelten.

Along the beautiful river Mosel, one can experience the history of over 2000 years in some of the oldest cities of Germany.

When arising from the river Col de Bussang in France, the river Moselle only resembles a small rivulet. But because of the many tributary rivers joining it, the rivulet soon develops into an impressive stream. After nearly 186 miles it finally meets Germany and Luxembourg in the border triangle area where the river Moselle forms a historically important, natural border. The river has received its name by the Celts who settled in this region 500 years BC. During the Gallic War, Romans conquered the

Malerischer Blick auf den Jugendstilort Traben-Trarbach an der Mosel.
Picturesque view of Traben-Trarbach, a town in the style of Art Nouveau at the river Moselle.

Im Gallischen Krieg eroberten die Römer die keltisch besiedelten Gebiete um die Mosel, darunter auch den wichtigsten Stamm der Treverer, und gliederten sie in ihre Provinz Gallia Belgica ein. Sie übernahmen den keltischen Namen des Flusses „Mosea" und latinisierten ihn zu Mosella. Kaiser Augustus gründete 16 n. Chr. Trier als „Augusta trevorum" – „die Stadt des Augustus im Land der Treverer". Die Römerstadt Trier, die somit die älteste deutsche Stadt darstellt, ist die erste Station der Mosel auf deutschem Boden. Durch das hier vorherrschend mediterrane Klima, das die Römer an ihre Heimat erinnerte, fühlten sie sich in der Moselregion sehr wohl, wovon zahlreiche

areas settled by Celts along the river Moselle, including the most important tribe of the Treverians, and integrated them into the Roman Province Gallia Belgica. They took the Celtic name of the river "Mosea" and Latinised it to "Mosella". In 16 A.D., Emperor Augustus founded Trier, which was called "Augusta trevorum" at those times – "the city of Augustus in the country of the Treverians". The Roman city Trier, which thus is the oldest city of Germany, was the first station of the river Moselle on German ground. Due to the dominating Mediterranean climate of the area around the river Moselle, the Romans were reminded of their home and felt comfortable in this region,

Das Amphitheater in Trier bot nach seiner Fertigstellung um 100 n. Chr. ca. 20.000 Besuchern Platz.
The amphitheatre in Trier, built around 100 AD, offered space for about 20,000 visitors.

Prachtbauten wie das Amphitheater, die verschiedenen Thermen, die Aula Palatina sowie das römische Stadttor Porta Nigra zeugen.
Trier, das in seiner damaligen Ausdehnung fast dreimal so groß wie das römische Köln war, diente als wirtschaftlicher Mittelpunkt diesseits der Rheingrenze sowie als Handels- und Sammelplatz landwirtschaftlicher Produkte. Weiterhin hatten die Generalsteuereinnehmer mit ihrem großen Stab und der Stadthalter der Provincia Belgica hier ihren Sitz. Weinanbau und -handel florierten in dieser Zeit ebenso wie das Töpfer- und Tuchgewerbe. Es entstanden bedeutsame Manufakturen und die Villae Rusticae, die Agrarbetriebe, aber auch prachtvolle Villae Urbanae. Eine große Zahl von Resten

which is demonstrated by the great number of impressive buildings that can be found here such as the amphitheatre, the various thermal baths, the Aula Palatina and the Roman town gate Porta Nigra.
Trier, which was at that time nearly three times as big as the Roman Cologne, served as economic centre on this side of the Rhine border. It was also an important trading centre and collecting point of agricultural products. Furthermore, the general tax collectors and their numerous staff members, as well as the governor of the Provincia Belgica were located here. At that time, wine-growing and –trading flourished, just as the pottery and cloth industry. Several important manufactories and

Der Keller unter der Arena ist heute noch erhalten.
The cellar underneath the arena is still in good condition.

derartiger römischer Niederlassungen ist heute noch entlang der Mosel zu finden.
Wenn die Mosel auch meist als Wasserweg verwendet wurde, so bot sie durch ihre variierenden Wasserstände keine Garantie für sichere Transporte. So legten die Römer schon damals parallel zur Mosel Straßen und Wege für die Beförderung von Gütern an. Die berühmte "Roemische Weinstrasse" entstand. Dennoch war die Mosel als wichtige Wasserstraße unverzichtbar, ließen sich doch ohne große Anstrengungen schwere Waren und sogar Truppen in weit entfernte Regionen befördern. Somit konnte man weiterhin lukrative Handelsgeschäfte mit befreundeten Germanenvölkern

Villae Rusticae, Roman farms, but also magnificent Villae Urbanae came into existence. Today, a great number of remains of those Roman settlements can still be found along the river Moselle.
Although the river Moselle was mostly used as waterway, it did not guarantee safe transport due to its varying water levels. Therefore, the Romans constructed roads that run parallel to the river Moselle for the transport of goods. On this occasion, the famous "Roman wine road" was built. Nevertheless, the river Moselle still was an essential waterway as it offered the possibility to easily transport heavy goods and even troops to far-off regions.

Der Alte Krahnen, ein Steinbau aus dem Jahre 1413, steht am Krahnenufer auf der rechten Moselseite in Trier.
The "Alte Krahnen" ("Old Tower Crane"), a stone building from 1413, is situated on the "Krahnenufer" ("Crane banks") on the right bank of the river Mosel in Trier.

betreiben und problemlos die römischen Siedlungen im Norden versorgen. Indem sie durch ihre Größe und Breite für feindliche Truppen eine nur schwer zu überwindende Barriere bildete, fungierte die Mosel auch als natürliche Grenze zu den noch nicht römisch besetzten Gebieten.

Während einer fast 200-jährigen Friedenszeit herrschte ein enormer Aufschwung mit stetig steigenden Einwohnerzahlen. Man errichtete zahlreiche imposante Gebäude, die noch heute als prächtige Ruinen von der Blütezeit Augusta Trevorums künden. Die Ruine der mächtigen, damals sehr prunkvoll ausgestatteten Barbarathermen, die zur Zeit ihrer Errichtung (im 2. Jh. n. Chr.) das zweitgrößte Badehaus im

Thus, profitable business could still be made with friendly Germanic tribes and the Roman settlements in the North could be easily supplied. Due to its size and latitude the river Moselle constituted an obstacle to hostile forces that was hard to overcome. Thus, the river also served as natural border to the regions that were not yet occupied by the Romans.

During a nearly 200 years lasting period of peace an enormous boom guaranteed a continuously increase of population. Numerous impressive buildings were constructed. Still today, their magnificent ruins speak of the prosperity of Augusta Trevorums. The ruins of the luxuriously designed Barbara thermal baths, which were at the time of their

Imposante Überbleibsel aus Römischen Zeiten: Die Kaiserthermen in Trier.
Impressive remains from Roman times: The "Kaiserthermen" ("Emperor baths") in Trier.

gesamten Römischen Reich waren, sowie das Amphitheater, dessen Auditorium ursprünglich 20.000 Zuschauer fassen konnte, dienen heute als bemerkenswerte Zeitzeugen des Reichtums, der Macht und der bedeutenden Rolle, die Trier während der Kaiserzeit im Imperium Romanum inne hatte.

Auch das um 180 n. Chr. errichtete Stadttor, das man seit dem Mittelalter Porta Nigra („Schwarzes Tor") nennt, ist als eine der wohl beeindruckendsten Ruinen erhalten.

Seit 273 n. Chr. ist Trier Bischofssitz, wovon der Dom als älteste Bischofskirche Deutschlands Zeugnis ablegt. Er gehört zum UNESCO-Weltkulturerbe und spiegelt eine über 1600 Jahre alte Kunst-, Kultur- und Architekturgeschichte wider.

construction (in the 2nd century A.D.) the second biggest bathing house in the whole Roman Empire, as well as the amphitheatre, whose auditorium could originally accommodate 20,000 spectators, still bear witness to the wealth, the power and the important role that Trier owned during the times of the Roman Empire.

One of the most impressive ruins that can be visited today is the town gate of Trier, which was constructed in 180 A.D. and which is known as "Porta Nigra", the black gate, since the Middle Ages.

Since 273AD Trier has been a diocesan town, indicated by the cathedral being the oldest bishop's church in Germany. It belongs to the UNESCO world heritage and documents over

Die Porta Nigra, ein ehemaliges römisches Stadttor, ist das bekannte Wahrzeichen Triers.
The Porta Nigra, a former Roman city gate, is the famous emblem of Trier.

Mit dem Einfall der Germanen in das Römische Reich und der Verwüstung Triers im Jahre 273 durch die Alemannen war ein Wendepunkt in der Geschichte erreicht. Um das Reich sichern und verteidigen zu können, teilte man es in Ost- und Weströmisches Reich. Trier wurde Hauptstadt des Weströmischen Reiches (295 n Chr.).
Neben den großartigen, berühmten Ruinen von Prachtbauten, ist entlang der Mosel auch eine Vielzahl kleinerer Überbleibsel römischer Architekturkunst zu bestaunen.
In der Gemeinde Longuich gibt es eine originale Villa Urbana zu besichtigen. Villae Urbanae gab es im Imperium Romanum wie Sand am Meer. Sie dienten wohlhabenden Gutsfamilien als luxuriöse Anwesen. Auch in der Villa Urbana von Longuich sind noch Reste der Badeanlage

1600 years of architectural, cultural and art history.
With the invasion of the Germanic tribes into the Roman Empire and the devastation of Trier by the Alemanni in 273, another turning point in history was reached. To be able to defend the Empire, the Romans divided it up into an Eastern and a Western part. Trier became capital of the West Roman Empire (295 A.D.).
Among the magnificent famous ruins and buildings, one can also enjoy the sight of numerous smaller remains of Roman architecture along the river Moselle.
In the small community of Longuich, an original Villa Urbana is open for visitors. At the times of the Roman Empire, there were plenty

Die Villa Urbana in Longuich war ehemals ein luxuriöses Römer-Anwesen.
The Villa Urbana in Longuich was once a luxury Roman estate.

erhalten, die, wie im Römischen Reich üblich, aus frigidarium und caldarium (Heiß- und Kaltbad) bestand. Die früheren Bewohner schienen sogar über eine Wand- und Bodenheizung verfügt zu haben, was neben den aufwendigen Wandmalereien und Verzierungen aus Glas und Marmor ein deutlicher Hinweis auf ihren Reichtum sein könnte. Das Interessante bei dieser Villa Urbana ist, dass sie nicht die erste Villa war, die an diesem Ort errichtet worden ist. Offenbar befand sich an ihrem Standort zuvor noch eine weitaus weniger noble Villa Rustica, ein landwirtschaftlicher Betrieb. Schlendert man ein wenig östlich der Villa entlang, so findet man ein ebenfalls sehr beeindruckendes

of these Villae Urbanae. They served wealthy landowners and their families as luxurious mansions. In the Villa Urbana in Longuich the remains of the former bathing complex, which consisted of the frigidarium and caldarium (hot and cold baths) as it was common in the Roman Empire, are still preserved. The former inhabitants seemed to even have had a wall and floor heating, which, combined with the extravagant wall paintings and the ornaments made of glass or marble that can be found here, could be a hint to their prosperity. Especially interesting about this Villa Urbana is the fact that it was not the first Villa to be erected at this place. Apparently, there once existed a

Neben dem edlen Marmorboden (rechts) gehörte auch eine Fußbodenheizung (links) zur Ausstattung der Villa Urbana .
Apart from the precious marble floor (left), a floor heating (right) was part of the interior of the Villa Urbana.

Relikt der Römerzeit vor: einen Sarkophag, der im vierten Jahrhundert ein kleines Mädchenskelett barg.

In Detzem an der „Roemischen Weinstrasse" kann man einen nachgebildeten Meilen- bzw. Leugenstein begutachten, nach dem auch der Ort selbst benannt ist (10. Leugenstein). Eine Leuge entsprach einer Länge von 2 - 3 Kilometern.

Im ältesten Weinort Deutschlands, Neumagen-Dhron, befinden sich das Römerweinschiff und das Grabmal eines vermögenden Kaufmanns aus dem 2. bis 4. Jahrhundert.

Eine weitere Villa aus Römerzeiten ist in Mehring zu begutachten: Es handelt sich um far less noble Villa Rustica, a farm, at this site. Taking a stroll along the eastern part of the Villa, one will find another very impressive relict of the Roman era: a sarcophagus, which held a small skeleton of a girl in the 4th century.

In Detzem at the Roman Wine Road visitors can examine a reproduced mile, or Leugen, stone, which gave the town its name (the tenth Leugen stone). One Leuge was approximately equal to a length of 1 to 2 miles.

In the oldest wine resort of Germany, Neumagen – Dhron, the "Roman wine ship" and the tomb of a wealthy merchant from the 2nd to 4th century are well worth seeing.

Schon zu Zeiten der Römer wurde in solchen Fasskellern Wein aufbewahrt.
In these cellars wine has been stored since the Roman era.

Another villa from the Roman era is open for public visitors in Mehring: This manor house of a court was preserved and partly reconstructed. The building, originating from the middle of the 2nd century, was built after the model of a characteristic Gallo-Roman architectural design – with two avant-corps to structure the façade and a colonnade. This building as well was partly destroyed during the invasions of Germanic tribes. Afterwards, it was inhabited by Germanics for a long time until it was abandoned, probably in the 5th century.

The nearby Kenn, too, offers its visitors an impressive relict from the Roman era: the Roman cellar consisting of three rooms. Originally, it was part of a villa from the middle of the 2nd

das Herrenhaus eines Hofes, das bewahrt und zum Teil wieder aufgebaut wurde. Das Gebäude, das aus der Mitte des 2. Jahrhunderts stammt, war damals nach einer typischen gallo-römischen Konstruktionsweise errichtet worden - mit zwei Avantkorps zur Gliederung der Fassade sowie einem Säulengang. Auch dieses Gebäude ist bei den Germaneneinfällen teilweise zerstört worden. Danach wurde sie eine Zeit lang von Germanen bewohnt bis sie vermutlich im 5. Jahrhundert aufgegeben wurde.

Auch im nahe gelegenen Kenn kann man ein

Sehenswert ist die Altstadt von Bernkastel-Kues mit seinen Giebelfachwerkhäusern aus dem 17. Jahrhundert.
Definitely worth seeing is the city centre of Bernkastel-Kues with its gabled frame houses from the 17th century.

spannendes Relikt aus der Zeit der Römer bestaunen - den Römerkeller mit drei Räumen. Ursprünglich war er Bestandteil einer Villa aus der Mitte des 2. Jhs. Überbleibsel von Marmor- und Sandsäulen, Wandmalerei und die Plastik einer Najade, ein über Bäche, Flüsse und Quellen wachender weiblicher Naturgeist, zeugen noch heute von einer erhabenen Ausstattung und Gestaltung des Anwesens und dem Reichtum seiner Bewohner.

Die Römer sind für ihre fortschrittlichen Bewässerungssysteme, die sie mit viel Aufwand für die Versorgung ihrer Städte mit Trink- und Badewasser anlegten, bekannt. Die berühmtesten Beispiele in Deutschland sind wohl die Wasserleitung Ruwertal für die Wasserversorgung Triers sowie die Eifelwasserleitung für die Versorgung Kölns. Darüber hinaus errichteten sie Wasserleitungen zu Villae Urbanae und Rusticae. So lieferte beispielsweise das unterirdische Bewässerungssystem Qanat von Pölich aus Wasser an eine römische Niederlassung im Moseltal. Bei Ausgrabungen stieß man sogar auf Reste des Badetraktes eines Herrenhauses. Die über 400 m lange, antike Wasserleitung aus Schiefer ist mit einem Alter von mittlerweile 1800 Jahren noch intakt und trägt auch heute noch zur Versorgung der Gegend mit frischem Wasser bei. Neben Besichtigungen römischer Bewässerungssysteme in Mehring und Longuich ist die Begutachtung dieses Reliktes unbedingt zu empfehlen.

Im Archäologiepark „Römische Villa Borg" fühlt man sich regelrecht in die Zeit des Imperium Romanums zurückversetzt, wenn man

century. Today, remains of the pillars made of marble or sand and the sculpture of a naiad, a female natural spirit who is watching over rivulets, rivers and springs, still show how luxuriously the mansion was once furnished and designed and prove the wealth of its owners.

The Romans are especially renowned for their advanced irrigation systems, which they constructed under high effort to supply their towns with drinking and bath water. The most famous examples that can be found in Germany are the aqueduct Ruwertal, responsible for the water supply of Trier, and the Eifel aqueduct for the supply of Cologne. Moreover, the Romans constructed aqueducts that led to Villae urbanae and rusticae. The subterranean irrigation system Qanat, for example, supplied a Roman settlement in the Moselle valley with water from Pölich. During excavations, even the remains of the bathing area of a mansion were discovered. The antique water pipe made of slate measures over 437 yards and despite its age of 1800 years still is intact today, supplying the region with fresh water. Apart from visits to the Roman irrigation systems in Mehring and Longuich this relict is also worth seeing.

In the archaeological park "Roman Villa Borg" visitors will find themselves taken back in time to the era of the Roman Empire. The impressive Roman mansion with its working bath, a tavern including a kitchen and various Roman gardens are all open for public.

The Emperor`s palace in Konz, former residence of the Emperor Valentinian I. (364-375), is well worth a visit.

das imposante römische Herrenhaus mit funktionsfähigem Bad, einer Taverne mit Küche und unterschiedlichen römischen Gartenanlagen besichtigt.

Der Kaiserpalast in Konz, in dem Kaiser Valentinian I. (364 – 375) residierte, stellt ein lohnenswertes Ausflugsziel dar.

Sehenswert ist auch das mittelalterliche Fachwerkstädtchen Bernkastel-Kues. Ein Verweis auf den berühmten Namenspatron Nikolaus von Kues, vielen besser bekannt als Cusanus, darf hier nicht fehlen. Der große Theologe, geniale Philosoph und Mathematiker prägte nicht nur eine Zeit, sondern besiegelte durch seine

Another destination worth an excursion is the medieval town Bernkastel-Kues with its half-timbered houses. The town was named after the famous Nikolaus von Kues, commonly known as Cusanus. The great theologian, brilliant philosopher and mathematician did not only influence a whole era but his writings marked the end of medieval thinking. As a reformer and humanist philosopher, he represents the intellectual father of both modern theology and modern philosophy. Today, he is still celebrated as he is name patron to projects, such as the "Cusanus-Werk" of the Catholic Church, an Episcopal study sponsorship

In a picturesque surrounding enclosed by vineyards and directly situated at the river Moselle lies Bernkastel-Kues.

Schriften das Ende mittelalterlichen Denkens. Als Reformer und humanistischer Philosoph ist er sowohl der geistige Vater der modernen Theologie als auch der Philosophie der Neuzeit. Noch heute ehrt man ihn durch Namensgebungen, wie beim „Cusanus-Werk" der Katholischen Kirche, einer bischöflichen Studienförderung für Hochbegabte. In seinem Wohnhaus ist ein Museum eingerichtet, dessen Besuch sehr empfehlenswert ist. Aber nicht nur das Schauen ist Erleben, sondern auch das Schmecken und Riechen. So gehört die „Älteste Weinstube" anno 1640 zu den ältesten und renommiertesten Lokalen der Region. Mitten im

for highly talented students. His house holds a museum which is worth visiting. But as we experience not only via visual impressions but also via our senses of smell and taste, Bernkastel-Kues has another highlight to offer: The "Älteste Weinstube" ('the oldest tavern') dates back to the year 1640 and belongs to one of the oldest and most renowned local pubs. Situated in the old centre of Bernkastel, it hosts the "Fairy Tale Hotel" (Maerchenhotel), an ideal residence to explore the western Moselle region.

Only a few miles further downstream you will find the Art Nouveau town Traben-Trarbach.

In malerischer Umgebung inmitten von Weinbergen und direkt an der Mosel liegt Bernkastel-Kues.

alten Ortskern von Bernkastel gelegen, beherbergt sie heute das Märchenhotel, welches ein idealer Aufenthaltsort ist, um die westliche Moselregion zu erkunden. Von hier aus liegt nur wenige Kilometer stromabwärts der Jugendstilort Traben-Trarbach. Als protestantische Enklave und zweitgrößte Weinhandelsstadt Europas (nach Bordeaux) ergab es sich, dass besonders die Geschäfte mit Preußen florierten und der Gemeinde einen immensen Wohlstand brachten. Anfang des 20. Jahrhunderts entstanden viele neue Gebäude, die im Stile dieser Zeit reich ornamentiert und gestaltet sind. Vom Ortskern aus windet sich die Straße in engen Serpentinen hinauf in den Hunsrück, einem Teil des Rheinischen Schiefergebirges. Der Hunsrück wurde schon früh besiedelt und zeigt mit zahlreichen Funden aus der Römerzeit, dass er vollständig erschlossen war. Die Ausoniusstraße ist vielleicht der bekannteste Beweis und als Wanderweg überaus reizvoll. Ein römischer Wachturm bei Dill und Niedersohren illustriert die Geschichte ganz vorzüglich. Der Name kommt von einem römischen Dichter, der über diese Straße nach Trier reiste und seine Eindrücke in dem Gedicht „Mosella“ verewigte. Wechselvolle Geschichte paart sich mit gelebten oder erzählten Erinnerungen an „Früher“. Doch kehren wir noch einmal zurück zur Mosel, zu dem lieblichen aber auch mächtigen Städtchen Traben-Trarbach, den dortigen Steillagen und dem vorzüglichen Lagenwein und fahren weiter flussabwärts. Bald erreichen wir die Stadt Koblenz. Sie liegt am Zusammenfluss von Mosel und Rhein. Seit der Zeit der Römer

A protestant enclave and second biggest wine-trading city of Europe (Bordeaux is number one), the parish grew incredibly wealthy as trade with Prussia flourished. Consequently in the beginning of the 20th century, a lot of new buildings that were elaborately designed and ornamented in the contemporary style were constructed. (Many Art Nouveau elements decorate the drawbridge that houses a restaurant and is an emblem of Traben-Trarbach at the Moselle.) Yet let us focus on living nature and leave the stony ornaments behind. Starting in the city centre, a winding road leads us upward into a region called Hunsrueck, a part of the Rhenish slate mountains.

Early settlements and countless findings from Roman times show that the area was well developed. The Ausoniusroad, probably the most renowned of Roman relics, serves as a very appealing hiking trail. A Roman watchtower near Dill and Niedersohren brilliantly illustrates local history. A Roman poet lent the road, along which he travelled to Trier, his name. He immortalized his impressions in a poem called "Mosella". Changeful history couples with lived or recounted memories of the past.

Let us return once more to the Moselle and the lovely yet powerful town of Traben-Trarbach, its steep vineyards and excellent wines and move on further downstream. Soon we reach the city of Koblenz, situated at the confluence of the river Rhine and the river Moselle.

Since Roman times Koblenz has been of great strategic importance because of its exposed

Das Geburtshaus von Cusanus in Bernkastel-Kues, ein Renaissancebau aus dem 16. Jahrhundert.
The birth house of Cusanus in Bernkastel-Kues, a Renaissance building from the 16th century.

hat die Stadt in ihrer exponierten Lage große strategische Bedeutung. An einer Landzunge, direkt an der Mündung der Mosel in den Rhein, liegt das „Deutsche Eck" mit einem monumentalen Kaiser- Wilhelm-Denkmal. Unweit davon erinnert das Deutschherrenhaus an den Deutschen Ritterorden, der sich 1216 hier ansiedelte. Auf der anderen Rheinseite liegt die Festung Ehrenbreitstein, eine von den Trierer Kurfürsten vor rund 1.000 Jahren angelegte Burganlage. Sehenswert ist auch die Kaiserin-Augusta-Anlage, eine schöne Uferpromenade des Gartenbaukünstlers Peter-Joseph Lenné, sowie die Basilika St. Kastor. Hier verhandelte Ludwig der Fromme 842 über die Teilung des Fränkischen Reichs.

position. Sitting on a headland directly at the estuary of the Moselle as it joins the Rhine there is the 'Deutsche Eck' with a monumental Kaiser Wilhelm memorial.

Not far from there, the 'Deutschherrenhaus' is a reminder of the German Order of Knights that settled here in 1216. On the other side of the Rhine you can see the fortress Ehrenbreitstein, a stronghold built roughly a thousand years ago by the electors of Trier. Well worth seeing are also the 'Kaiserin-Augusta-Anlage", a beautiful waterfront of the landscape gardener and artist Peter-Joseph Lenné and the basilica St. Kastor. In the latter Ludwig the Pious negotiated the partition of the Frankish Empire.

Am deutschen Eck in Koblenz treffen Rhein und Mosel aufeinander.
River Rhine and Moselle meet at the "Deutsche Eck" ("German corner") in Koblenz.

CULTURE & CASTLES
HISTOHOTELS
HISTORIC HOTELS of GERMANY

Zu Gast im ODENWALD

Ein Reise(ver)führer zu historischen Stätten, Sehenswürdigkeiten und Paradiesen im Naturpark Odenwald

wtv

Der HÖERHOF

Gastgeber/host: Sabine Kogge

Hessen

Aufwendig restauriertes „Schlösschen von Idstein" mit einmaligem Ambiente am Rande der Altstadt der einstigen Residenzstadt Idstein.

Thoroughly restored, small „Castle of Idstein" with unique ambience, located at the edge of the historic city centre of the former residential town Idstein.

Obergasse 26
65510 Idstein im Taunus
Hessen
Tel: +49 6126 50026
Fax: +49 6126 500226
www.hoerhof.de
info@hoerhof.de

Hotel ★★★★
Restaurant ★★★★

Das Restaurant -****Hotel HÖERHOF befindet sich inmitten der grünen Hügel des Taunus. Das 1620 - 1626 erbaute Schlösschen steht in der malerischen Altstadt der einstigen Residenzstadt Idstein. Nach stilgerechten Renovierungen bietet der Renaissancebau heute 14 klassisch eingerichtete Zimmer und wunderbare Möglichkeiten, sich zu entspannen und zurückzuziehen. Der Charme des über 400 Jahre alten Fachwerk-Ensembles besteht in der liebevollen und detailgetreuen Fassaden-Renovierung sowie in der persönlichen Führung durch die Gastgeberin. Perfekte Funktionalität und liebevolle Gastlichkeit komplettieren das elegante Ambiente des Anwesens. So ergänzen sich traditionelle Gemütlichkeit und moderner Komfort zu einem harmonischen Ganzen. Komfort und Tradition schaffen im Restaurant -****Hotel HÖERHOF ein einmaliges Ambiente zum Wohlfühlen und die Seele baumeln lassen. Fünf verschiedene Tagungsräumlichkeiten ▸

The historic restaurant and hotel HÖERHOF is surrounded by the green hills of the Taunus mountains. The small castle, situated in the historic center of Idstein, a former seat of royal power, was built in the beginning of the 17th century. After authentic renovations, today the renaissance-building offers 14 classically furnished, bedrooms en-suite. The charming timberframe building in connection with the hostess' lovely and personal way and manner makes you find calm and serenity for both body and soul. Perfect functionality and caring hospitality complement the hotel's elegant ambience and create a harmonious unity. The picturesque court yard and outdoor beer garden invite you to linger. Far away from the daily hustle and bustle the Gutsstube and the exquisite cuisine invite you to ▸

Angebot/facility

95-110 €

120-135 €

A/S 125-150 €

2-45

Idstein
5 km

Frankfurt/
Main
35 km

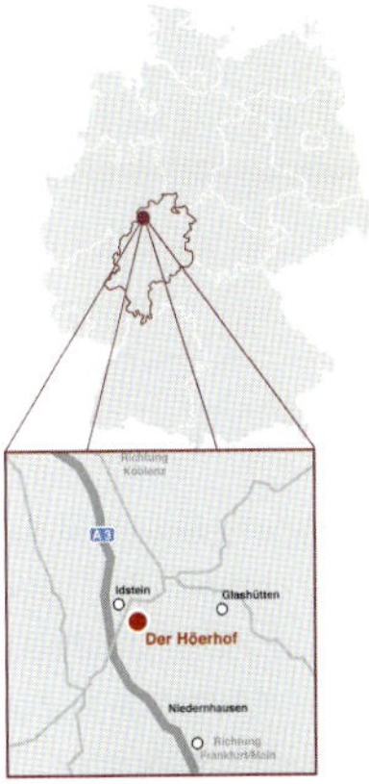

für 2 bis 45 Personen bieten den Rahmen für kreative Einfälle und Diskussionen.

Der HÖERHOF steht für Lebensfreude und sinnlichen Genuss. Über das Jahr verteilt werden vielerlei Veranstaltungen organisiert, stets in Verbindung mit kulinarischen Hochgenüssen. Alljährlich im Juni findet das Idsteiner Jazzfestival statt mit diversen Bühnen, Künstlern und einem vielfältigen Rahmenprogramm. Küchenchef Daniel Schönberger kreiert dazu mit seinem Köche-Team raffinierte Speisen aus sorgfältig ausgesuchten Rohstoffen und frischen Zutaten, die man dazu auch à la carte in der Gutsstube genießen kann, deren unbeschreiblich besonderer Raumeindruck nicht zuletzt durch den gusseisernen Kaminofen, das bleiverglaste Fenster auf der Nordseite oder die rustikale Holzdecke bestimmt wird.

relish the carefully selected specialities and wonderful assortment of complementing wine. In the HÖERHOF comfort and tradition create a unique atmosphere to feel good and truly relax.

Five different conference rooms for 2 to 45 people provide the ideal work setting for creative ideas and discussions.

The HÖERHOF stands for joie de vivre and sensual pleasure. During the whole year a wide variety of events and celebrations, always in combination with ultimate culinary delights, are organized. Every year in July the Idsteiner Jazzfestival takes place with a diversity of stages, artists and a multifaceted framework programme. On this occasion head chef Daniel Schönberger and his team of top-class chefs create refined tasty dishes out of carefully selected, first-class quality and fresh ingredients. Guests also have the chance to enjoy those delicious meals à la carte in the "Gutsstube", which impresses with an indescribable outstanding room appearance. Especially the cast-iron chimney, the stained glass window on the northern site and the rustic wooden ceiling are eyecatchers.

In der näheren Umgebung:

Idstein: Killingerhaus (Stadtmuseum), Idsteiner Badewelten (Wellness, SPA, Sauna und Fitness), Golf Park Idstein (größte 18-Loch Golf-Oase des Rhein-Main-Gebietes); **Eltville (33 km):** Rheingau, Kloster Eberbach (Drehort von „Im Namen der Rose"); **Wiesbaden (24 km):** facettenreiche (hessische) Landeshauptstadt mit großen Prachtstraßen, kleinen Altstadtgassen und idyllischen Plätzen; **Limburg (31 km):** Limburger Dom, Burgmannenhaus, Alte Lahnbrücke (Via Publica).

In the surrounding area:

Idstein: Killingerhaus (municipal museum), Idsteiner Badewelten, Golf Park Idstein (biggest 18-hole-golf course of the Rhine-Main-Area); **Eltville (21 miles):** Rheingau, Monastery Eberbach (Filming location of „The name of the Rose"); **Wiesbaden (15 miles):** diverse and colourful state capital of Hesse with wide grand boulevards, narrow alleyways of the oldtown and idyllic squares; **Limburg (19 miles):** Limburg Cathedral, Burgmannenhaus, 750 years old Lahn bridge (Via Publica).

TIPP

Im Freilichtmuseum Hessenpark in Neu-Anspach/Taunus (33 km) können Sie entdecken, wie unsere Vorfahren gelebt, gearbeitet und gefeiert haben. Vom nordhessischen Gutshof über das mittelhessische Tagelöhnerhaus bis zum südhessischen Wirtshaus – an über 100 Gebäuden können Sie nachvollziehen, wie sich Bauen und Wohnen in den Regionen seit 400 Jahren entwickelt haben. Besonders beeindruckend im Hessenpark sind die traditionellen ländlichen Handwerke, Geräte und Werkstätten, die in zahlreichen Vorführungen erlebbar gemacht werden.

In the open-air museum Hessen park in New-Anspach/Taunus (21 miles) you can discover the way our ancestors used to live, work and celebrate. Starting from northhessian family estates, middlehessian day laborer's houses to the southhessian pubs/inns – seeing over 100 historic buildings, you can keep track of the development of construction and housing in the area in the past 400 years. One particularly impressive sight in the Hessen park is the traditional rural craftsmanship, instruments and devices, which are demonstrated in a very vivid way.

Herrenhaus Barthélemy

Gastgeber/host: Rosemarie Eifler-Bollen, Clemens Bollen

Repräsentatives Landhaus des ehemaligen französischen Magazinverwalters der Festung Landau, heute ein Boutiquehotel im Charme der Provence.

Representive country house of the former French Storeroom Administrator of the Fortress Landau, which today is a boutique hotel with the charm of the Provence.

Bergstraße 4
76835 Gleisweiler
Rheinland-Pfalz
Tel.: +49 6345 953022
Fax: +49 6345 953023
www.herrenhaus-barthelemy.com
mail@herrenhaus-barthelemy.com

Hotel ★★★★

1802 übernahm Isaac Barthélemy, der Magazinverwalter der Festung Landau, das bereits seit 1619 als Wohnhaus genutzte Anwesen. Ort und Hof gehörten in der Folgezeit zu Frankreich. Nachdem 1870 die Gesellschafterin von Johanna Barthélemy („Jenny") Haus und Hof geerbt hatte, verblieb das Anwesen über 100 Jahre im Familienbesitz, bevor es weiterveräußert wurde.

Die heutigen Gastgeber entdeckten das charmante Herrenhaus 2007, kauften es und setzten es behutsam wieder instand. Das, was sie vorfanden, passte zu ihrer frankophilen Leidenschaft. Jedes Zimmer und jede Suite ist überraschend anders. Farben, Stoffe und Accessoires bilden mit den alten, sorgfältig restaurierten Möbelstücken aus der Zeit von Barthélemy eine harmonische Einheit.

Die Gäste spüren die bezaubernde Würde des alten Hauses und die Freude und Begeisterung, mit denen die Gastgeber es zu neuem ▸

In 1802 Isaac Barthélemy, Storeroom Administrator of the Fortress Landau , resumed the property, which already had been used as residential house since 1619. In the following period, the town and court belonged to France. After being inherited by the associate Johanna Barthélemy ("Jenny"), town and court remained in family ownership for over 100 years, before it was resold and vacant for a long time.

In 2007 the present owners discovered, bought and repaired the charming manor house gently. The house matched their francophile passion perfectly. Each room and suite looked surprisingly different. Colours, fabrics and accessories combined with old, carefully restored pieces of furniture from the period of Barthélemy form a harmonious unit.

Guests can sense the house's adorable dignity, ▸

Angebot/facility

90-115 €

110-135 €

A/S 80-140 €

Landau 10 km
Neustadt 15 km
Mannheim 50 km

Karlsruhe/Baden-Baden 80 km
Frankfurt/Main 120 km
Stuttgart 120 km

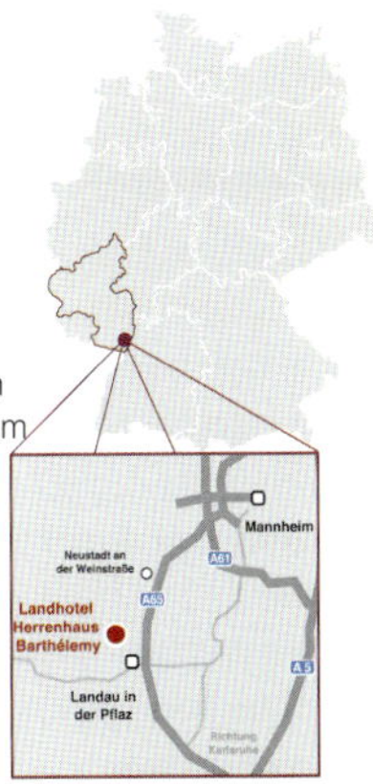

Leben erweckten. Dem Zauber des Kaminfeuers, dem Knistern der Flammen und dem Duft von würzigem Holz können sie sich ebenso wenig entziehen, wie dem Charme der bemalten Decke oder den herrlichen Sandsteinböden.

Im Garten laden große und kleine Sitzplätze, wunderschöne Holzbänke und helle Sonnenschirme zur Siesta ein: unterm Weinlaub der überdachten Terrasse des alten Gartenhauses, im geheimnisvollen Wäldchen oder unter der Magnolie im Remisenhof.

Wenn der Wind zunimmt und leichter Regen fällt, wird das Grün im Garten noch intensiver und Lavendelduft steigt in die Nase. Die Remisen-Sauna ist dann aufgeheizt, die Gäste haben ausgiebig Zeit, endlich den Roman zu lesen, für den ihnen bisher die Zeit fehlte. Wenn die Sonne herauskommt, lesen Sie einfach im Garten weiter, oder genießen die himmlische Ruhe und das behagliche Umfeld des Landhotels, ganz so, als wären Sie in einem Maison d`hôtes der Provence!

such as the delight and enthusiasm, with which the hosts brought the old house to life.

They can neither detract from the magic of the chimney fire, the crackling sound of the flames and the spicy scent of the wood, nor from the charm of the ceiling painting or the sandstone floors. In the garden, big and small seating-acomodations, lovely wooden benches and light parasols invite the guests to take a siesta: You can retreat below the climbing vine leaves of the roofed terrace of the old summer house, in the mystical small forest or below the magnolia in the yard.

When the wind is getting stronger and it is raining lightly, the garden's green seems to become more intense and a pleasant fragrance of lavender rises to the nose. During this time the sauna is heated up and the guests can finally spend their time reading a novel for what they might not have found the time before. If the sun shows its friendly face, you can carry on reading in the garden or just relax and enjoy the heavenly quiet as well as the cozy environment of the country hotel, just as if you were staying in a Maison d`hôtes of the Provence.

In der näheren Umgebung:

Gleisweiler: romantisches Winzerdorf mit Zehnthof, Fachwerkhäusern, Sonnentempel; **Villa Ludwigshöhe (10km):** Sommerresidenz des bayerischen Königs Ludwig I. mit Max Slevogt-Galerie; **Hambacher Schloss (20km):** Wahrzeichen der deutschen Demokratie mit Dauerausstellung und guter Sicht ins Rheintal; **Speyer (25km):** Unesco-Weltkulturerbe Kaiserdom mit Krypta, jüdisches Viertel, Fischmarkt, Alte Münze, Altpörtel.

In the surrounding area:

Gleisweiler: romantic wine village with Zehnthof, half-timbered houses, sun temple; Villa Ludwigshöhe (6 miles): The summer residence of the Bavarian King Louis I. with a gallery of Max Slevogt; **Castle Hambach (12 miles):** landmark of the German Democracy with a permanent exhibition and a great view over the Rhine valley; **Speyer (16 miles):** UNESCO World Heritage imperial cathedral with crypt, jewish district, fish market, „Alte Münze", Old Gate „Altpörtel".

TIPP

Als echte Institution gilt Chawwerusch in Herxheim, das freie professionelle Theater „von Leuten für Leute", immer nah an den Menschen und ihrer aktuellen Erlebniswelt, manchmal irritierend, aber stets mit einem Augenzwinkern. Vielfach ausgezeichnet inszeniert das Theater regionale Geschichte und Geschichten, Klassiker wie Goethes Faust oder Shakespeares Hamlet aus "verrückten" Perspektiven.
Theatersaal in Herxheim bei Landau
Reservierung
Tel.: +49 7276 5991

Chawwerusch in Herxheim, the free theatre with a professional claim „created by people for people" is quite an institution. Sometimes confusing, but always with a tongue in cheek, it is close to the people and their actual current experiential world. The theatre, which has received multiple awards, stages local history and stories, classics like Goethe's Faust or Shakespeare's Hamlet from a "crazy" perspective.
Theatre hall in Herxheim near Landau
Reservation-Phone +49 7276 5991.

Kloster Hornbach

Gastgeber/host: Christiane und Edelbert Lösch

Ehemalige Benediktinerabtei des Missionsbischofs Pirmin bei Zweibrücken ist heute ein stilvolles Klosterhotel und Refugium für besinnlich erholsame Auszeiten.

Former Benedictine-abbey of the missionary and bishop Pirmin close to the French border, today a classy monastery-hotel and a retreat for contemplative and recreative times.

Im Klosterbezirk
66500 Hornbach
Rheinland-Pfalz
Tel: +49 6338 910100
Fax: +49 6338 9101099
www.kloster-hornbach.de
hotel@kloster-hornbach.de

Hotel ★★★★★
Restaurant ★★★★★

Entspannen können die Gäste in Zimmern mit den unterschiedlichsten Einrichtungsstilen: afrikanischer, asiatischer, mediterraner, aus den Klöstern des Mittelmeerraums stammender Stil sowie „Pure Style", ausgehend von der Glaubensgemeinschaft der Shaker. Die Klosterschänke mit Biergarten bietet ein Angebot regionaler Speisen, das Restaurant Refugium geradlinige Küche aus erstklassigen Produkten. In der ehemaligen Abtskapelle der Mönche steht ein Standesamt für Trauungen zur Verfügung.

Das heutige Kloster Hornbach wurde 742 vom Heiligen Pirmin als Benediktinerkloster gegründet. Die sanfte Hügellandschaft der südwestlichen Pfalz entsprach dem Ideal der ▸

The guests are able to relax in rooms furnished in the most varied styles: Ethno, Asian, Mediterranean based on the Mediterranean monasteries, as well as "Pure Style" originating from the Shaker religious community. The restaurant „Klosterschänke" with beer garden offers regional cooking and the restaurant Refugium spoils you with light, Mediterranean cuisine using only first class products. In the monks former Abbots Chapel a registry office is available for weddings.

The present day Hornbach Monastery was established in 742 by St. Pirminius as a Benedictine monastery. The gentle hilly landscape of the ▸

Angebot/facility

ab 118 €

ab 179 €

A/S ab 225 €

10-100

Mo./Di. Gourmet-restaurant

Zweibrücken 8 km

Zweibrücken 6 km

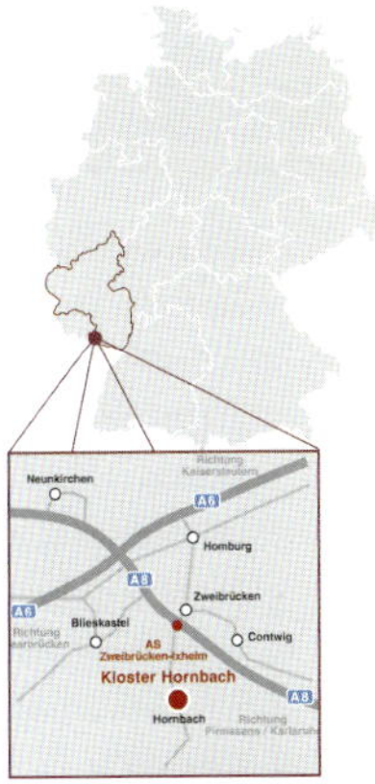

Mönche für einen Ort der Besinnlichkeit und inneren Einkehr. Das Kloster erfuhr in den folgenden Jahrhunderten eine bewegte Geschichte: von der Blüte einer klösterlichen Wirkungsstätte bis hin zum fast völligen Verfall. Nach mehrjähriger Restauration und Renovierung konnte im Mai 2000 die einstige Klosterruine als Hotel eröffnet werden. Im Museum Historama sowie im Kräutergarten des Urvaters der Botaniker, Hieronymus Bock, der als Lehrer und Prediger in Hornbach im 16. Jahrhundert gelebt hat, kann man die Spuren der Vergangenheit entdecken.

southwest Palatinate provided the monks ideal location for a sanctuary of contemplation and introspection. In the following centuries the monastery's history was changeable: from the blossoming of a small monastery to almost becoming completely derelict. After several years of restoration and renovation, the former monastery ruin was ready to be opened as a hotel in May 2000. Traces of the past can be discovered in the Historama Museum as well as in the herb garden of the founding Father of Botany, Hieronymus Bock, who lived in Hornbach in the 16th century as a teacher and preacher.

In der näheren Umgebung:

Bitche (15 km): Citadelle aus dem 17. Jahrhundert mit ehemaliger Festungsanlage, Garten des Friedens; **Fischbach (30 km):** Biosphärenhaus mit Baumwipfelpfad; **Gersheim (12 km):** römische Ausgrabungen; **Pirmasens (25 km):** Schuhmuseum im Alten Rathaus; **Rodalben (30 km):** Bärenhöhle in größter natürlicher Felsenhöhle der Pfalz; **Zweibrücken (8 km):** Wildrosengarten mit mehr als 3.000 Sorten; **Shoppingideen:** Outlets in Zweibrükken, Pirmasens, Rodalben, Mettlach.

In the surrounding area:

Bitche (9 miles): Citadel from the 17th century with former fortification, Garden of the Peace; **Fischbach (19 miles):** Biosphere House with treetop path; **Gersheim (7 miles):** Roman excavations; **Pirmasens (15 miles):** Shoe museum in the old town hall; **Rodalben (19 miles):** Bear cave in the largest natural rock cave in the Palatine; **Zweibrücken (5 miles):** Wild rose garden with more than 3.000 species; **Shopping ideas:** Outlets in Zweibruecken, Pirmasens, Rodalben, Mettlach.

TIPP

Mit einer vollgetankten „Ente", dem klassischen 2CV, einem reich bestückten Picknickkorb, Sonnenschirm und Decken geht es vom Kloster Hornbach zur nur zwei Kilometer entfernten französischen Grenze. Als Ausflugsziele bieten sich die wildromantischen Nordvogesen mit ihren Burgen und Sandsteinfelsen, die Museen des Bitcher Lands oder der Region Moselle sowie ein Abstecher ins zirka 90 Kilometer entfernte Straßburg an. Für das französische Lebensgefühl beim Stopp zwischendurch sorgen Baguette, Brie, Pâté und ein Gläschen Rotwein für den Beifahrer.

A fully fueled Citroën 2CV with a well-stocked picnic basket, sunshade and blankets takes you from Kloster Hornbach to the French border, which is only two kilometers away. The wild and romantic Vosges with their castles and sandstoned rocks, the museums of the Bitcher Land or the Moselle region are possible excursion destinations. Strasbourg is about 90 kilometers away and worth a detour, too. Baguette, Brie, pâté and a glas of red wine for the co-driver provide for the French sense of life.

LÖSCH für Freunde

Gastgeber/host: Stefanie Welsch und Olivier Fabing

Rheinland-Pfalz

Ausgezeichnet als bestes neues Hotel in Europa ist das Landhaus „LÖSCH für Freunde" mit seinem unkonventionellen Gästekonzept ein modernes Refugium.

Awarded best new hotel in Europe, the country house "LÖSCH für Freunde" is a modern hideaway with a unique, unconventional guest concept.

Hauptstraße 19-21
66500 Hornbach
Rheinland-Pfalz
Tel.: +49 6338 910100
Fax: +49 6338 9101099
www.loesch-fuer-freunde.de
info@loesch-fuer-freunde.de

Hotel ★★★★★
Restaurant ★★★★★

Die Atmosphäre und Herzlichkeit, die "Seele" des Hotels machen das „LÖSCH für Freunde" zu einer neuen Stilikone der Hotellerie und gleichzeitig zu einem individuellen Rückzugsort, großzügig und zum Wohlfühlen, eben wie bei guten Freunden. Am 19. Mai 2011 eröffneten die Besitzer des renommierten Hotels Kloster Hornbach und Gastgeber mit Leib und Seele das Landhaus „LÖSCH für

Freunde". Hier übernachten Gäste in 15 individuell gestalteten Zimmer und Suiten, die klangvolle Namen tragen wie "Land und Meer" oder "Mein Atelier". Ihre Einrichtung ist auf das jeweilige Thema abgestimmt. Auch für Familienfeste oder Tagungen bie- ▸

The atmosphere and warmth, the soul of the hotel characterise the "LÖSCH für Freunde" ("LÖSCH for friends") as a new style icon of hotel business and at the same time provide the country house with the calm ambience of an individual retreat, spacious and comfortable, just as at your good friends' house. On the 19th May 2011 the owners of the renowned hotel cloister Hornbach ("Kloster Hornbach") and hosts with heart and soul opened the country house "LÖSCH für Freunde". Up to 15 guests can stay here, accommodated in 15 individually designed rooms or suites which carry names as melodious as "Land and Sea" (Land und Meer) or "My ▸

Angebot/facility

ab 183 €

ab 148-168 €

A/S ab 158-208 €

2-25

Zweibrücken Hbf 8 km

Zweibrücken 6 km

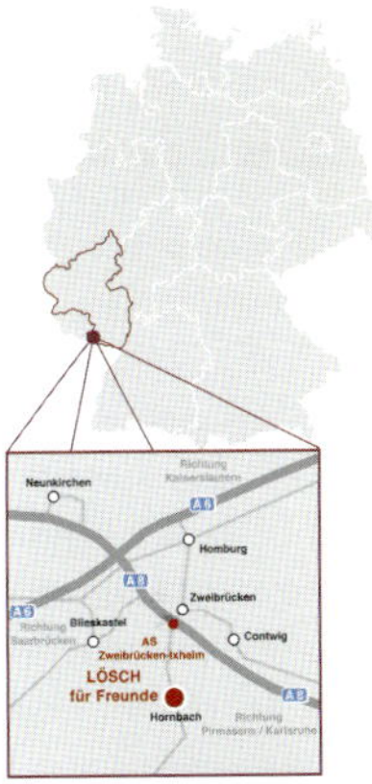

tet das Landhaus einen einzigartigen Rahmen. Hier sind Gruppen bis zu 30 Personen ganz unter sich, denn Gäste können das Haus auf Anfrage komplett mieten und es sich in privater Atmosphäre gemütlich machen.
Dieses stilvolle Haus mag man gar nicht Hotel nennen, weil es eigentlich ein sehr großzügiges Wohnhaus ist, elegant und einladend, anregend, aber auch gemütlich: Mit einer großen, bequemen Lounge, in der Gäste Tee trinken oder Wein, mit einem großen Esszimmer direkt neben einer offenen Küche, so dass Sie dem Koch über die Schulter schauen können, mit Wellness-Bereich und Tabaklounge. Persönlicher Service durch die Gastgeber und der gesellige Austausch der Gäste, unter anderem bei gemeinsamen Mahlzeiten an einer großen Tafel, werden hier großgeschrieben. Alle Bereiche des Landhauses stehen den Besuchern offen. Das gilt auch für die gemeinschaftliche Küche. Hier können Interessierte mit dem Koch und Gastgeber Olivier Fabing, der zuvor schon als Chefpatissier im Kloster

Atelier" (Mein Atelier). The interior is adjusted to the particular theme.
The country house also provides an ideal framework for family celebrations or business meetings. Groups of up to 30 people can be on their own at the "LÖSCH für Freunde" as the country house can be booked entirely on request, thus offering its guests a private, cosy atmosphere.
This stylish house you would not want to call a hotel as it actually is a spacious home, elegant and inviting, inspiring but also homely: With a large comfortable lounge that invites guests to have a cup of tea or a glass of wine. With a large dining room directly next to the open kitchen so that you will be able to watch the chef at work. And moreover also with a Spa area and a tobacco lounge.
Personal service by the hosts and communication among the guests, for instance during the shared mealtimes at a long table, also belong to the country house's premises. All parts of the house are open to its guests, including the kitchen. Interested visitors will be able to talk shop with

Hornbach tätig war, fachsimpeln oder selbst zum Kochlöffel greifen. Die Sauna-Oase auf dem Dach des Hauses bietet einen Panoramablick auf die malerische Landschaft der Südwestpfalz und das benachbarte Kloster Hornbach.

Der Preis für eine Übernachtung in einem Themenzimmer enthält die „Gaumenfreuden". Diese bestehen aus einem üppigen Frühstück, hausgemachtem Kuchen und herzhaften Snacks am Nachmittag und einem mehrgängigen Abendessen an der großen Küchentafel mit Apéritif, Wein und Wasser. Zwischendurch stehen den Hausgästen außerdem Softgetränke, Wasser, Tee, Kaffee und Obst zur Verfügung.

chef and host Olivier Fabing, who was head patissier at cloister Hornbach before, or to cook by themselves if they fancy to. The sauna area on the roof top of the building offers a fantastic panoramic view of the picturesque landscape of the South-western Pfalz and the neighbouring cloister Hornbach.

The price of one overnight stay in a themed room also includes culinary treats ("Gaumenfreuden"). These consist of a lush breakfast, home-made cake and hearty snacks in the afternoon as well as of a multi-course dinner at the large kitchen table with aperitif, wine and water. In between the meal times guests of the house may have soft drinks, water, tea, coffee and fruits for free.

TIPP

Nur 15 km von Landhaus „LÖSCH für Freunde" entfernt liegt das französische Städtchen Bitche, eingebettet in die faszinierende Landschaft der Nordvogesen. Neben dem weitläufigen Naturpark, der den Ort umschließt, finden Besucher hier auch eine Vielzahl an Gärten, die zu einem Spaziergang einladen. Bekanntestes Merkmal der Stadt ist die Zitadelle, welche erstmals im Jahre 1680 erbaut wurde. Nach ihrer Zerstörung während mehrerer Aufstände wurde die Burg im 18. Jahrhundert schließlich wieder errichtet und beherbergt heute ein Museum, das neben Ausstellungen auch architektonische Rundgänge auf dem Burggelände anbietet.

Situated only 9 miles from the country house "LÖSCH für Freunde" the small French town Bitche lies embedded in the fascinating landscape of the Northern Vosges. Apart from the extensive national park that encloses the town, visitors will find numerous gardens that invite to take a stroll. The most renowned feature of Bitche is the citadel that was built in 1680. After its destruction during several uprisings the fortress was reconstructed in the 18th century. Today it hosts a museum which offers guided tours on the castle grounds and exhibitions worth seeing.

Relief von 1794

Schafhof Amorbach

Gastgeber/host: Vera und Herbert Ullrich

Schafhof Amorbach, ehemaliges Klostergut, inmitten des Naturparks Bayerischer Odenwald.

Schafhof Amorbach, a former monastery in the heart of the fascinating Bavarian Odenwald Nature Park.

Schafhof 1
63916 Amorbach
Bayern
Tel: +49 9373 97330
Fax: +49 9373 4120
www.schafhof.de
rezeption@schafhof.de

Hotel ★★★★★
Restaurant ★★★★★

Inmitten des traumhaft schönen Naturparks Bayerischer Odenwald liegt der Schafhof Amorbach, ein ehemaliges Klostergut. Die komfortablen Zimmer im luxuriös-ländlichen Stil offenbaren eine Symbiose aus Tradition und zeitgemäßer Modernität. Das Gourmet-Restaurant „Abt- und Schäferstube" bietet moderne französische Küche auf Sterneniveau, das Restaurant „Benediktinerstube" ländlich mediterrane Spezialitäten.

Das ehemalige Klostergut Amorhof der Benediktinerabtei Amorbach, der heutige ▸

The Schafhof of Amorbach, a former monastery, is situated in the heart of the fascinating Bavarian Odenwald Nature Park. The comfortable rooms in the luxurious rustic style reveal a traditional and modern symbiosis. The Abbott and Shepherd Parlour gourmet restaurant offers modern, first class French cuisine, whilst the Benedictine Parlour restaurant offers rural Mediterranean specialities. The former Amorhof Monastery of the Amorbach Benedictine Abbey, which became today's 'Schafhof', was mentioned for the first ▸

Angebot/facility

129 €

148-193 €

A/S 233-308 €

12-120

Schäferstube Mo./Di. Bendiktiner-stube Mi./Do.

Amorbach 3 km

Frankfurt/Main 85 km

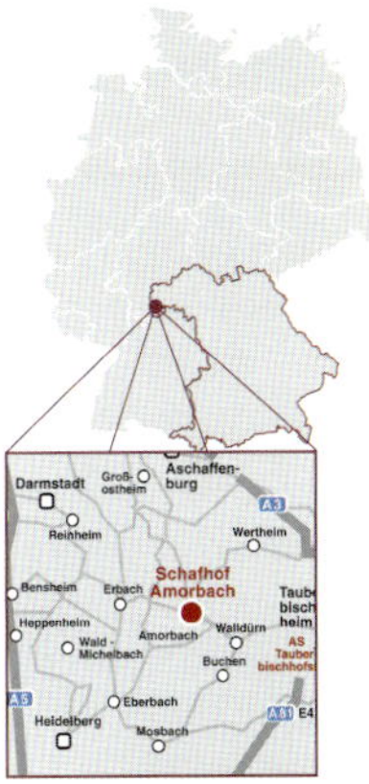

Schafhof, wurde 1446 erstmals urkundlich erwähnt. 1721 und 1974 liebevoll renoviert, übernachtet man heute in den alten Gemächern der Mönche oder den kleinen gemütlichen Zimmern des ehemaligen Klosterspeichers. Wundersam zurückversetzt in eine andere Zeit machen Tradition und Ausstrahlung den Schafhof zu einem Ort für Individualisten und Liebhaber ausgefallener Szenerie. Ein idealer Platz fernab der Großstadthektik, wo man in Ruhe arbeiten, tagen und sich erholen kann. Für entspannende, wohlige Momente sorgen die erlesenen Produkte und Anwendungen des Vital & Beauty Refugiums.

time in records in 1446. Lovingly restored in 1721 and 1974, today overnight stays in the old living quarters of the monks or the small cosy rooms of the former loft of the monastery are possible. Wondrously set back in time, tradition and charisma establish the 'Schafhof ' as a retreat for individualists and lovers of unusual scenery. An ideal place, far away from the hustle and buzzle of the city, where you can work in peace, hold meetings and recuperate. Not only do the exquisite products and exercises of the 'Vital & Beauty' retreat provide for relaxing, pleasant moments, so do the numerous sports activities.

In der näheren Umgebung:

Amorbach (5 km): Besichtigung der ehemaligen Benediktinerabtei; **Miltenberg (14 km):** Weinprobe auf dem Weingut, Ausflugsschifffahrt auf dem Main; **Buchen-Eberstadt (29 km):** Besuch der Eberstadter Tropfsteinhöhle und des Elfenbeinmuseums; **Aschaffenburg (45 km):** Automuseum mit der größten Sportwagensammlung der Welt; **Glashofen-Neusaß (20 km):** Golf-Schnupperkurs bei der Golfakademie Ergül Altinova; **Miltenberg, Walldürn (20 km), Michelstadt (23 km):** Spaziergang im historischen Städtchen.

In the surrounding area:

Amorbach (3 miles): Visit to the historic Benedektinerabtei; **Miltenberg (9 miles):** Wine tasting on the vineyard, boat excursion on the River Main; **Buchen-Eberstadt (18 miles):** Visit to the Eberstadt stalactite cave in Buchen-Eberstadt and the ivory-museum; **Aschaffenburg (28 miles):** Automobile Museum with the world's largest sports car collection; **Glashofen-Neusaß (12 miles):** Golf trial training course at the Erguel Altinova Golf Academy; **Miltenberg, Walldürn (12 miles), Michelstadt (14 miles):** Visit the small, historical town.

TIPP

Der Schafhof Amorbach bietet ganzjährig besondere Aktivitäten an, die Sie an der Rezeption erfragen sollten, z. B. Bogenschießen in der Feierscheune oder im Freien, geführte Wanderungen, in den Wintermonaten auch mit Fackeln, Empfang mit Fruchtbowle an den Teichen, im Winter wärmende Lagerfeuer mit Punsch, Besichtigung der Abteikirche in Amorbach mit anschließendem Orgelkonzert.

The Schafhof of Amorbach offers all year round special activities, which you should inquire about at reception, e.g. archery in the leisure activity barn or in the open air, organised walks, also with torches during the winter months, reception with punch at the ponds, warming campfire with mulled wine in the winter, guided tour of the abbey church in Amorbach followed by an organ concert.

Klöster und ihre Güter

Monasteries and their properties

Stadtbildprägend: die mächtige Klosterkirche in Armorbach.
Landmark of Armorbach: the impressive monastery church.

das Kloster Amorbach und das Kloster Hornbach

Amorbach monastery and Hornbach monastery

Klöster haben eine lange und bewegende Geschichte, nicht nur als Orte der Frömmigkeit und kontemplativen Lebensweise für Nonnen und Mönche, sondern auch als Orte der Bildung und Wissenschaft sowie eine nicht zu verachtende ökonomische Bedeutung für die jeweilige Region.

Heute ein beliebtes Ausflugsziel für Besucher aus der ganzen Welt, zeugt das Kloster Amorbach von einer Geschichte, die bis auf das 8. Jahrhundert zurückgeht. Als eines von vier Benediktinerklöstern kam ihm die Aufgabe zu, ein bis dahin unbesiedelte Waldgebiet zu erschließen. Die im Kloster lebenden Mönche befass-

Monasteries have a long and eventful history not only as places of contemplative life style and piety for nuns and monks but as places of education and science. Moreover, they are of noticeable economic importance for the particular region they are situated in.

Today a popular tourist attraction for people from all over the world, Amorbach monastery bears witness to a history that dates back to the 8th century. As one of the four Benedictine monasteries it was assigned the task to develop a forest area that had been unsettled until then. The monks who were living in the monastery started to clear the extensive

Blick auf das Konventsgebäude des ehemaligen Klosters Amorbach vom Seegarten aus.
View of the convent building of the former Amorbach monastery from the lake garden.

ten sich in damaliger Zeit mit der Rodung des ausgedehnten Waldareals – eine Aufgabe, die über mehrere Jahrhunderte zu den Ämtern des Klosters Amorbach zählte. Ebenso sollten sie die Region Ostfranken missionieren und die Verbreitung des Ideals eines einheitlichen christlichen Reiches beschleunigen.

Doch nicht nur die Übernahme religiös-bildender Missionarsämter und landwirtschaftlicher Arbeit prägen die Geschichte des Kloster Amorbach: Auch als Zentrum für Kultur, Wissen und Forschung verfügte das Kloster über enorme Bedeutung. In der Bevölkerung waren Nonnen und Mönche fast die einzigen, die des Lesens und Schreibens mächtig waren. Mönche vervielfältigten bedeutsame Bücher, indem sie diese handschriftlich kopierten und erhielten

woodland- a task that became one of the monastery's duties for many centuries. Furthermore, they were supposed to proselytise the region of Ostfranken and to spread the ideal of a united Christian empire.

But not only taking charge of missionary functions for religious education and performing agricultural work characterise the history of Amorbach monastery: It was also an important centre for culture, science and research. At those times nuns and monks were nearly the only ones in the general public that were able to read and write. Thus monks duplicated important books by copying the writings by hand and therewith preserved the literary works for posterity.

Barocke Pracht in der Klosterkirche Amorbach.
Baroque splendour in the monastery church Amorbach.

die literarischen Stücke somit für die Nachwelt. Die Amorbacher Traditionsnotizen, gelten als eine der bedeutendsten Informationsquellen zur mittelalterlichen Geschichte des östlichen Odenwaldgebietes.

Doch obwohl das Kloster Amorbach als kulturelles Zentrum der Region eine ungemeine Bedeutung besaß, gewährte es über Jahrhunderte nur dem Adel freien Zutritt. Erst ab dem 15. Jahrhundert standen die Tore auch anderen Bevölkerungsschichten offen – eine Wende, welche durch die Wiedereinführung der ehemaligen Benediktiner Klosterordnung herbeigeführt wurde. Im selben Jahrhundert gelang es schließlich auch, das Kloster von seinen vorherigen finanziellen Schwierigkeiten zu bereinigen. Somit schuf man Raum für neue Investi-

The Amorbach donation notices ("Armorbacher Traditionsnotizen") belong to the most important sources of information on the medieval history of the eastern Odenwald territory.

Even though Amorbach monastery plays a significant role as cultural centre of the region it only granted the nobility entry for many centuries. It was not until the 15th century that the monastery's gates were opened for other social classes, too – a turning point that was caused by the reintroduction of the former Benedictine monastery order. In the same century the monastery could finally be freed from its former financial difficulties. Thus space was created for new investments and soon a mill and a bakery were built. When the Peasants'

Ehemaliges Klostergut "Amorhof" der Benediktinerabtei Amorbach von 1446.
Former monastery property "Amorhof" of the Benedectine abbey Amorbach from 1446

tionen und ließ bald darauf eine hauseigene Mühle sowie ein Backhaus errichten. Als 1524 der Bauernkrieg ausbrach, erstürmten und plünderten aufständische Bauern Abtei und Kloster. Wenig später, während des Dreißigjährigen Krieges, fiel Kloster Amorbach erneut Besetzung und Plünderungen anheim. Die Lage verschärfte sich so stark, dass man schließlich das Kloster für einige Zeit aufheben musste.

Nach einer turbulenten Zeit jahrzehntelanger Kriege, hatte sich die Landschaft um das Kloster Amorbach verändert: Viele Orte der Region waren nun besiedelt und nahmen dem Kloster seine wirtschaftliche Grundlage, sodass ab 1650 seine wirtschaftliche Bedeutung abnahm und entsprechend auch die Anzahl der Klosterbewohner.

War started in 1524, the cloister and abbey were stormed and looted by revolting farmers. Shortly after, during the Thirty Years' War, Amorbach monastery was again conquered and looted. The situation became so severe that the monastery finally had to be closed for some time. After a turbulent period of tumults and war the landscape around the monastery had changed: Many places were now populated which thus diminished the economic basis of the monastery. Therefore, its economic importance decreased from 1650 onwards and in the course of this development the number of its inhabitants shrank.

Kräutergarten und das Wissen um die Nutzung und Wirkung von Heil- und Nutzpflanzen gehören seit jeher zum Standardrepertoire der Klöster und ihrer Güter.
Herb gardens and the knowledge of use and effect of medicinal and crop plants have been part of the standard repertoire of monasteries and their properties.

Die Säkularisierung und Schließung des Klosters erfolgte im Jahre 1803. Seitdem werden seine Gemäuer vom Fürstenhaus Leiningen bewohnt, dem das Kloster und verschiedenen Ländereien als Ausgleich gegen von Napoleon annektierte Besitztümer in der Vorderpfalz zugesprochen wurde. Die Klosterkirche wurde künftig evangelisch-lutherische Hofkirche genutzt und beheimatet seit 1859 die evangelische Pfarrgemeinde Amorbach. Der Schafhof, das ehemalige Klostergut der Benediktinermönche, beherbergt heute ein angenehm elegantes Landhotel .

Ein weiteres ehemals bedeutendes Benediktinerkloster ist das Kloster Hornbach in Rheinland-Pfalz. 741 vom heiligen Pirminius gegründet, der hier auch gestorben und begraben ist,

In the year 1803 Amorbach monastery was finally secularised and closed. Since then its buildings are inhabited by the Princely family of Leiningen who received the monastery and additional land property as compensation for annexation of property in the Vorderpfalz region by Napoleon. From then on the monastery church was used as Evangelical -Lutheran court church and hosts the Evangelical parish of Amorbach since 1859. The sheep farm ("Schafhof"), former monastery property of the Benedictine monks, hosts a comfortable elegant country hotel today.

Another formerly important Benedictine monastery can be found in Rhineland-Palatinate: Hornbach monastery was founded by in741 by St. Priminius, who also died there and was

Abendstimmung im Kloster Hornbach.
Evening ambience at Hornbach monastery.

Im säkularisierten Kloster Hornbach wird die Tradition, Reisende und Gäste aufzunehmen und zu bewirten, gepflegt und zeitgemäß interpretiert.
At the secularised Hornbach monastery the tradition to receive and host guests and travellers is maintained and interpreted in a contemporary way.

verfügte es bis ins 14. Jahrhundert über einen weitreichenden Einfluss und trug im großen Maße zur Entwicklung Oberlothringens bei. Es war nachweislich an zahlreichen Dorfgründungen beteiligt.

Bis 1230 übte das Kloster das Münzrecht aus, das ihm von Kaiser Heinrich V. verliehen worden war. Schon früh baute man eine Klosterschule, die die Ausbildung adeliger Kinder in Geisteswissenschaften und Sprachen zum Zweck hatte. Fürsten und Adelige der Region hielten hohe Stücke auf das Kloster Hornbach, das dadurch erhebliche Sonderrechte zugesprochen bekam.

buried on the monasterial grounds. Until the 14th century the monastery had a far reaching influence in the region and played an important role in the development of Oberlothringen. It was involved in numerous village foundings.

Until 1230 the monastery exercised the right to mint coins – a privilege granted by Emperor Henry V.. Early on a monastery church was built which had the purpose to educate children of aristocratic families in humanities and languages. Counts and noblemen from the region thought highly of Hornbach monastery which thus was granted privileges.

Einfach aber komfortabel: die Pilgerzimmer in der alten Klosterremise.
Simple but comfortable: the pilgrim guest rooms in the old monastery shed.

Klostergarten in Hornbach: erholsame Ruhe in inspirierender Umgebung.
Monastery garden in Hornbach: relaxing calm in inspiring surroundings.

Die umfangreiche Bibliothek und Schreibstube lässt die hohe Bedeutung erahnen, die dieses Kloster als wissenschaftliches Zentrum der Region inne hatte.

Nach der Auflösung des Klosters durch Verfügung Napoleons, verfielen die Gebäude im Laufe der Jahrzente und Ruinenreste wurden bis Ende des 20. Jahrhunderts nur noch partiell genutzt.

Nach einer aufwendigen Rekonstruktion beherbergt es heute das Hotel Kloster Hornbach, in dem der Geist der Benediktiner erkennbar weht und das einen Aufenthalt in Hornbach zu einem unvergesslichen Erlebnis macht.

The extensive library and study gives an idea of the great importance the monastery had as scientific centre for religion.

After the dissolution of the monastery by orders of Napoleon, the buildings forfeited throughout the centuries and remains of its ruins were only partly used until the end of the 20th century.

After the monastery was restored and reconstructed under high effort, it now hosts the Hornbach monastery Hotel (Hotel Kloster Hornbach), in which the spirit of the Benedictines can still be felt and which will make your stay in Hornbach an unforgettable experience.

Die Hotellobby im Kreuzgang, so empfängt Kloster Hornbach seine Gäste.
Hotel lobby in the cross-coat - here Hornbach monastery welcomes its guests.

landrover.de/ ourplanet
UNVERGLEICHLICHER LUXUS.
DER RANGE ROVER.
Der Range Rover – eines der vollständigsten und vielseitigsten Luxus-Allradfahrzeuge der Welt. Der neue 4,4-Liter TDV8 Turbodiesel macht ihn noch leistungsfähiger und noch wirtschaftlicher. Ein Auto, das Ihnen höchsten Komfort bietet – selbst auf Reisen und Ausflügen durch unwegsames Gelände. Weitere Informationen erhalten Sie gebührenfrei über das Land Rover Service Center unter 0800 1088500.
RANGE ROVER

www.landrover.de
ANGE ROVER
LAND ROVER

Von Zapfenpflückern und Wildkirschen
Of cone pickers and wild cherries

In Deutschland gibt es etwa hundert Zapfenpflücker, die einem der am wenigsten bekannten und gleichzeitig skurrilsten Berufe nachgehen. Dabei hängt von ihnen der Erfolg der gesamten Forstwirtschaft ab. Zapfenpflücker reisen als Selbstständige während der Saison mit dem Wohnwagen von Ernteplatz zu Ernteplatz. Die meisten sind hauptberuflich noch in einem anderen grünen Beruf tätig, etwa als Forstwirt oder Baumpfleger. Die Saison der Zapfenpflükker ist kurz und strapaziös.

Sie ernten den Baumsamen, der zur Aufforstung von Wäldern benötigt wird. Darüberhinaus übernehmen Zapfenpflücker auch spezielle Aufgaben wie etwa das Pflücken von Wildkirschen für spezialisierte Brennereien, wie die Edelobstbrennerei Ziegler in Freudenberg am Main.

Die seltenen winzigen Wildkirschen für den Ziegler Wildkirsch Nr. 1 werden von Zapfenpflückern geerntet, die die Standorte in Steinbrüchen oder versteckten Waldlichtungen der weit verstreuten Wildbäume kennen.

Da diese Bäume teilweise bis zu 30 Meter hoch sind, können die Früchte nicht von Hand gepflückt werden, sondern die kuriose Zunft der Zapfenpflücker klettert mit Steigeisen die mächtigen Stämme hoch, nahe der Baumkronen werden dann Schüttelseile befestigt und kurz darauf „regnet" es Wildkirschen.

n Germany, there are about 100 cone pickers who are working in one of the least known but at the same time most bizarre jobs.

Nevertheless, the success of the whole forestry depends upon them. During the season cone pickers travel as self-employed workers with their trailers from one place of harvest to the next. Most of them have a full-time occupation in other „green" jobs, such as forester or arborist. The season of the cone pickers is short and exhausting.

They harvest tree seeds which are needed for the afforestation of the woods. Moreover, they take on other special tasks such as pikking wild cherries for specialised distilleries as the "Edelobstbrennerei" (distillery for fine fruit) Ziegler in Freudenberg am Main.

The rarely found tiny wild cherries for the "Ziegler wild cherry no 1" ("Ziegler Wildkirsch Nr 1") are harvested by cone pickers who know the locations in quarries or hidden clearings of the wide spread wild cherry trees.

As these trees are usually up to 32.8 yards high, their fruits cannot be picked by hand: The cone pickers climb up the massive trunks with crampons, fasten ropes to shake close to the treetop and shortly after wild cherries are falling down to the ground.

The cone pickers of the Ziegler distillery only deliver excellent products. The wild grown

Wildkirschbaum in voller Blüte.
Wild cherry tree in full bloom.

Die Zapfenpflücker der Brennerei Ziegler liefern nur exzellente Ware ab. Die wild gewachsenen Früchte sind natürlich gereift - ohne künstlichen Dünger - und haben dadurch ein besonders intensives Aroma.

Nach der Eingangskontrolle werden die Früchte von Hand sortiert, von Blattwerk, Stielen und Ästen befreit, entsteint und entkernt. Anschließend wird die Maische in extra dafür gebauten kühlbaren Rührwerktanks bei konstant 18 °C gegärt.

Gebrannt wird nach dem Doppelbrandverfahren: Rohbrand, Feinbrand. Aus dem Herzstück des Feinbrandes wird der Ziegler Edelbrand gewonnen und mit Wasser aus der eigenen Quelle auf Trinkstärke gebracht.

fruits are naturally ripened – without artificial fertilisers – and thus have an especially intensive aroma.

After the examination of the incoming cherries, the fruits are sorted by hand, freed from leaves, roots and branches, stoned and cored. Afterwards, the mash is fermented at a constant temperature of 64 °F in agitator tanks which can be cooled and have been constructed especially for this procedure.

Afterwards a double distillation process consisting of raw and fine distillation is used to distil the liquid. From the heart of the fine spirit the Ziegler fine eau de vie ("Edelbrand") is generated and by use of water from the distillery's own well diluted to drinking quality.

Die Zapfenpflücker der Brennerei Ziegler kennen ihre „geheimen" und ergiebigen Plätze, an denen Wildkirschen gedeihen.
The cone pickers of the Ziegler distillery know the "secret" and fruitful spots where they can find wild cherries.

Ziegler seit 1865
Freudenberg
DIE ESSENZ DER FRÜCHTE.
No 1
WILD
KIRSCH
No 1
WILDKIRSCH
LIKÖR
20% vol.
0,35l
DEUTSCHES
ERZEUGNIS
www.brennerei-ziegler.de

Hotel Palmenwald Schwarzwaldhof

Gastgeber/hosts: Radka Titova

Baden-Württemberg

Elegantes Kurhotel im Stil der Gründerzeit und des Jugendstils in Freudenstadt.

Elegant health resort in Wilhelminian and Art Nouveau style in Freudenstadt.

Lauterbad-Str. 56
72250 Freudenstadt
Baden-Württemberg
Tel.: +49 7441 88870
Fax: +49 7441 8887111
www.palmenwald.de
booking@palmenwald.de

Hotel ★★★★★
Restaurant ★★★★★

Das Hotel Palmenwald gilt als eines der Symbole von Freudenstadt. Die gemütlichen Salons und die 83 eleganten Zimmer und Suiten, die teilweise mit Balkonen oder Terrassen ausgestattet sind, bilden zusammen mit dem weitläufigen Areal den passenden Rahmen für einen erholsamen Aufenthalt. Mit dazu bei tragen zum einen die Köstlichkeiten aus Küche und Keller, die je nach Wetterlage im Palmensaal oder auf der Sonnenterrasse mit einem phantastischen Blick auf Freudenstadt und den Schwarzwald serviert werden.

Die Individualität des Hauses besticht mit seiner einzigartigen aufwendig wieder hergestellten Innenausstattung, in der reichen Sammlung von Originalgemälden und mit seinem luxuriösen ▸

The Palmenwald Hotel is considered as one of the symbols of Freudenstadt. The cosy salons and the 83 elegant rooms and suites, some of which with balconies or terraces, and the spacious grounds form a convenient setting for a pleasant stay. The delights from kitchen and cellar, which are served either, depending on the weather, in the palm hall or on the sun terrace with a fantastic view of Freudenstadt and the Black Forest contribute to a refreshing and unforgettable holiday.

The individuality of the hotel captivates its visitors with its unique interior design, which was restored under great effort, with a rich collection of original paintings and with its luxurious ROSEN ▸

Angebot/facility

94-101 €

174-198 €

A/S 196-440 €

bis 140

Freudenstadt 1,5 km

Stuttgart 85 km

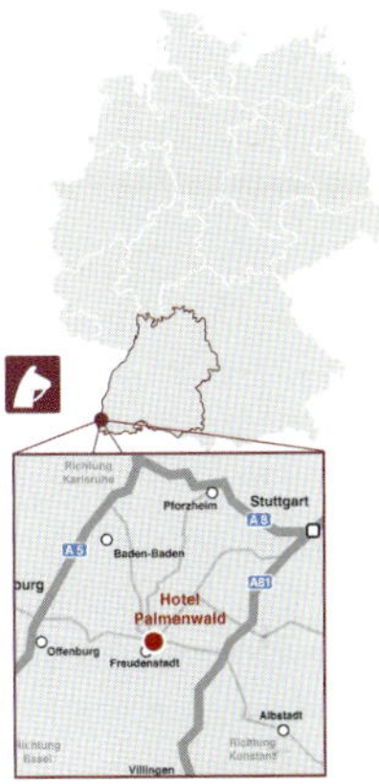

ROSEN SPA, erfüllt vom zärtlichen Duft der bulgarischen Rose und den Verlockungen des Orients.

Hotel „Palmenwald" wurde im Jahr 1895 als Kurhaus vom angesehenen Unternehmer und Sozialreformator Paul Lechner aus Stuttgart erbaut. Der romantische Jugendstil und das heilende Klima von Freudenstadt verwandelten es rasch in einen bevorzugten Ferienplatz.

Rund 100 Jahre nach seiner Erbauung und nach einer bewegten Geschichte wechselvoller Nutzungen - während des Ersten und Zweiten Weltkriegs wurde das Gebäude z.B. als Militärlazarett benutzt; aus dieser Zeit sind an den Wänden der unterirdischen Hotelräume einzigartige Zeichnungen von Soldaten erhalten - erstrahlt das palaisartige Gebäude seit 2010 wieder in neuem alten Glanz der Gründerzeit und des Jugendstils.

SPA, which attracts guests with the sweet scents of Bulgarian rose and the temptations of the orient.

The Palmenwald Hotel was built in 1895 as "Kurhaus Palmenwald", a spa hotel, by the renowned entrepreneur and social reformer Paul Lechler from Stuttgart. The romantic style of the Art Nouveau and the healthy climate of Freudenstadt soon led to its development into a popular holiday destination.

Approximately 100 years after its construction and its eventful history of multiple uses – during World War I and II, the building served as military hospital; even today, unique drawings by soldiers from this era can still be found on the walls of the subterranean hotel rooms - the palace resembling building shows its former glory in styles of the Wilhelminian and Art Nouveau era again since 2010.

In der näheren Umgebung:

Rund um den Kienberg: 8,6 km langer Rundweg (2 Stunden Gehzeit), führt in Serpentinen und durch eine üppige Fauna zum Kienberg, dem Hausberg Freudenstadts, hinauf; unterwegs Skulpturen, Besucherbergwerk, Friedrichsturm und Wetterwarte; **Freudenstadt:** größter Marktplatz Deutschlands mit Winkelhakenkirche; **Baden-Baden (40 km):** „Sommerhauptstadt Europas" mit Festspielhaus, Theater, Museum Frieder Burda, Fabergé Museum, Brahmshaus, Casino, römische Badruinen, Galopprennbahn, Kloster Lichtenthal, ausgedehnten Parks und schönen Geschäftsstraßen.

In the surrounding area:

Around the mountain Kienberg: circular path of 8 miles (2 hours of walking) leads in serpentines and through rich fauna directly up to Kienberg, the local mountain of Freudenstadt; on the way you will also come across sculptures, an exhibition mine, the tower Friedrichsturm and a weather station; **Freudenstadt:** biggest market square of Germany with the Winkelhaken church; **Baden-Baden (24 miles):** "summer capital of Europe" offering a festival hall, theatre, the Frieder Burda museum, the Fabergé museum, the house of Brahms, a casino, the ruins of Roman baths, a racecourse, Lichtenthal cloister, a large park and lovely shopping streets.

TIPP

Gleich hinter dem Hotel beginnt der Aufstieg zum höchst gelegenen, 1985 angelegten Rosenweg Deutschlands. Die neue, durch das Hotel Palmenwald geförderte "Rose von Kazanlak", eine Duftrose, die seit dem 16. Jahrhundert im Rosenanbaugebiet nahe der bulgarischen Stadt Kazanlak gezüchtet wird, hat bis zu 200 cm lange biegsame Triebe, die einen überhängenden Strauch bilden, mittelgroße hellrosa gefüllte Blüten in Büschen mit leicht zerzauster Mitte sowie einen lieblich süßen Duft. Auf einer Länge von 2 km führt der Weg an insgesamt über 1.000 Strauchrosen vorbei.

Just behind the hotel buildings you will find the ascent to the highest situated rose trail of Germany which was constructed in 1985. The Palmenwald Hotel especially supports the new "rose of Kazanlak", a scented rose that has been bred in a rose growing area close to the Bulgarian town Kazanlak since the 16th century. It has long, flexible sprouts which can measure up to 78.7 inches and which form an overhanging bush, middle-sized bright pink filled blossoms in bushes with a slightly tousled centre and a lovely sweet scent. The trail leads 1.24 miles past a variety of over 1,000 bush roses.

Landhaus Mühle

Gastgeber/hosts: Katja Nowak und Rolf Pochert

Baden-Württemberg

Charmantes Landhotel in einmalig schöner Ortsrandlage über dem Ostufer des Schluchsees.

Charming countryside hotel in a unique location overlooking the eastern shore of Lake Schluchsee

Unterer Mühlenweg 13
79859 Schluchsee
Baden-Württemberg
Tel: +49 7656 209
Fax: +49 7656 982192
www.landhaus-muehle.de
info@landhaus-muehle.de

Hotel ★★★★
Restaurant ★★★★

An der Ostseite des Schluchsees liegt das Landhaus Mühle, ein über 500 Jahre altes Schwarzwaldhaus. Der Bach, der das Mühlrad antrieb, plätschert noch heute an der Terrasse vorbei, durch die angrenzenden Wiesen hinunter zum See. Die ehemaligen Wohnräume des Mühlenhofes wurden von den Gastgebern in gemütliche Salons verwandelt. Die „Alte Stube" wurde zum neuen „Wohnzimmer" des Landhauses und lädt zum gemeinsamen

Lesen, Spielen oder Fernsehen ein. In der rustikalen „Ofenstube" wird das Frühstück serviert und aus der „Alten Küche" wurde ein Raucher-Refugium. Die im Landhaus Stil eingerichteten Zimmer laden zu einem erholsamen Aufenthalt ein. ▸

The country house mill, (Landhaus Mühle), a 500-year-old traditional Black Forest house is situated on the eastern side of Lake Schluchsee. The brook that used to drive the millwheel is still plashing, and after passing the terrace meanders gently through the adjoining meadows into the valley and down to the lake. The former living quarters in the courtyard of the mill were converted to comfortable parlours by the hosts. The „Old Snuggery" became the new living room of the country house, inviting you to watch TV, play games or to read a book in company.

Breakfast is served in the „Oven Snuggery" and the „Old Kitchen" was turned into a retreat ▸

Angebot/facility

75-90 €

135-170 €

A/S 165-190 €

5-20

Bahnhof Schluchsee
2 km

Zürich Kloten
76 km
Basel-Moulhouse
92 km
Karlsruhe 160 km
Stuttgart-Echterdingen 169 km
Frankfurt 312 km
München 387 km

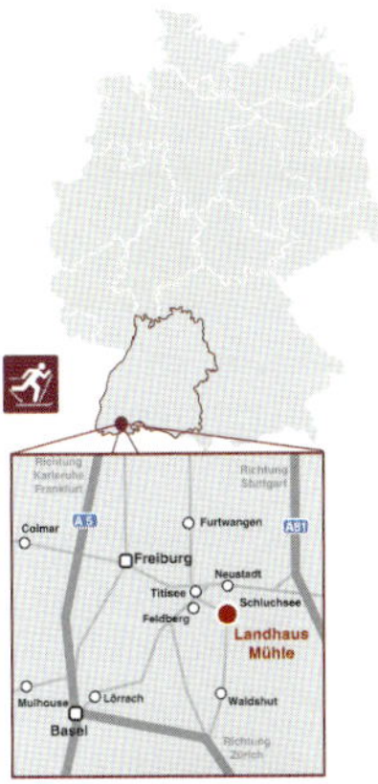

Bei schönem Wetter empfängt ein weitläufiger Naturgarten die Landhaus-Gäste. Auf bereit stehenden Liegen kann man es sich bequem machen oder die Beine im Mühlbach kühlen, wozu die Gastgeber eigens eine kleine Badestelle angelegt haben.

Die gourmetverdächtige Landhausküche speist sich ausschließlich aus frischen Produkten der Region. In den Töpfen von Rolf Pochert werden daraus wunderbare Gerichte, die – je nach Wunsch und Wetter – auf der Sonnenterrasse oder vor dem Kamin im Restaurant, dem ehemaligen Hauptraum der Mühle, serviert werden.

Die Umgebung der alten Landhaus Mühle bietet vielfältige Möglichkeiten zum Wandern, Walken, Radfahren oder Langlaufen: Wanderwege und Loipen beginnen direkt am Haus!

for smokers. The cosy rooms, furnished in a country house style, invite you to enjoy a pleasant and relaxing stay.

In beautiful weather a spacious uncultivated natural garden awaits you. You can lie down on one of the couches or cool your legs in the Mühlbach where the hosts built a sweet bathing place. The gourmet country house cuisine only uses fresh products of the region. In the pots of Rolf Pochert, these are transformed into marvellous dishes which are served – depending upon weather and personal choice – on the sun terrace or in front of the fire-place in the restaurant, the former main area of the mill. The surroundings of the old country house mill offer various possibilities for walking, cycling or cross-country skiing: trails and cross-country ski run start directly at the house!

In der näheren Umgebung:

Schluchsee: Kurort Schluchsee am Ufer des gleichnamigen größten Schwarzwaldsees auf 930 bis 1.300 Meter Höhe; Badesee und Wassersportzentrum; alte Handwerkskunst im Vogelhaus; Skilift im Ortsteil Fischbach; Erlebnisbad „AQUA FUN"; **Todtmoss (27 km):** barocke Wallfahrtskirche; Schaubergwerk; Museum "Heimethus" in einem 250 Jahre alten Schwarzwaldhaus; „Hausberg" Hochkopf (1.263 m ü.d.M), bei gutem Wetter Alpenpanorama; **Titisee /Neustadt (21 km):** Uferpromenade; Holzmaskenschnitzerei; Eisenbacher Uhrmacherhandwerk (7 km nordöstlich von Titisee); **Feldberg (21 km):** höchster Berg im Schwarzwald (1.493 m ü.d.M) im Naturpark Hochschwarzwald.

In the surrounding area:

Lake Schluchsee: Health resort Schluchsee on the banks of the largest Black Forest lake of the same name, at 1017 to 1421 yards above sea level; one of the cleanest lakes to swim in and centre of water sport in the black forest; old craftsmanship in the bird house; Ski lift in Fischbach; Experience bath "AQUA FUN"; **Todtmoss (17 miles)**: baroque pilgrimage church; mine-museum; Museum "Heimethus" in a 250 year old Black Forest house; mountain "High head" (1381 yards) with an excellent view over the alps if the weather permits it; **Titisee/Neustadt (13 miles)**: lakeside promenade; mask carver; watchmaking in Eisenbach (5 miles northeast of Titisee); **Feldberg (13 miles)**: highest mountain in the Black Forest (1632 yards) in the Black Forest natural park.

TIPP

Einen Ausflug zum ehemaligen Benediktinerkloster St. Blasien und die Besichtigung des im frühklassizistischen Zopfstil erbauten Domes, der städtebaulichen Dominante des Ortes St. Blasien, sollten Sie sich nicht entgehen lassen. 1783 als Abteikirche eingeweiht, misst die Kuppel des beeindruckenden Baues in ihrer Gesamthöhe 62 Meter. Mit einer Spannweite von 36 Metern war sie zu diesem Zeitpunkt die drittgrößte Kuppelkirche Europas.

Do take a trip to the former Benedictine monastery of St. Blaise, and visit the cathedral built in early Louis XVI style. Inaugurated in 1783 as an abbey church, the cupola of this impressive building is 67 yards high. At the time it was the third biggest dome in Europe. With a wingspan of 40 yards it is still one of the biggest cupolas in Europe.

CHAMPAGNE

ALFRED GRATIEN

Epernay

Champagner aus dem Hause Alfred Gratien hat eine lange Tradition und ist sich - allen Massen- und Modetrends zum Trotz - bis heute treu geblieben: Ein "handgemachter" Champagner, der für Qualität und Einzigartigkeit steht.

Rigorose Auswahl der Trauben, traditionelle Vinifikation, freiwillige Begrenzung auf 250.000 Flaschen pro Jahr und Achtung des Terroirs: Diese Prinzipien und die Tatsache,

Champagnes from Alfred Gratien have a lengthy tradition and, disregarding the mass-produced ethos and fashions of modern times, still remain true to that tradition today. What you get is a "hand-crafted" champagne that represents quality and uniqueness.

Rigorous selection of grapes, traditional winemaking methods, voluntarily limited production to 250,000 bottles per year, respect ▸

dass er zu den letzten "handgefertigten" Champagnern überhaupt zählt, verhelfen Alfred Gratien zu seiner großartigen Qualität und machen ihn genauso einzigartig wie die historischen Häuser von Culture & Castles | HISTOHOTELS.

Dafür steht Kellermeister Nicolas Jaeger. Genauso wie sein Vater und seine Vorfahren bewahrt er bereits in der vierten Generation die Einzigartigkeit des Champagners. Jedes Jahr sorgt er für die besten Cuvées aus den Sorten Chardonnay, Pinot Noir und Pinot Meunier. Akribisch und strikt achtet er auf Einhaltung der Gärung in den typischen Holzfässern und garantiert so ganz persönlich eine gleichbleibend hohe Qualität und das unvergleichliche Aroma. ▸

Champagne Alfred Gratien
30, rue Maurice Cerveaux
B.P. 3
51201 EPERNAY Cedex - France

Tel.: +33 3 26543820
Fax.: +33 3 26545344

contact@alfredgratien.com
www.alfredgratin.com

Cuvée Brut Classique

Der Stil von Alfred Gratien zeigt sich in diesem großen Klassiker. Die raffinierte Zusammensetzung wird vom fruchtigen Pinot Meunier, verbunden mit der Eleganz des Chardonnay, dominiert.

Farbe: hellgold, sehr schön
Mousseux: feinperlig, sehr lang anhaltend
Bukett: Zitrusfrüchte, Mango, Pfirsich und Aprikose
Mundaroma: Herrliches Gleichgewicht von aromatischer Kraft und der Frische exotischer Früchte
Harmonie: raffinierter Verschnitt, in dem sich die Eleganz des Chardonnay mit dem fruchtigen Pinot Meunier und dem Durchhaltevermögen des Pinot Noir verbindet Das ist die Kunst der Champagnerherstellung
Alkohol: 12,5 % vol

Cuvée Paradis Brut Rosé

Weich und fruchtiger Rosé Champagner des Hauses Alfred Gratien

Farbe: helles, lachsfarbenes Kupfer
Mousseux: sehr feinperlig, sehr lang anhaltend
Bukett: fein, sich entfaltend, dominiert von Orangenschalen, Trockenfrüchten und Lebkuchen
Mundaroma: prickelnd, von Orangenschalen, die sich in Noten von Erdbeer- und Himbeersorbets verlieren
Harmonie: ein kräftiger, zarter und harmonischer Rosé. Der Vorgeschmack auf das Paradies
Alkohol: 12,0 % vol

Service

Alfred Gratien erhalten Sie in den Culture & Castles | HISTOHOTELS, im gehoben Fachhandel und in ausgewählten Lebensmittelabteilungen der Warenhäuser. Weitere Bezugsquellen in Ihrem näheren Postleitzahlenbereich erfahren Sie über vertrieb@henkell-sektkellerei.de.

In diesen kleinen, nur 228 Liter fassenden Eichenfässern findet die erste Gärung statt und gibt dem Champagner einen sehr geschmackvollen, ausbalancierten Stil. Alfred Gratien ist eines der letzten Unternehmen, das diese Tradition beibehalten hat! Auf diese Weise bleibt das Aroma der Trauben und des Terroirs erhalten und der Wein behält auch mit zunehmendem Alter seine Frische.

Bei Alfred Gratien lagern die Jahrgänge mit verdrahteten Korken. Die Durchlässigkeit und Flexibilität des Korkens lassen kleine Mengen Sauerstoff leichter eindringen, was für eine gelungene Reifung des Champagners unerlässlich ist, denn ein guter Champagner wird nicht "hergestellt", er wird "erschaffen". Dank der weinigen Struktur eignen sich die Champagner von Alfred Gratien für eine lange Lagerung.

for the land - these principles and the fact that it is one of the last few remaining "hand-crafted" champagne producers in the world are the secret behind the outstanding quality of Alfred Gratien champagne and the factors which make it as unique as the historic houses of Culture & Castles | HISTOHOTELS.

Our cellar master, Nicolas Jaeger, makes it his business to ensure that things stay that way.

Following in the footsteps of his father and his forefathers, he represents the fourth generation to preserve the uniqueness of our champagnes.

Every year, he ensures that we have the very best cuvée of Chardonnay, Pinot Noir and Pinot Meunier grape varieties. He is meticulous and strict in the way he oversees

the fermentation of the wines in traditional wooden casks. In this way, he personally guarantees consistently high quality and an incomparable aroma.

The first fermentation takes place entirely in small 228 litre oak casks (champagne casks) and gives the champagne a vinous, flavoursome, balanced style. Alfred Gratien is one of the last remaining wine-makers to maintain this tradition.

At Alfred Gratien, the vintages are sealed with wired corks before being placed in the cellar. The permeability and flexibility of the cork allows small amounts of oxygen to penetrate into the wine, a process which is essential for successful maturation. Tasting these wines is an unforgettable moment in the life of any wine connoisseur.

Champagne is not "manufactured", it is "created". Only the best grapes are selected for the composition of Alfred Gratin cuvées. Thanks to their vinous structure, champagnes from Alfred Gratien lend themselves to long periods of cellaring.

Champagne Alfred Gratien
30, rue Maurice Cerveaux
B.P. 3
51201 EPERNAY Cedex - France

Tel.: +33 3 26543820
Fax.: +33 3 26545344

contact@alfredgratien.com
www.alfredgratin.com

Cuvée Brut Classique

This great classic clearly shows the style of Alfred Gratien. It's a refined blend dominated by fruity Pinot Meunier combined with the elegance of Chardonnay.

Colour: Light-gold, very beautiful
Sparkle: Fine, extremely long-lasting mousse
Bouquet: Citrus fruits, mangos, peaches and apricots
Palate: A wonderful balance of aromatic strength and the freshness of exotic fruits
Overall impression: A refined blend in which the elegance of the Chardonnay melds with the fruitiness of the Pinot Meunier and the enduring flavour of the Pinot Noir. That is the art of champagne production
Alcohol: 12.5% vol.

Cuvée Paradis Brut Rosé

The only rosé champagne from Alfred Gratien, soft and fruity.

Colour: Light, salmon-pink copper colour
Sparkle: Very fine, very long-lasting mousse
Bouquet: Delicate, slowly unfolding, dominated by the flavour of orange peel, dried fruits and gingerbread
Palate: Tingling flavours of orange peel, melding into notes of strawberry and raspberry sorbet
Overall impression: A strong, delicate and harmonious rosé. A foretaste of paradise!
Alcohol: 12.0 % vol.

Service

You can purchase Alfred Gratien in the Culture & Castles | HISTOHOTELS, in highly specialised trade and in well-chosen food departments of the department stores. You find out other sources of supply in your closer zip code area about vertrieb@henkell-sektkellerei.de.

Grandhotel Römerbad

Gastgeber/hosts: Sandra Kunert & Vladimir Saal

Baden-Württemberg

Traditionsreiches Grandhotel und kultureller Mittelpunkt des Luft- und Mineralwasserkurortes Badenweiler.

Traditional Grand Hotel and cultural centre of the Spa and mineral water resort Badenweiler.

Schlossplatz 1
70410 Badenweiler
Baden-Württemberg
Tel: +49 7632 700,
Fax: +49 7632 70200
www.hotel-roemerbad.de
roemerbad@lbbhotels.com

Hotel ★★★★
Restaurant ★★★★

Das Grandhotel Römerbad hat nicht nur eine glanzvolle Vergangenheit, sondern ist zugleich ein Kulturdenkmal von besonderer Bedeutung. Ob kleine Nachtmusik im Hofsaal oder große Denker im literarischen Salon – hier wird Kultur gelebt. Schließlich trägt das Grandhotel seit dem Jahre 1825 den Beinamen „Kultur-Residenz". Die Vierflügelanlage, deren imposanter Innenhof 1880 mit einer prachtvollen Kuppel überdacht und von offenen Galerien mit gläsernen Jugendstil-Balustraden umrundet wurde, bietet 76 Zimmer und Suiten sowie andere großzügige Räumlichkeiten, die einen angenehmen Aufenthalt sowie herrliche Ausblicke ins Rheintal und die im nahen Frankreich liegenden Vogesen ermöglichen.

Die Küche ist badisch mediterran bis international, wobei der Küchenchef und sein Team mit Lust und Leidenschaft alle Register der feinen Küche ziehen.

Das Grandhotel Römerbad liegt inmitten einer herrlichen Urlaubslandschaft mit vielfältigen Angeboten aller denkbaren Sport- und ▸

Grand Hotel Römerbad has not only a glamorous past, but is a cultural monument of particular historical and art-historical importance. Whether little serenade in the yard hall or great poets and thinkers in the literary salon – here culture is lived. After all, the Grand hotel has also esteemed the title „culture residence" („Kulturresidenz") since 1825.

The four-wing complex of the Grand Hotel Römerbad, whose impressive courtyard has been roofed with a magnificent cupola roof in 1880 and is circled by open galleries with vitreous art nouveau balustrades, offers 76 rooms and suites as well as other spacious facilities that will make your stay a comfortable experience and that give you the chance to enjoy a wonderful view over the Rhine Valley and the Vosges mountains in nearby France. ▸

Angebot/facility

88-225 €

152-290 €

A/S 184-410 €

2-200

Müllheim (Baden) 7 km

Freiburg 39 km
Basel, Mulhouse 39 km

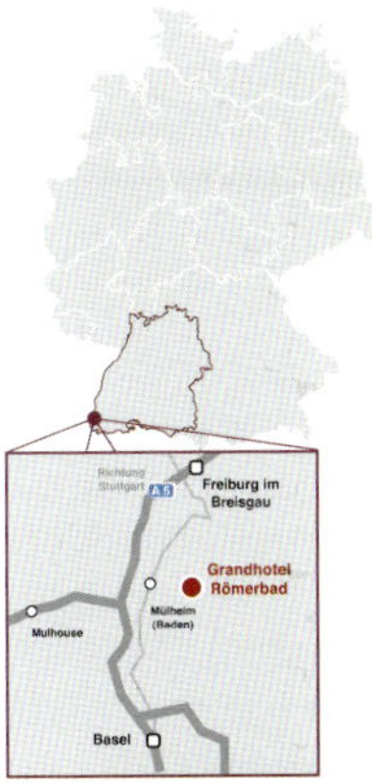

Freizeitmöglichkeiten. Zwölf schön gelegene Golfplätze bieten in der näheren Umgebung den Hotelgästen eine Greenfee-Ermäßigung. Vielfältige Kunst- und Kulturveranstaltungen unterhalten die Gäste im Haus und im parkähnlich angelegten Kurort Badenweiler. Südländisches Flair umfängt die Gäste auch in der Außenanlage sowie im angenehm warmen Thermalwasserpool.

Auch die klassischen Seiten des Hauses werden von den Gästen sehr geschätzt, bei entspannter Zeitungslektüre oder erstklassischer Pianomusik im Salon. Und selbst am späten Abend, wenn charmante Barkeeper in der englischen Kult-Bar „Caesar" farbenfrohe Drinks in Cocktailgläser zaubern, kommt mit frischer Live-Musik Bewegung ins Grandhotel Römerbad.

The cuisine at Grand Hotel Römerbad is regional, Mediterranean up to international as the executive chef and his team pull out all the stops of fine cuisine with zest and passion.

The Grand Hotel is situated amidst a fantastic vacation region with a range of activities to offer of all imaginable sports. In addition 12 beautiful golf courses in the surrounding area hotel guests a greenfee-discount. A variety of art- and cultural events entertain the guests at the hotel and in the park-like Spa town of Badenweiler.

The guest will be surrounded by a pleasant Mediterranean flair in the outdoor area of the hotel as well as in the pleasantly warm thermal water pool.

Moreover, guests also appreciate the hotel's classic aspects, while unstressed newspaper reading or listening to first class piano music. And when at night charming barmen perform colourful magic in cocktail glasses in the English cult bar „Caesar", then a real drive comes up when live music is played at the Grand Hotel Römerbad.

In der näheren Umgebung:

Parkanlagen des Kurortes Badenweiler: englischen Landschaftsgarten mit artenreichem Baumbestand, Mammutbäumen, malerischem Schwanenweiher, Hildegard-Garten mit Heilkräutern nach Vorgaben der Hildegard von Bingen, Gutedel-Garten; **Sulzburg im Breisgau (9,5 km):** Landesbergbaumuseum in der alten Stadtkirche des Resedenzstädtchens; **Steinen (26 km):** Vogelpark mit Falkneranlage.

In the surrounding area:

Parks of the Spa town Badenweiler: English landscape garden with species-rich tree population, giant redwood trees, picturesque swan pond, Hildegard garden with medicinal herbs according to the instructions of Hildegard von Bingen, Gutedel garden; **Sulzburg in Breisgau (6 miles):** national mining museum in the old church of the residence town; **Steinen (16 miles):** bird park with falconry centre.

TIPP

400 Jahren Leben im Schwarzwald sind in Gutach (84 km), im Freilichtmuseum Vogtsbauernhof, im wahrsten Wortsinne zu erleben. Sechs voll eingerichtete Eindachhöfe, ein Tagelöhnerhaus sowie zahlreiche Nebengebäude: Mühlen, Sägen, Speicher, Kapelle und Leibgedinghaus stehen beispielhaft für die Architektur und Wirtschaftsweise seiner jeweiligen schwarzwälder Herkunftsregion. In dem Hofladen des Vogtbauernhofes sind allerlei Handarbeiten sowie Literatur rund um den Schwarzwald zu erwerben, im Museumsrestaurant „Zum Hofengel" genießt man kulinarische Köstlichkeiten der Region.

400 years of life in the Black Forest can be experienced literally in the open air museum Vogts farm ("Freilichtmuseum Vogtsbauernhof") in Gutach (52 miles). 6 completely furnished one roof farms, a day labourer's house as well as numerous neighbouring buildings: mills, sawmills, storehouses, a chapel and a retirement cottage present the architecture and way of farming of the particular Black Forest region they originated from. In the farm shop of the Vogts farm you can buy various handmade articles as well as literature on the Black Forest. The museum's restaurant "Zum Hofengel" is the perfect location to enjoy culinary treats from the region.

Pfaffenkeller

Gastgeber/host: Claude F. Gysin-Spitz

Altes Pfarr- und Domänenhaus mit Feinschmeckerrestaurant, himmlischen Gästezimmern und einer Bio-Lebensmittel-Manufaktur.

Old rectory and domain house with gourmet restaurant, heavenly guest rooms and a organic food manufactory.

Rathausstr. 9
79400 Wollbach-Kandern
Baden-Württemberg
Tel.: +49 7626 9774290
Fax: +49 626 97742999
www.pfaffenkeller.de
info@pfaffenkeller.de

Hotel ★★★★
Restaurant ★★★★

Mitten im Ortskern von Wollbach, nur 15 Kilometer von Basel entfernt, liegt der Pfaffenkeller, das ehemalige Pfarr- und Domänenhaus des Ortes. Im Rahmen einer Totalsanierung des im Jahr 1618 datierten Haupthauses, bei der ausschließlich baubiologisches Material zum Einsatz kam, wurde das Aussehen von 1860 wieder hergestellt. Es beherbergt nun ein Feinschmeckerrestaurant und neun charmante Zimmer und Suiten mit einem unverwechselbaren Stil, der die charakteristische Tradition der Gegend harmonisch mit modernem Komfort verbindet.

Über dem renovierten Sandstein-Türgewand ▸

In the center of the small village Wollbach and only 9 miles from Basle is this beautiful former presbytery and manor house Pfaffenkeller situated. The main House was in 1618 built and in 1860 restored. A complete renovation in witch purely biological material was used is now finished. It houses a fine gourmet restaurant and nine charming guest rooms and suites with a ▸

Angebot/facility

95-190 €

125-280 €

A/S 125-280 €

Restaurant Montag

Badischer Bahnhof Basel 15 km

Basel 25 km

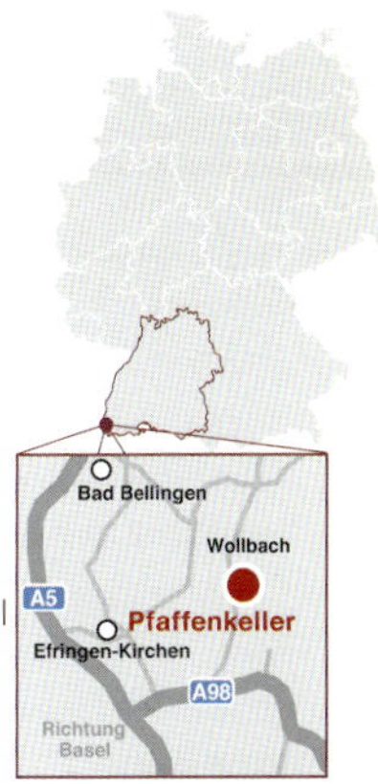

weisen die Wappen auf die einstige Bedeutung des mehr als 390 Jahre alten Gebäudeensembles hin. Rechts geht es die Treppe hinauf in die gemütlichen Zimmer und Suiten, geradeaus an der Küche vorbei in die gepflegten Gaststuben. Der saisonale Rhythmus der Natur bestimmt die Gerichte, bei denen ausschließlich frische Produkte aus den eigenen Obstgärten, Gemüsekulturen und Kräutergärten sowie regionaler Bio-Erzeuger Verwendung finden. Gute, alte bäuerliche Gastgeber-Tradition also, fortgelebt mit einer persönlichen, modernen Note.

distinctive style that combines the typical tradition of the area in harmony with modern comforts.

Over the renovated sandstone door, refers the coats of arms to the former meaning of the more than 390 years old building. Right it goes upstairs into the cosy rooms and suites, straightforward at the kitchen past into the maintained guest rooms. The seasonal rhythm of nature dominates the dishes, which excludes fresh products of the own vegetable cultures, fruit and herb gardens as well as those of other regional organic producers. Good, old rural host tradition thus.

In der näheren Umgebung:

Bauernhausmuseum Schneiderhof (15 km): Zeugnis traditionellen bäuerlichen Lebens im Originalzustand; **Vogelpark Steinen (11 km):** über 1.000 Vögel in 300 Arten sind hier zu besichtigen; Greifvogel-Vorführungen mit Adlern, Falken und Eulen; **Bad Bellingen (12 km):** exklusives Thermalbad Balinea Thermen; **Schloss Bürgeln (17 km):** eindrucksvoller Barockbau von 1762, in dem täglich Führungen und gelegentlich auch Konzerte stattfinden; **Weil am Rhein (16 km):** Vitra Design Museum mit wechselnden Ausstellungen; Hallenbad Laguna Badeland mit großzügiger Saunalandschaft; **Basel (18 km):** gepflegte Altstadt am Rhein, Einkaufsmöglichkeiten, lauschige Grünanlagen, Museen von Weltruf, Galerien, Theater, Kleinkunstbühnen und Konzertveranstaltungen.

In the surrounding area:

Farmhouse museum Schneiderhof (9 miles): Certification of traditional rural life in the original; **Bird park Steinen (7 miles):** over 1.000 birds in 300 kinds are to be visited here; Grab bird demonstrations with eagles, falcons and owls; **Bad Bellingen (7 miles):** exclusive thermal bath Balinea hot springs; **Schloss Bürgeln (11 miles):** impressive baroque building of 1762, in which daily guidance and occasionally also concerts take place; **Weil on the Rhine (10 miles):** Vitra Design museum with changing exhibitions; singular indoor swimming pool Laguna bath country with a generous sauna landscape; **Basel (11 miles):** Well-tended historic centre on the Rhine, shopping options, secluded green open spaces, museums with an international reputation, galleries, theatres, cabarets and concert events.

TIPP

Von Mai bis Oktober kann man mit der Kandertalbahn, einem historischen Dampflockzug, auf einer Strecke von 13 km von Haltingen ins Töpferstädtchen Kandern fahren. Die Fahrt führt durch die liebliche Landschaft des Kandertals. Am Bahnhof in Kandern ist das Depot der Bahn ganzjährig zu besichtigen. Neben Erläuterungen zu den Fahrzeugen und Informationen zur Geschichte der Bahn, kann den Mitarbeitern des Vereins bei ihren Unterhaltungsarbeiten an den Fahrzeugen über die Schulter geschaut und der umfangreiche Maschinenpark des Vereins besichtigt werden. Infos auf: www.kandertalbahn.de

From may to october one can drive with a historical steam locomotive of the Kandertal railway, on a distance from 8 miles from Haltingen to the pottery city Kandern. The trip leads by the lovely landscape of the Kandertal. At the station in Kandern the depot of the railway is to be visited all year round. Apart from explanations concerning the vehicles and information about the history of the railway, you can watch the coworkers of the association with its maintenance work on the vehicles and visit the extensive machinery of the association. Timetable and further information: www.kandertalbahn.de

Schwarzwald

The Black Forest

Die barocke Sonnenuhr in St. Blasien ist ein besonderes Schmuckstück: Sie verkündet neben der Uhrzeit auch den jeweiligen Monat.
The baroque sundial in St. Blasien is a special gem: It does not only tell the time but also the respective month.

eine deutsche Idylle mit kulturellen Edelsteinen

German idyll with cultural gems

Denkt man an den Schwarzwald, assoziiert man unweigerlich Schinken, Torte und Kuckucksuhren. Man denkt an dunkle Wälder, Förster und Trachtenmädel mit Bollenhut. Der Schwarzwald ist der Inbegriff deutscher Idylle und gesunder Natur. Hauptreisegrund ist Wandern und aktive Erholung. Hier zählen die Stille und Einsamkeit des Hochwaldes mehr als die pulsierenden Adern einer Weltmetropole. Doch neben bergigen Wäldern, traumhaften See- und Flusslandschaften und liebenswürdigen Kurorten bietet der Schwarzwald auch eine interessante Museumslandschaft mit sehenswerten Sammlungen und mitreißenden Veranstaltungen,

The Black Forest is invariably associated with ham, gateau and cuckoo clocks. It also makes you think of dark woods, forest wardens and girls in traditional costume with the typical big hats. For many, the Black Forest is the embodiment of German idyll and untouched nature. Hiking and active recreation are the main reasons for visiting. Here, the quiet and solitude of the timber forest are preferable to the vibrant restlessness of a metropolis. The Black Forest is a holiday region that stands for deep relaxation and recuperation and an area that became famous for its almost stoic continuity. Eco tourism might well have been invented here.

Der Feldberg, Wahrzeichen und höchste Erhebung des Schwarzwalds.
View of the Feldberg, landmark and highest elevation of the Black Forest.

insbesondere in den Sommermonaten. Im Schwarzwälder Freilichtmuseum Vogtsbauernhof kann die historische Lebens- und Arbeitsweise im Schwarzwald in originalen Höfen, Mühlen, Scheunen und Wohnstuben nacherlebt werden. Das Freilichtmuseum besteht aus historischen Bauernhöfen, die von ihrem ursprünglichen Standort abgebaut und hier mit viel Mühe und Liebe zum Detail wieder aufgebaut wurden. Durch eine Vielzahl von Nebengebäuden wie Speichern, Backhäusern, Mühlen etc. gibt das Museum einen

The open-air museum Vogts farm (Vogtsbauernhof), which is located in the Black Forest, offers its visitors a fascinating insight into the historical local way of living and working on original farms, mills, in barns and in sitting rooms. The museum consists of historic farms that have been removed from their original location and were reconstructed under great effort and with great devotion on the grounds of the museum. Numerous outbuildings such as store houses, bakehouses and mills give a detailed insight into life and work of the

Das Schwarzwälder Freilichtmuseum Vogtsbauernhof zeigt, wie im Schwarzwald in den letzten 400 Jahren gewohnt, gelebt und gearbeitet wurde.
The open-air museum Vogtsbauernhof lets visitors experience how people lived and worked in the Black Forest during the last 400 years.

umfassenden Einblick in das Leben und Arbeiten der Schwarzwälder Bauern im 16. und 17. Jahrhundert.

In Triberg, einem Städtchen mit dem höchsten Wasserfall Deutschlands befindet sich ein weiteres Schwarzwaldmuseum. Auch dieses Museum möchte dem Besucher die Lebens- und Arbeitsweise im Schwarzwald näher bringen. Auf 1600 m^2 Ausstellungsfläche werden dem Besucher originale Schaustücke aus vier Jahrhunderten von A bis Z geboten – von Trachten über Uhren bis hin zu

Black Forest farmers during the 16th and 17th century.

In Triberg, the town with the highest waterfall of Germany, you will find another Black Forest museum, which also aims at giving its visitors an understanding of life and work in the Black Forest. On 1913 yards^2 exhibition space, one can marvel at original exhibits of 4 centuries ranging from A to Z – traditional costumes, clocks and even mineral mines, just to mention a few of them, display the rituals, manners of dress, daily routines, way of working,

Filigrane Holzarchitektur und internationale Bildhauersymposien zeugen im Schwarzwald von einer ausgeprägten Handwerkskunst.
Finely wrought wood architecture and international sculptor symposia depict the distinctive craftsmanship that can be found in the Black Forest.

Mineralienstollen wird man im Schwarzwaldmuseum umfassend über Bräuche, Kleidungsstile, Tagesabläufe, Arbeitsweisen, Ernährungsgewohnheiten sowie über Gewerbe und die unterschiedlichsten Sparten des Handwerks im Schwarzwald, wie die Uhrmacherei und die Flechterei, informiert. Ein Groß-Diorama der Schwarzwaldbahn begeistert vor allem die kleinen Beuscher.

Das Deutsche Uhrenmuseum in Furtwangen bringt dem Besucher die Geschichte der Zeitmessung, angefangen bei der Bestimmung der Zeit durch Sonnenuhren bis hin zur präzisen Messung durch Atomuhren, näher, wobei der Schwerpunkt insbesondere auf der handwerklichen und industriellen Uhrenproduktion im Schwarzwald liegt.

Im Deutschen Phonomuseum St. Georgen erfährt man Wissenswertes über die Geschichte und Entwicklung der Phonoindustrie. Es sind historische Phonographen aber auch Geräte und Methoden der modernen Unterhaltungstechnik zu bewundern.

Im Schwarzwälder Trachtenmuseum, im Konventgebäude des ehemaligen Kapuzinerklosters Haslach, können Besucher die Geschichte und Entwicklung der Volkstrachten im Schwarzwälder Raum nachvollziehen und wertvolle Originaltrachten begutachten.

Immer im Frühling und im Herbst findet das Schwarzwald Musikfestival statt. Historische Baudenkmäler wie der Dom St. Blasien oder die Alpirsbacher Klosterkirche, aber auch moderne Werkshallen werden dafür zu Konzertsälen umfunktioniert. Es finden sogar Open

eating habits as well as the industry and several branches of craft, such as watchmaking and braiding, in the Black Forest. A great diorama of the Black Forest Railway especially fascinates all little visitors.

The German clock museum in Furtwangen exhibits the history of time measurement, starting with the determination of time by sundials and ending with the precise measurement by atomic clocks. The museum's focus is clearly set on manual and industrial clock production in the Black Forest.

In the German Phonograph museum St. Georgen visitors can learn more about the history and development of the phonograph industry. The exhibition holds historic phonographs as well as gadgets and methods of the modern entertainment technology.

The Black Forest Folk Costume museum, situated in the convent building of the former Capuchin monastery Haslach, documents the history and development of the local traditional costumes from the Black Forest region and

Dom St. Blasien mir seiner imposanten, dem Petersdom in Rom nachempfundenen Kuppel.
St. Blasien cathedral with its impressive cupola that has been constructed after the model of St. Peter's Basilica in Rome.

Air Konzerte in schöner Umgebung statt, bei denen eine romantische Atmosphäre herrscht. Wer im idyllischen Landhaus Mühle, über dem Ostufer des Schluchsees, die sprichwörtliche Schwarzwälder Gastfreundschaft genießt, für den ist es nur ein Katzensprung zu den Domfestspielen, die in jedem Sommer in der atemberaubenden Kulisse des Dom St. Blasien stattfinden, auf dem sich die drittgrößte Kuppel Europas befindet.
Hinter dem im Jugendstil erbauten Hotel Palmenwald in Freudenstadt eröffnet sich der

exhibits valuable original traditional costumes. During spring and autumn time, the annual Black Forest music festival takes places. Historical monuments such as St. Blasien cathedral or the Alpirsbacher cloister church and modern factory buildings serve as venues for the concert. Even Open Air concerts take place in beautiful surroundings with a romantic atmosphere. If you are residing at the idyllic Landhaus Mühle, just above the east banks of Lake Schluchsee, and enjoying the hospitality of the Black Forest people, you will find it only a

Der Schluchsee, Wasserreservoir und Wasserparadies für Urlauber
Lake Schluchsee, water reservoir and water paradise for tourists.

Zugang zum höchst gelegenen Rosenpfad Deutschlands.

Reist man weiter in den weltbekannten Kurort Baden-Baden, sollte man sich weder die Staatliche Kunsthalle noch das erste Fabergé Museum entgehen lassen. Baden-Baden zählt zu den besterhaltenen Kurorten Deutschlands. Als Wahrzeichen der Stadt gilt das Kurhaus mit dem berühmten „Casino Baden-Baden". Das Kunstmuseum Frieder Burda präsentiert Werke der Klassischen Moderne und zeitgenössischer Kunst in einem

stone's throw to the cathedral festival, which takes place every summer in the fascinating scenery of St. Blasien cathedral, whose dome is the third biggest in Europe.

Just behind the Palmenwald Hotel, which was designed in the Art nouveau style, one can find the access to the highest "Rose trail" (Rosenpfad) of Germany. Traveling further to the world-famous health resort Baden-Baden you should neither miss the State Art Gallery (Staatliche Kunsthalle) nor the first Fabergé museum. Baden-Baden is one of the

Rosengarten auf Schloss Bürgeln, Kluckert mit Blick in die Rheinebene.
Rose garden at Bürgel Castle, Kluckert with view of the Rhine valley.

preisgekrönten, von Richard Meier entworfenen Gebäude. Auch das Museum für Kunst und Technik des 19. Jahrhunderts ist unbedingt einen Besuch wert.
Im idyllischen Erholungsort Badenweiler erwartet das literarische Museum „Tschechow-Salon", das dem russischen Schriftsteller Anton Pawlowitsch Tschechow gewidmet ist, seine Besucher. Das Museum zeigt mit Bildern, Texten, Briefen und anderen Zeitzeugnissen interessante Aspekte im Leben und Wirken des brillanten Autoren auf. Auch die Ruine der Burg Baden und das Großherzogliche Palais sind einen Besuch wert. Die erste

best preserved health resorts of Germany. The city's landmarks are its spa rooms with the famous "Casino Baden-Baden". The art museum Frieder Burda, situated in an award-winning building designed by Richard Meier, exhibits works of classic modernism and contemporary art. Another museum worth visiting is the museum for art and technology from the 19th century.
In the idyllic health resort Badenweiler you will find the literary museum "Tschechow-Salon", which is dedicated to the Russian writer Anton Pawlowitsch Tschechow. The museum offers a fascinating insight into the life and work of

Blick bis zu den Vogesen vom Badenweiler Burgberg auf Weinberge und ins Rheintal.
View of the Vosges, vineyards and the Rhine valley from Badenweiler castle hill.

Etage des Kunstpalais beherbergt eine Galerie, in der wechselnde Ausstellungen stattfinden. Im Café im Erdgeschoss finden regelmäßig Matineen und Kulturabende mit hervorragender Kunst und Musik statt. Darüber hinaus bietet das Kunstpalais Workshops für Musik an und das Grandhotel Römerbad brilliert mit hochkarätiger Musik und Diskussionsveranstaltungen als kultureller Mittelpunkt des Ortes.

In Basel, der Stadt mit der höchsten Galeriendichte, lockt das Kunstmuseum Basel als älteste Kunstsammlung der städtischen Sammlungen weltweit sowie als größtes schweize-

the brilliant author – its exhibits include a range of pictures, texts, letters and other historical documents. The old ruins of Baden Castle and the Grand-Ducal Palais (Großherzogliches Palais) are well worth seeing. On the first floor of the Art Palais (Kunstpalais) you will find a gallery, which holds changing exhibitions. The café on the groundfloor is venue to regular matinees and cultural evenings with impressive art and music. Furthermore, the Art Palais offers several workshops for music and the Grand Hotel Römerbad, the cultural centre of the town, charms its visitors with top-class music and debating events.

Die Holzbrücke in Bad Säckingen ist mit 203,7 Metern die längste gedeckte Holzbrücke Europas und verbindet die deutsche mit der schweizer Seite über den Rhein.
The wooden bridge in Bad Säckingen measures 222.7 yards and is the longest covered wooden bridge in the whole of Europe. It connects Germany and Switzerland across the Rhine.

risches Kunstmuseum mit atemberaubenden Sammlungen von Kunst der Renaissance sowie des 19. und 20. Jahrhunderts. Auch die private Fondation Beyeler, die Gemälde und Plastiken der klassischen Moderne ausstellt, sowie das Museum für Gegenwartskunst, in dem Kunstwerke aus den Jahrzehnten ab 1960 zu besichtigen sind, zählen zu bedeutenden Kunstsammlungen. Dem Antikenmuseum, dem Cartoonmuseum und dem Papiermuseum Basel sollte man unbedingt einen Besuch abstatten.

Die staatlichen Museen des Kantons Basel gehen auf den Kauf der privaten Sammlungsbestände der Buchdruckerfamilie um

In Basel, the town with the highest frequency of galleries, the art museum Basel is well worth a visit as it has the oldest art collection of the town collections worldwide and the biggest Swiss art museum with fascinating collections of art from the renaissance and the 19th and 20th century. The private Foundation Beyeler, which exhibits paintings and sculptures from classic modernism, and the museum for contemporary art, which offers its visitors numerous works of art from 1960 onwards, are counted to important art collections. The antique museum, the cartoon museum and the paper museum Basel are well worth visiting.

Malerische Häuser in Laufenburg am Rhein
Picturesque houses in Laufenburg at the river Rhine.

Basilius Amerbach, der ein leidenschaftlicher Kunst- und Naturaliensammler war, („Amerbach-Kabinett") im Jahre 1661 zurück. Sie stellen die älteste durchgängig bestehende Museumssammlung des bürgerlichen Gemeinwesens dar. Die umfangreiche und umfassende Museumslandschaft, deren Wurzeln, wie beschrieben, bis ins 16. Jahrhundert zurückreichen, ist identitätsstiftender Bestandteil der Kultur dieser Stadt

Das Vitra Design Museum in Weil am Rhein widmet sich der Möbelgestaltung und der Innenarchitektur. Die große Sammlung gibt einen umfassenden Einblick in Gestaltungsabläufe, von der Rohskizze bis hin zu den

The state museums of the canton Basel can be traced back to the purchase of the "Amerbach-Kabinett" in 1661, the private collections of the book printer family around Basilius Amerbach, who was a passionate collector of art and natural produce. These collections constitute the oldest continuously existing museum collection of the civil community. The large museum landscape, whose roots date back, as mentioned above, to the 16th century, is a distinguishing characteristic of the town's culture.

The Vitra Design Museum in Weil at the river Rhine documents the design of furniture and interior design. The extensive collection gives

fertigen Produkten. Schon allein der von dem amerikanischen Architekten Frank O. Gehry entworfene futuristische Museumsbau ist ein Erlebnis.

Wer sich danach der ländlichen Ruhe und kulinarischen Hochgenüssen zuwenden möchte, der ist im nur 14 Kilometer entfernten Pfaffenkeller Wollbach bestens aufgehoben.

a detailed insight into the design processes, from the first drafts to the finished product. The museum's building was designed by the American architect Frank O. Gehry and thus is a special sight for its visitors.

If you are looking for rural peace and culinary treats afterwards, the Pfaffenkeller Wollbach, which is only 9 miles away, will be the perfect place for you.

Denkmal für Anton Tcheschow und Hildegard von Bingen Garten in Badenweiler
Monument to Anton Tcheschow and Hildegard von Bingen Garden in Badenweiler.

Schloss Amerang

Gastgeber/host: Giulia Freifrau von Crailsheim-Larisch, Ortholf Freiherr von Crailsheim

Bayern

Mittelalterliche Rundburg mit beeindruckendem Arkadenhof auf einem Hügel über Amerang im bayerischen Voralpenland.

Medieval castle with an impressive arcade yard up on a hill above Amerang in the Bavarian Prealps.

Schloss 1
83123 Amerang
Bayern
Tel.: +49 8075 91920
Fax: +49 8075 919233
www.schlossamerang.de
info@schlossamerang.de

Hotel ★★★★

Schloss Amerang wurde 1072 erstmals urkundlich als Edelsitz erwähnt. Im 16. Jahrhundert bauten die im Exil lebenden Herren von Verona, die Scaliger, einen trapezförmigen Arkadenhof in die alte gotische Burg. Seit über 700 Jahren und seit über 23 Generationen ist das Schloss nicht nur Familienwohnsitz, sondern auch Stätte herausragender kultureller Ereignisse und Feierlichkeiten.

Die geräumigen Zimmer auf Schloss Amerang wurden sehr persönlich und jeweils individuell von der gastgebenden Baronin Crailsheim eingerichtet und verfügen über unterschiedliche Bettengrößen, vom französischen bis zum klassischen Ehebett.

Besucher auf Schloss Amerang, egal ob diese für nur eine Nacht oder für zwei Wochen ▸

Amerang Castle was first mentioned in a document as a manor house in 1072. During the 16th century the lords of Verona, the Scaliger who lived in exile, ordered to build a trapezium shaped arcade yard into the old gothic castle. For over 700 years and over 23 generations the castle has not only been the family residence but also centre of outstanding cultural events and festivities.

The spacious rooms in Amerang Castle were furnished by the hosting Baroness Crailsheim herself in a very individual way and are equipped with beds in different sizes ranging from three quarter beds to classic double beds. The Lords of the Castle always regard their visitors as personal ▸

Angebot/facility

105 €

165 €

A/S 180-240 €

Bad Endorf 11 km

München-Erding 75 km

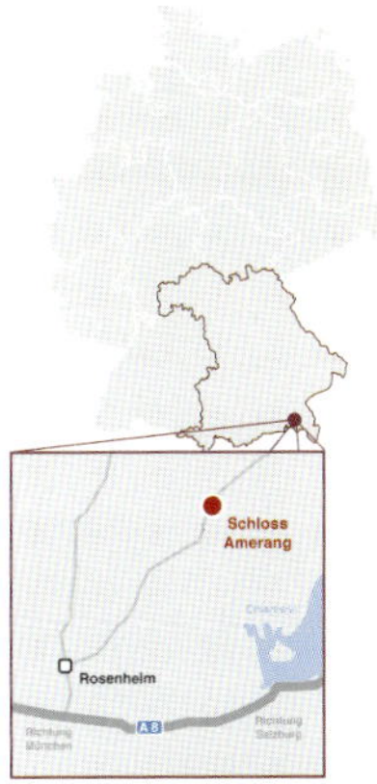

bleiben, sind immer auch persönliche Gäste der Schlossherren. Schloss Amerang versteht sich mehr als Privathaus, denn als ein Hotel im üblichen Sinne. Im Herzen des Chiemgaus gelegen, ist das Schloss ein besonderer Ausgangspunkt für einen abwechslungsreichen Urlaub. 33 Seen und die Chiemgauer Alpen liegen direkt vor der Haustür.

Direkt am Schloss gibt es ein Arboretum und einen Lehrobstgarten. Auch der Ort Amerang bietet einige Sehenswürdigkeiten sowie ein Bauernhausmuseum und ein Museum für Automobilgeschichte. Ausflüge zum Bummeln und Shoppen führen nach Wasserburg, Salzburg und München oder in sehenswerte Städte wie Prien, Rosenheim und Traunstein rund um den Chiemsee, das Bayerische Meer.

guests, whether they are just staying for one night or even for two weeks. Castle Amerang regards itself more as a private house than a hotel in the usual kind of way. Situated in the heart of Chiemgau, the Castle is an ideal starting point for a holiday full of variety. 33 lakes and the Chiemgau Alps are just a stone's throw away.

Right by the castle there is an arboretum and a teaching orchard. The small town Amerang also offers a lot of sights, such as a farmhouse museum and a museum for automobile history. In order to shop, relax or take a stroll, visitors can go on trips to Wasserburg, Salzburg or Munich or even to other cities well worth seeing like Prien, Rosenheim and Traunstein, situated in the area around Lake Chiemsee - the Bavarian Sea.

In der näheren Umgebung:

Wasserburg am Inn (13 km): sehenswerte Altstadt auf einer vom Inn umflossenen Halbinsel; **Chiemsee (18 km):** Bayerisches Meer mit Fraueninsel und Herreninsel mit Schloss Herrenchiemsee von Ludwig dem II; **Rosenheim (24 km):** mediterrane Einkaufsstadt an Inn und Mangfall, mit weitläufigen Plätzen, pastellfarbenen Häusern, Arkaden und imposanten Zwiebeltürmen; **Traunstein (34 km):** pulsierender Mittelpunkt des Chiemgaus mit stattlichen Bürgerhäusern, idyllischen Straßen und Plätzen und atemberaubendem Blick auf die Chiemgauer Alpen.

In the surrounding area:

The Moated Castle at the river Inn (8 miles): Worth seeing historic city center on a peninsula surrounded by the river Inn; **Chiemsee (11 miles):** Bavarian Sea with the islands Fraueninsel and Herreninsel with the Castle Herrenchiemsee of Louis II; **Rosenheim (15 miles):** Mediterranean shopping city situated at the rivers Inn and Mangfall, with extensive squares, pastel-coloured houses, arcades and imposing onion-domed towers; **Traunstein (21 miles):** Vibrant centre of Chiemgau with noble middle-class houses, idyllic streets and squares and a breathtaking view over the Chiemgau Alps.

TIPP

Aktivurlaub mit (oder ohne) Pferd! Im neu erbauten Gestütsstall, nur 5 Minuten vom Schloss entfernt, stehen den Pferden der Gäste Außenboxen mit Gummimatten und Späneeinstreu zur Verfügung. Im Sommer wird das Frühstück im Garten serviert. Gerne organisieren die Gastgaber auch ein Reitpicknick. Halle, Galoppbahn und Geländestrecken stehen auch den Gästen zur Verfügung. Gäste, die lieber golfen, angeln oder Tennis spielen, sind ebenfalls in nur fünf Minuten am Ziel.

Activity holiday with (or without) horse! In the newly built stud farm, only 5 minutes away from the Castle, outside boxes with rubber mats and span are available for the guests' horses. During the summer the breakfast is served in the garden. The hosts also love to organise picnics for the horses and riders. The riding hall, the race track and the cross-country course are also at the guests' disposal. Guests who prefer golfing, fishing or playing tennis will need only five minutes to reach their destination.

Idyllische Morgenstimmung am Chiemsee mit Blick auf die Voralpen.
Idyllic morning atmosphere at Lake Chiemsee with view of the Prealps.

Der Chiemgau und das Bayerische Meer

Chiemgau and the "Bavarian Sea"

Immer wieder findet man in Deutschland Gegenden, die Archetypen eines ländlichen Klischees zu sein scheinen. Besonders prädestiniert ist Bayern, da vor allem Lederhose, Gamsbart, Kirchturmzwiebel und Heimatfilmblick für viele die Insignien der Idylle sind. Und es gibt einen Landstrich, der alle diese Faktoren erfüllt: der Chiemgau in Oberbayern. Die Voralpenlandschaft ist durch die letzte Eiszeit geprägt. Hier stagnierte der Vortrieb, so dass beim langsamen Abschmelzen zahllose Hügel, Täler und vor allem Seen übrig blieben. Durch die vom Eis vor sich hergeschobenen Schutt- und Geröllhaufen sind nicht nur ansehnliche Berge entstanden, sondern wurden auch eine Vielzahl von Bodentypen und Gesteinsarten mitgebracht. Das

Many regions in Germany seem to be archetypes of rural cliché. Especially predestined is Bavaria, as Lederhose, Gamsbart, onion shaped church steeples and lovely, pastoral views are the epitome of idyllic beauty for many people. One region in particular embodies all these aspects: the Chiemgau with the Lake Chiemsee, nicknamed the Bavarian Sea.

These foothills of the Alps have been shaped by the last Ice Age. Here, the strong push of the glaciers stagnated and the slowly melting ice created innumerable hills, valleys and above all else, lakes. Pushing aside huge amounts of debris and detritus, the ice not only created formidable mountains but also transported a multitude of different rock and

Die 15,5 Hektar große und autofreie Straueninsel liegt malerisch im Chiemsee.
Covering 38.75 acres, the car-free Fraueninsel is situated picturesquely in Lake Chiemsee.

macht die Landschaft sehr abwechslungsreich und die Flora und Fauna vielfältig. Aber es gibt auch andere Erklärungsmodelle, darunter die Theorie vom Chiemgau-Impakt. Demnach soll im 2. bis 5. Jahrhundert v.Chr. ein Komet in einer Höhe von 70 km über dem Gebiet explodiert sein, dessen Trümmer mit der Gewalt von 8000 Hiroshimabomben Menschen und Natur vernichteten. Diese Aufsehen erregende Theorie ist relativ aktuell und natürlich stark umstritten. Das CIRT (Chiemgau Impact Research Team) hat seit Oktober 2009 ein kleines Museum eingerichtet, was in keinem Reiseführer steht. Die permanente Ausstellung befindet sich in Grabenstätt, im Außengebäude des Rathauses in der Schlossökonomie.

Für diese Landschaft ist das Gut Ising als Station ideal. Das Hoteldorf ist ein historisch gewachsenes Ensemble aus 3 Bauernhöfen und 7 Häusern und damit in seiner Struktur einzigartig in Deutschland. Die Landidylle paart sich hier mit den vielfältigsten Sportmöglichkeiten wie Polo und Reiten, Golfen, Tennis und natürlich Segeln, Wandern und Radeln. Gut Ising liegt leicht erhöht, aber direkt am zentralen Punkt des Chiemgaus, dem Chiemsee, einem über 80 km² großen Gewässer, welches auch „bayerisches Meer" genannt wird. Es ist der drittgrößte See in Deutschland und das vielleicht beliebteste Erholungsgebiet Bayerns. Der Artenreichtum ist beeindruckend: rund 1.300 Pflanzen-, 300 Vogel- und 30 Fischarten sind hier beheimatet. Besonders reizvoll ist der Chiemsee auch durch seine drei berühmten Inseln; Fraueninsel, Herreninsel und Krautinsel.

soil types. Thus the scenery competes with flora and fauna for diversity. Nevertheless other explanations for the evolution of the Chiemgau have been thought of, such as the Chiemgau impact theory. It states that between 200 and 500 BC a comet exploded about 44 miles above the region in the atmosphere and its pieces extinguished all life with the force of 8.000 Hiroshima bombs. This sensational theory is pretty recent and highly controversial. In October 2009, the CIRT (Chiemgau Impact Research Team) opened a small museum that is not mentioned in the guidebooks. The permanent exhibition is in Grabenstaett, in an outbuilding of the town hall in the Schlossoekonomie.

Gut Ising is an ideal base for enjoying this scenery. The hotel village, a historically grown ensemble, consists of three farms and seven houses and is unparalleled in Germany. The rural idyll also offers many possibilities for leisure and sports such as polo, horse riding, golf, and of course, sailing, walking and cycling. Gut Ising finds itself in a slightly elevated position directly at the most central point of the Chiemgau, on the shores of Lake Chiemsee. The lake covers 50 sq miles and is nicknamed 'Bavarian sea'. It is Germany's third biggest lake and might well be the most popular of all Bavarian recreation areas. With its round about 1,300 plant species, 300 bird species and 30 species of fish, the region around Lake Chiemsee offers an extraordinary biological diversity.

Furthermore, on the lake you will find three

Die Insel Herrenchiemsee ist mit ihrer Fläche von 238 ha die größte der drei Chiemseeinseln. Jahrhundertelang war die Insel im Besitz von Kloster Herrenchiemsee, das nach der Säkularisierung in das Alte Schloss Herrenchiemsee umgestaltet wurde. Nach dem Vorbild des Schloss Versailles in Paris ließ der bayerische Märchenkönig Ludwig II. das Neue Schloss Herrenchiemsee errichten.

very popular islands: the Fraueninsel, the Herreninsel and the Krautinsel.

The island "Herrenchiemsee" or "Herreninsel" has a total area of 595 acres and thus is the biggest of the three islands on Lake Chiemsee. For many centuries, the island was owned by the cloister "Herrenchiemsee", which was redesigned into the Old Castle Herrenchiemsee after secularisation.

Das ehemalige Augustiner-Kloster steht auf der Insel Herrenchiemsee.
The former Augustinian monastery is located on the island Herrenchiemsee.

Es war das letzte Bauprojekt Ludwigs des II., der auch schon das Schloss Neuschwanstein errichten ließ. Mit dem Tod des Königs 1886 beendete man die Bauarbeiten am Schloss. Bis heute bleibt das Gebäude unvollendet.

Die Insel Frauenchiemsee oder Fraueninsel ist geprägt vom 782 gegründeten Benediktinerinnenkloster Frauenwörth, das als Wallfahrtsort für Irmgard von Chiemsee, die Schutzheilige des Chiemgaus, dient. Die Insel besticht durch ihre landschaftliche Einzigartigkeit sowie durch die Gastfreundschaft ihrer Bewohner, die Räucherfischspezialitäten und Töpfereierzeugnisse herstellen.

Im Gegensatz zu ihren Nachbarinseln ist die Krautinsel unbewohnt. Im Sommer lassen die um den Chiemsee niedergelassenen Bauern ihr Vieh hier weiden. Im Mittelalter diente die Insel den Nonnen des Benediktinerinnenklosters als Anbaugebiet von Gemüse und Kräutern.

Das verträumte Luft- und Kneippkurörtchen Prien am Chiemsee, von dem man einen herrlichen Ausblick auf die „Krampenwand" hat, ist mit seinem malerischen und ländlichen Ortsbild der Inbegriff Oberbayerns. Die farbenfrohen Gebäude stechen mit ihren kostbaren Verzierungen sofort ins Auge. Vom Hafen aus kann man die Herren- und Fraueninsel problemlos erreichen.

Die angrenzenden Chiemgauer Berge (Hochfelln, Hochgern, Hochplatte und Kampenwand) geben der Region den besonderen Reiz. Natürlich ranken sich allerlei Gerüchte, Legenden und Anekdoten um den See. So soll auf der Herreninsel ein Mönch spuken, den

The New Castle Herrenchiemsee was constructed after the model of Versailles castle in Paris, under order of the Bavarian fairytail King Ludwig II. This was the last construction project of King Ludwig II., who had already redesigned Neuschwanstein Castle. With the King's death in 1886, construction work on the castle was determined. Until today, the building remains incomplete.

The island "Frauenchiemsee" or "Fraueninsel" is characterised by the Benedictine monastery "Frauenwörth" that was founded in 782 and which is a place of pilgrimage for Irmgard von Chiemsee, the patron of Chiemgau. The island offers a beautiful scenery and charms its visitors with the smoked fish specialities, products of the local pottery and the hospitality of its residents.

In contrast to its neighbour islands, the island Krautinsel is uninhabited. During the summer, farmers from areas around Lake Chiemsee let their cattle graze on the island. In the Middle Ages, it served the nuns of the Benedictine monastery to grow vegetables and herbs.

The idyllic health and Kneipp spa resort Prien at Lake Chiemsee offers a splendid view of the "Krampenwand" and represents the perfect example of a town in Upper Bavaria with its picturesque rural appearance. The first to notice are the colourful buildings with their numerous precious decorations. From the harbour of the town one can easily reach the Herren- or Fraueninsel.

Imposing neighbours, the Chiemgau mountains (Hochfelln, Hochgern, Hochplatte and

Habgier und Geiz zu Lebzeiten dazu verurteilten, jede Nacht nach Schätzen in den Kellern und Gewölben des Klosters zu suchen. Bis auf den heutigen Tag ist es daher möglich, ihm gramgebeugt aber mit irr flackernden Augen zur mitternächtlichen Stunde im Kreuzgang zu begegnen. Opfer sind bisher nicht zu beklagen, zumindest ist dies nicht überliefert. Eine zweite „Tatsache" betrifft die Krautinsel. Komisch ist es ja schon, dass zwischen der schönen Herren- und Fraueninsel eine nur den Schafen und dem Gestrüpp vorbehaltene dritte Insel existiert.

Kampenwand) add a particular appeal. Obviously many rumours and anecdotes have grown up around the lake. On Herreninsel a monk, sentenced by his own greed and meanness, is said to haunt the cellars and vaults every night, looking for treasures. Until this very day you might meet him as he walks in the cloister at midnight, grief-stricken, wild eyes flickering madly. No victims are yet to be mourned – at least nothing has been recorded.

Another matter concerns the 'islands of weeds', Krautinsel. It is indeed curious that

Der Westwind zaubert eine ganz eigene Stimmung am Chiemsee bei Chieming.
The west wind conjures up a peculiar atmosphere over the lake at Chieming.

Exponierte Behausung für Vögel.
Exhibited home for birds.

Doch der Grund ist natürlich ein Fluch und eine Strafe Gottes. Die beiden Klöster Herrenwörth und Frauenwörth umschließen dieses verschwiegene Plätzchen, welches abtrünnige und die Gelübde der Keuschheit brechende Nonnen und Mönche besuchten, um ungezügelt ihre Lust zu leben. Als Strafe wurde die einst grüne Insel unfruchtbar und die sündigen Diener Gottes wurden auf den Grund des Sees verbannt, wo sie auch heute noch in stürmischen Nächten ihr Unwesen treiben. Manches Fischerboot ist schon gekentert, weil die ungezügelte Lust der Untoten die Wellen türmte. Aber es gibt natürlich auch die Geschichten von Seligen und Heiligen der katholischen Kirche, so die Irmgardlegende, die eine einstige Äbtissin in hellem Glanz einer sich aufopfernden und durch die göttliche Gnade unterstützten Frau beschreibt. Es war Nacht, der Donner grollte, Blitze durchhellten gespenstisch die Dunkelheit und ein Orkan peitschte die Wellen des Chiemsees. Ein Fischer verlor die Orientierung und war hilflos den entfesselten Naturgewalten ausgeliefert. Um die Sache noch brisanter zu machen, stand seine Frau, natürlich ein kleines Kind auf dem Arm, am Strand und wartete ängstlich auf ihren Mann. Die selige Irmgard, mutig und entschlossen, bestieg ein Boot, um den Fischer zu retten. Da ließ der Himmel ein helles Licht über Frauenwörth erstrahlen und somit den Fischer nach Hause finden. Der feste Glaube und das Gottvertrauen der frommen Irmgard hatten die Gnadentat ermöglicht. Solcherlei Phänomene gibt es überall, auch gleichen sie sich in Aussage und Deutung. Dennoch

this island, lying between beautiful Herren- and Fraueninsel, is only the abode of sheep and undergrowth. The cause of course is a curse and divine punishment. The two monasteries Herrenwoerth (monks) and Frauenwoerth (nuns) enclose this discreet little place that was visited by apostate nuns and monks who broke their vows of celibacy to freely indulge themselves in their lust. As a punishment the once fertile island grew barren and the sinful servants of God were banished to the bottom of the lake. They are still up to mischief in stormy nights and many a fisherman's boat has capsized because of the unbridled lust of the undead towering up the waves.

Yet there are also legends of Blessed and Saints of the Catholic Church, for example the legend of St. Irmgard that depicts a former abbess in the bright glory of a woman who sacrifices herself and is saved and aided by God's mercy.

It was late at night, thunder rolled, lightening lit up the eerie darkness and a hurricane lashed the waves of Lake Chiemsee. A fisherman had lost orientation and drifted across the lake helplessly, at the mercy of the raging elements. To make things even worse, his spouse, a small infant in her arms, stood on the shore, waiting anxiously for her beloved husband. Blessed Irmgard, courageous and decisive, got into a boat to save the fisherman. Lo and behold a bright light shone straight from the heavens upon Frauenwoerth and the fisherman, recovering his sense of direction,

sind sie Bestandteil fester Riten und Gebräuche. Erst 2003 wurden nach umfangreicher DNA-Analyse die Gebeine und der Schädel der Seligen Irmgard von Buchau in einem gläsernen Sarg in der Klosterkirche Frauenwörth zusammengeführt und jedes Jahr am 16. Juli begeht man den Irmgardstag. Die katholische Kirche hat viele solcher Anekdoten auf Lager. Auch die Kirche zu St. Salvator ist aus einer Legende entstanden. Eine Frau, die schwere Schuld auf sich geladen hatte, entschloss sich, dennoch die heilige Kommunion zu empfangen. Als sie jedoch die Oblate in der Hand hielt, verlor sie den Mut und die Reue über ihre Sünden verbot ihr, die Oblate zu essen. Angsterfüllt ging sie nach Hause, bestrebt, die Hostie loszuwerden. In einem unbeobachteten Moment tat sie es. Sie legte sie auf einer grünen Wiese mitten in das frische Gras. Doch kaum, dass sie den Boden berührte, verschwand sie auch schon in ihm. Über dieses Wunder mehr als beunruhigt, eilte die Frau zu ihrem Pfarrer, gestand ihm alles und geleitete ihn zu der Stelle. Heute steht, wie könnte es anders sein, hier eine Kirche deren Altar exakt die entsprechende Stelle markiert.

Auch Märthyrergeschichten wie die des Hl. Koloman und Liebesgeschichten aller Art werden erzählt. Doch wenn man vom Gut Ising aus die Lieblichkeit der Gegend erlebt und die Wegkreuze bei anbrechender Dämmerung als gute Geister des Heimweges dankbar begrüßt, so kann man vieles glauben, was einem bis vor kurzem noch unvorstellbar war.

Zur Erkundung des westlichen Chiemgaus

found his way home. Pious Irmgard's unshakable faith and unbreakable trust in God were answered with this act of mercy. Such phenomenon exist everywhere, their message and interpretation always similar. They are part of generations old rituals and traditions. As recent as 2003, the bones and skull of Blessed Irmgard von Buchau were put in a glass coffin in the church of convent Frauenwoerth after laboriously analysing their DNA and on 16th July there is held the annual celebration of St.Irmgard's Day.

The Catholic Church has many such anecdotes in store. The church of St.Salvator was also founded on a legend. Despite carrying heavy guilt, a woman decided to receive Holy Communion. Holding the Host in her hand, she lost courage and, tortured by bitter remorse, was unable to eat it. Filled with fear she went home and tried to think of a way to get rid of it. In a quiet moment she put it onto the fresh grass of a green meadow. As soon as the Host touched the ground it dissolved into the earth. Startled and upset by the miracle, the woman hurried to the local priest, confessed her sins and led him to the sacred spot. Today – and how could it be otherwise – the altar of St. Savator marks the exact place.

There are also stories of martyrs like that of St. Koloman and, of course, love stories. Yet if you taste the sweetness of the scenery around Ising Estate and gratefully greet the wayside crosses at dusk as good spirits of the way home you start to believe in many things that

bietet sich vor allem Schloss Amerang im gleichnamigen Ort an, das neben dem Schlossmuseum noch zwei weitere Museen vorzuweisen hat; das EFA Automobilmuseum und das Bauernhausmuseum Amerang. Als Inbegriff familiärer Tradition ist Schloss Amerang zugleich Zentrum gelebter Kultur. Das ganze Jahr über finden hier Musikevents wie z. B. der Operetten Frühling, Sommerkonzerte, Herbstnächte und Novemberkonzerte statt. Mit fast 50 Konzerten und 3 Großveranstaltungen im Jahr ist Schloss Amerang immer einen Besuch wert. Besonderes Highlight bildet das alljährliche Ritterfest, bei dem drei Tage lang gegessen, getrunken, gelacht und musiziert wird. Neben extravaganten Musikergruppen und spektakulären Showdarbietungen, kann man sich an bodenständiger Mittelalter-Comedy erfreuen. Auch für Kinder ist das Ritterfest ein Abenteuer-Spielplatz. Vielfältige Angebote sorgen dafür, dass es den Kleinen nicht langweilig wird.

Der Besuch des Ortes Wasserburg ist ein besonderes Erlebnis. Hier handelt es sich um Liebe auf den ersten Blick, ist man doch sofort überwältigt von der märchenhaften Insellage. Die Altstadt liegt nämlich auf einer Halbinsel, die fast vollständig von der Inn umflossen wird. Mit ihren bunten Mauern in Pastelltönen, prachtvollen Erkern und der gewaltigen Burg punktet die Stadt auf Anhieb. Älter als München, hat sie eine der bewegtesten Historien in Altbayern vorzuweisen. Wasserburg wurde von bayerischen Herzogtümern ständig umkämpft und rechtlich den großen Regierungssitzen

just a short while ago seemed unimaginable. For exploring the western parts of Chiemgau a visit to Amerang castle, which is situated in the town of the same name, is well recommendable. Apart from the castle museum, Amerang Castle offers two more museums: the EFA automobile museum and the farmhouse museum. As a perfect example of family tradition the castle is also centre of living culture. Throughout the whole year, various music events, such as the "spring time of the operettas", summer concerts, autumn nights and November concerts, take place at Amerang Castle. With nearly 50 concerts and three major events per year, it is well worth seeing. A special highlight is the annual Knight Festival, which promises three days of dining, drinking, laughing and music. Among extravagant music groups and spectacular performances, visitors can enjoy down-to-earth medieval comedy. Children will experience the Festival as an adventure playground. Various offers ensure that the little ones will not get bored.

The visit of the town Wasserburg is a special experience. At first sight, the town mesmerises its visitors with its beautiful, fairy-tale-like island location. The Old town of Wasserburg is situated on a peninsula, which is nearly completely surrounded by the river Inn. Its colourful walls in pastel shades, the gorgeous bays and the impressive castle belong to the town's attractive sights. As it even outdates Munich, Wasserburg has one of the most eventful histories in Old Bavaria to offer. It was permanently fought over by Bavarian

Schloss Amerang - ein Zentrum gelebter Kultur.
Amerang Castle - centre of lived

gleichgestellt. Durch die Innschifffahrt blühte hier der Salzhandel und die damit verbundenen Einnahmen brachten der Siedlung Wohlstand und Reichtum. Zudem hatte Wasserburg eine bedeutende Rolle als Handelsplatz für Produkte aus Italien, Österreich und dem Balkan inne.
Die kleine Stadt Rosenheim, an Inn und Mangfall gelegen, verzaubert ihre Besucher auf Anhieb mit ihrem sympathischen Charme, den sie mit ihren zartpastellenen Gebäudefassaden, den schon von weitem sichtbaren Türmen und den ausgedehnten Stadtflächen versprüht. Der besondere Reiz des Städtchens wird durch eine extravagante Verschmelzung aus alpenländischem und südländischem Esprit unterstrichen. Der Gast kann es sich hier so richtig gut gehen lassen: Neben hochqualitativen Kaffeespezialitäten kann man es sich in traditionellen Gasthäusern bei zünftigen Bierspezialitäten und schmackhaften Delikatessen aus der Region gut gehen lassen. Daneben können sich Kulturinteressierte in zahlreichen Museen, Galerien, Theatern und Konzerten beschäftigen. Besondere Highlights sind das alljährliche Herbstfest, das als eines der größten Volksfeste in ganz Bayern gilt, und der gemütlich-weihnachtliche Christkindlmarkt. Auch Naturliebhaber sind in Rosenheim gut beraten: Im prachtvollen Mangfallpark mit seiner traumhaften Auenlandschaft und einem großartigen Ausblick auf die Alpen und die Flüsse Inn und Mangfall kann man schön die Seele baumeln lassen.Auch Sportbegeisterte kommen in der Region um den Chiemsee voll auf ihre Kosten.
Im Urlaubsort Chieming finden von Frühjahr

dukedoms and legally on equal terms with the big residences of government. Because of the shipping traffic on the river Inn salt trade flourished in this area and the increasing incomes brought prosperity and wealth to the settlement. Furthermore, Wasserburg was an important centre for the trading of goods from Italy, Austria and the Balkans.
The small town Rosenheim, situated next to the rivers Inn and Mangfall, captivates its visitors with its pleasant charm: The tender pastel shades of the building facades, towers that can already be seen from the distance and its vast urban area are characteristic for this small town, which impresses with an extravagant combination of Alpine and Mediterranean esprit. Visitors can enjoy high-quality coffee specialities or relax in traditional inns and taste hearty beer specialities or delicious local delicacies. Furthermore, for people interested in culture Rosenheim offers numerous museums, galleries, theatres and concerts. Highlights are the annual autumn festival, which is renowned as one of the biggest festivals in Bavaria, and the cosy Christmas market. Nature lovers, too, will find a lot worth visiting in Rosenheim: The magnificent Mangfall Park with its beautiful green meadow grounds and its gorgeous view over the Alps and the rivers Inn and Mangfall are the perfect place to relax and enjoy the landscape. The region also has a lot to offer for sports enthusiasts.
The holiday resort Chieming is venue to several sports events from spring to autumn,

bis Herbst der Chiemsee-Triathlon sowie internationale Reitturniere statt. Hier hat man eine üppige Auswahl an Nordic Walking-, Radsport- und Wandermöglichkeiten. Eine Naturbeobachtungsstation gewährt einen unvergleichlichen Ausblick auf die Chiemgauer Berglandschaft.

Im Luftkurort Bernau kann man sich im Schießsport erproben, zu einer imposanten Ballonfahrt starten oder anderen Sportarten wie Skifahren, Snowboarden, Mountainbiken, Downhill, Eislaufen, Wandern, Klettern, Tennis oder Golfen nachgehen.

Und auf den Bergen laden die zahlreichen typischen bayerischen Almen mit ihren Almhütten, Gasthöfen und Sennereien stets zur Rast und einer zünftigen Brotzeit ein.

including the Chiemsee triathlon and various international equestrian tournaments. Visitors can choose between a wide range of outdoor activities such as Nordic Walking, mountain biking and hiking. A nature observation station offers a unique view over the Chiemgau mountain scenery.

The health resort Bernau offers the possibility to do shooting sport, to go on an impressive balloon ride or to do other sports such as skiing, snowboarding, mountain biking, downhill, ice skating, hiking, climbing, tennis or golf.

On the mountains, a range of typical Bavarian Alps with their Alpine huts, inns and Alpine dairies invite their visitors to rest and enjoy a hearty snack.

"Pferdeparkplätze" und andere interessante Details findet man im Chiemgau auf Schritt und Tritt.
You will come across places to "park" your horse and discover other interesting details at every corner of the Chiemgau.

Rent a Castle – Schlossherr oder Burgfräulein auf Zeit

Rent a castle – Become the temporary Lord or Lady

Refugien mit Kultur und Geschichte - Bei CULTURE & CASTLES | HISTOHOTELS kann man nicht nur besondere Urlaube verbringen, sondern auch ganze Schlösser und Burgen auf Zeit mieten.
Jedes HISTOHOTEL ist einzigartig, keines gleicht dem anderen. Jedes Haus kann mit einer langen Tradition, mit eigenen Mythen und Legenden aufwarten und mit jeweils einzigartiger Lage und Ausstattung. Und dennoch haben alle etwas gemeinsam: Es sind authentische Plätze mit altehrwürdigen Mauern an Orten, die durch ihre Vergangenheit leben und von ihren Hausherren beseelt und liebevoll erhalten werden, damit die Geschichte jedes Refugiums weiter geschrieben wird. **Burg oder Schloss als Eventlocation** - Sie suchen einen außergewöhnlichen Veranstaltungsort für eine Produktpräsentation, Ihr Firmenjubiläum, ein Seminar oder

Hideaways with culture and history - At Culture & Castles | HISTOHOTELS you can not only spend special holidays but also rent a whole castle or fortress for a certain period of time.
Each HISTOHOTEL is unique in its own way, none is similar to the other. Each hotel impresses with a long tradition, with its own myths and legends and with its unique view and interior. And yet they all have one thing in common: They are authentic buildings with ancient walls situated at places that live through their past and that are filled with spirit, love and soul by their owners, who tenderly take care of their preservation for that the history of the hideaway may be continued. **Fortress or Castle as event location** - You are looking for an extraordinary venue for

für ein Incentive? Für außergewöhnliche Momente bieten HISTOHOTELS mit Culture & Castles den passenden Rahmen.

Märchenhaft feiern im herrschaftlichen Ambiente - Hochzeiten, Geburtstage, Familienfeiern: Ob wildromantisch oder luxuriös, ob bodenständig oder exquisit, die HISTOHOTELS-Palette reicht von der mittelalterlichen Burg über den feudalen Herrensitz bis zum Märchenschloss. Ihre Gastgeber stehen Ihnen bei der Planung und Event-Organisation mit Rat und Tat hilfreich zur Seite und sind Garant dafür, dass Ihre Zeit als Schlossherr für Sie und Ihre Gäste zum unvergesslichen Event-Erlebnis wird.

Für weitere Informationen, persönliche Beratung und konkrete Angebote, entsprechend Ihren Vorstellungen, setzen Sie sich bitte direkt mit den Gastgebern der nachstehend aufgeführten Partnerhotels von Culture & Castles | HISTOHOTELS in Verbindung.

your product presentation, your company anniversary, a seminar or just for an incentive? HISTOHOTEL and Culture & Castles provide the ideal framework for any special moment.

Celebrating fairy-tale like in a grand ambience - Weddings, birthdays, family celebrations: Whether wild and romantic or luxurious, whether down-to-earth or exquisite - HISTOHOTELS offer a wide range from the medieval fortress to the feudal mansion or the fairy-tale castle. Your hosts will be glad to assist you with planning and organising the event and will guarantee that your time as Lord or Lady of the castle will be an unforgettable event experience for you and your guests.

For more information, personal advise and concrete offers please get in touch with the hosts of the following partner hotels of Culture & Castles | HISTOHOTELS.

★★★★

BURG BOETZELAER

Alte Wasserburg mit komfortablen Suiten und herrschaftlichen Gästezimmern, repräsentativen Sälen und Salons.

Gastgeber/host: Maximilian Freiherr von Wendt
Reeser Straße 247, 47546 Kalkar-Appeldorn

Tel.: +49 2824 977990; Fax: +49 2824 9779999

www.burgboetzelaer.de
info@burgboetzelaer.de

★★★★

HOTEL & SPA SCHLOSS LEYENBURG

Vorbildlich restauriertes Rokokoschloss und persönlich geführtes Hotel mit SPA am Niederrhein, umgeben von einem englischen Landschaftsgarten.

Gastgeberin/host: Inez van Tienhoven
Leyenburg 3, 47509 Rheurdt

Tel.: +49 2845 949921; Fax: +49 2845 949929

www.hotel-leyenburg.de
schloss@leyenburg.com

★★★★

SCHLOSS WISSEN

550 jähriger Herrensitz derer von Loë mit stilsicher eingerichteten Gästezimmern in der „Boye", in der früher die Angestellten der Betriebe lebten.

Gastgeber/host: Raphaël Freiherr von Loë
Schlossallee 21, 47652 Weeze-Wissen

Tel.: +49 2837 96190, Fax: +49 2837 961911

www.schloss-wissen.de
culture-castles@schloss-wissen.de

★★★★

SCHLOSSRUINE HERTEFELD

Deutschlands einzige bewohnbare Schlossruine, idyllisch gelegen am Niederrhein.

Gastgeber/host: Patricia Gräfin zu Eulenburg u. Hertefeld, Friedrich Graf zu Eulenburg u. Hertefeld
Hertefeld 1, 47652 Weeze

Tel.: +49 2837 2035

www.hertefeld.de
schloss@hertefeld.de

★★★★

HAUS BRÜCKHAUSEN

Malerisches Herrenhaus, eingerahmt von einer Gräfte, inmitten der münsterländischen Parklandschaft

Gastgeber/host: Freifrau Franziska von Twickel, Freiherr Franz von Twickel
Holling 6, 48351 Everswinkel-Alverskirchen

Tel.: +49 2582 277; Fax: +49 2582 659662

twickel-brueckhausen@t-online.de

★★★★

SCHLOSS LUDWIGSECK

Eine der letzten in Deutschland erbauten Wehrburgen; heute einladend charmantes chambres d'hôtes.

Gastgeber/host: Tanja von und zu Gilsa, Thilo von und zu Gilsa
36251 Ludwigsau

Tel.: +49 6670 205; Fax: +49 6670 1239

www.schloss-ludwigseck.de
casanier@t-online.de

★★★★

HERRENHAUS BARTHÉLEMY

Repräsentatives Landhaus des ehemaligen französischen Magazinverwalters der Festung Landau.

Gastgeber/host: Rosemarie Eifler-Bollen, Clemens Bollen
Bergstraße 4, 76835Gleisweiler

Tel.: +49 6345 953022; Fax: +49 6345 953023

www.herrenhaus-barthelemy.de
mail@herrenhaus-barthelemy.com

★★★★

SCHLOSS AMERANG

Mittelalterliche Rundburg mit beeindruckendem Arkadenhof im bayerischen Voralpenland.

Gastgeber/host: Giulia Freifrau von Crailsheim-Larisch, Ortholf Freiherr von Crailsheim
Schloss 1, 83123Amerang

Tel.: +49 8075 91920; Fax: +49 8075 919233

www.schlossamerang.de
info@schlossamerang.de

★★★★★

SCHLOSS LÜTGENHOF

Gastgeber/host: Katharina Stinnes

Ulmenweg 10
23942 Dassow

Tel.: +49 38826 8250
Fax: +49 38826 82522

www.schloss-luetgenhof.de
info@schloss-luetgenhof.de

Klassizistisches Schloss am Dassower See bei Lübeck, ideales Refugium für Hochzeiten, Familienfeiern, besondere Gesellschaften und Tagungen.

Neo-classical castle at Dassower Lake near Lübeck, ideal location for weddings, family celebrations, special parties and conferences.

★★★★★

SCHLOSS WENDORF

Gastgeber/host: Aikaterini Kasapidi, Johannes Butz

Hauptstraße 9
19412 Wendorf

Tel.: +49 38486 33660
Fax: +49 38486 336610

www.schlosshotel-wendorf.de
info@schlosshotel-wendorf.de

Exklusives Schlosshotel in bezauberndem Park, mit Gourmetrestaurant, Pferdesportarena sowie SPA und Beautycenter.

Exclusive castle hotel in a charming park, with gourmet restaurant, equestrian arena and SPA and Beauty Centre.

★★★★★

LANDHAUS LÖSCH FÜR FREUNDE

Gastgeber/host: Stefanie Welsch und Olivier Fabing

Hauptstrasse 19-21
66500 Hornbach

Tel.: +49 6338 910100
Fax: +49 6338 9101099

www.loesch-fuer-freunde.de
info@loesch-fuer-freunde.de

Ausgezeichnet als bestes neues Hotel in Europa ist das Landhaus „LÖSCH für Freunde" mit seinem unkonventionellen Gästekonzept ein besonderes Refugium.

Awarded best new hotel in Europe, the country house "LÖSCH für Freunde" is a special hideaway with a unique, unconventional guest concept.

★★★★

LANDHAUS MÜHLE SCHLUCHSEE

Gastgeber/host: Katja Nowak & Rolf Pochert

Unterer Mühlenweg 13
79859 Schluchsee

Tel.: +49 7656 209
Fax: +49 7656 982192

www.landhaus-muehle.de
info@landhaus-muehle.de

Charmantes Landhotel in einmalig schöner Ortsrandlage über dem Ostufer des Schluchsees.

Charming countryside hotel in a unique location overlooking the eastern shore of Lake Schluchsee.

Adressen

Kaufmannssinn und hanseatische Baukunst
Merchant trade and Hanseatic architecture

Europäische Route der Backsteingotik e.V.
Littenstraße 10, D-10179 Berlin
Phone +49 30 206132559
Fax +49 30 20613251
info@eurob.org, www.eurob.org

Tourismusverband Mecklenburg Vorpommern e.V.
Platz der Freundschaft 1, D-18059 Rostock
Phone +49 381 4030550
Fax +49 381 4030555
info@auf-nach-mv.de, www.auf-nach-mv.de

Welcome Center Lübeck (Touristbüro)
Holstentorplatz 1, D-23552 Lübeck
Phone +49 451 8899700
Fax +49 451 4091992
info@luebeck-tourismus.de
www.luebeck-tourismus.de

Tourismuszentrale Wismar
Am Markt 11
D-23966 Wismar
Phone +49 3841 19433
Fax +49 3841 2513091
touristinfo@wismar.de
www.wismar.de

Tourist-Information Schwerin
Am Markt 14, D-19055 Schwerin
Phone +49 385 59252 12/13/14
Fax +49 385 555094
info@schwerin.info
www.schwerin.com

Güstrow Tourismus e.V.
Franz-Parr-Platz 10, D-18273 Güstrow
Phone +49 3843 681023
Fax +49 3843 682079
info@guestrow-tourismus.de
www.guestrow-tourismus.de

Tourist-Information Rostock
Universitätsplatz 6 (Barocksaal)
D-18055 Rostock
Phone +49 381 2222
Fax +49 381 2601
touristinfo@rostock.de
www.rostock.de

Tourismuszentrale Stralsund
Alter Markt 9, D-18439 Stralsund
Phone +49 3831 24690
Fax +49 3831 246922
info@stralsundtourismus.de
www.stralsundtourismus.de

Fremdenverkehrsverein Greifswald und Land e.V.
Rathaus Am Markt, D-17489 Greifswald
Phone +49 3834 521380
Fax +49 3834 521382
greifswald-information@t-online.de
www.greifswald.de

Anklam-Information
Markt 3, D-17389 Anklam
Phone +49 3971 835154
Fax +49 3971 835175
info@anklam.de
www.anklam.de

Stadt Wolgast und Insel Usedom
Rathausplatz 10, D-17438 Wolgast
Phone +49 3836 600118
Fax +49 3836 233002
stadtinfo@wolgast.de
www.stadt-wolgast.de

Kultur- und Tourist-Information Neukloster
Rathaus Neukloster, Hauptstraße 27
D-23992 Neukloster
Phone +49 38422 44030
Fax +49 38422 44026
tourismus@neukloster.de
www.stadt-neukloster.de

Kunstsinn und Mäzenatentum – großartige Kunstsammlungen am Niederrhein Appreciation of art and Patronage Magnificent art collections on the Lower Rhine

Niederrhein Tourismus GmbH
Willy-Brandt-Ring 13, D-41747 Viersen
Phone +49 2162 817903
Fax +49 2162 8179180
info@niederrhein-tourismus.de
www.niederrhein-tourismus.de

Tourist-Information Duisburg
Königstraße 39, D-47051 Duisburg
Phone +49 203 285440
Fax +49 203 2854444
service@duisburg-marketing.de
www.duisburg.de

Museum Wasserburg Anholt
Schloss 1, D-46419 Isselburg-Anholt
Phone +49 2874 45353
Fax +49 2874 45356
museum@fuerst-salm.de
www.fuerst-salm.de

Adressen

Kröller-Müller Museum
Houtkampweg 6, NL-6731 AW Otterlo
Phone +31 318 591241
info@kmml.nl, www.kmm.nl

Museum Schloss Moyland
Am Schloss 4, D-47551 Bedburg-Hau
Phone +49 2824 951060
Fax +49 2824 951099
info@moyland.de
www.moyland.de

Museen Haus Lange und Haus Esters
Wilhelmshofallee 91-97, D-47800 Krefeld
Phone +49 2151 975580
Fax +49 2151 97558222
kunstmuseen@krefeld.de
www.kunstmuseenkrefeld.de

Tourist-Information Xanten GmbH (TIX)
Kurfürstenstr.9
D-46509 Xanten
Phone +49 2801 772200
Fax +49 2801 772199
info@xanten.de
www.xanten.de

Archäologiepark Xanten
Wardter Straße 1
D-46509 Xanten
Phone +49 2801 7120
apx.lvr.de

Garten der Erinnerung Duisburg
Springwall, D-47051 Duisburg
Phone +49 203 30550
post@innenhafen-portal.de
www.innenhafen-duisburg.de

MKM Museum Küppersmühle für Moderne Kunst
Innenhafen Duisburg, Philosophenweg 55
D-47051 Duisburg
Phone +49 203 30194811
Fax +49 203 30194821
office@museum-kueppersmuehle.de
www.museum-kueppersmuehle.de

Wilhelm Lehmbruck Museum
Friedrich-Wilhelm-Straße 40
D-47051 Duisburg
Phone +49 203 2833294
Fax +49 203 2833892

Museum Folkwang
Museumsplatz 1, D-45128 Essen
Phone +49 201 8845000
Fax +49 201 889145000
info@museum-folkwang.essen.de
www.museum-folkwang.de

Villa Hügel
Wohnhaus von Alfred Krupp von Bohlen und Halbach
Kulturstiftung Ruhr Essen
D-45133 Essen
Phone +49 201 616290
Fax +49 201 6162911
office@villahuegel.de
www.villahuegel.de

Museum zum Ruhrgebiet und Design Zentrum Nordrhein Westfalen in der Zeche Zollverein
Gelsenkirchener Straße 181, D-45309 Essen
Phone +49 201 246810
Fax +49 201 8543100
info@zollverein.de
www.zollverein.de

Kunstsammlung Nordrhein-Westfalen
Grabbeplatz 5, D-40213 Düsseldorf
Phone +49 211 8381204
Fax +49 211 8381209
service@kunstsammlung.de
www.kunstsammlung.de

Städtisches Museum Abteiberg. 27
Abteistraße 27, 41061 Mönchengladbach
Phone +49 2161 252637
Fax +49 2161 252659
mail@museum-abteiberg.de
www.museum-abteiberg.de

Stiftung Museum Kunstpalast
Ehrenhof 4-5 , D-40479 Düsseldorf
Phone +49 211 8990200
Fax +49 211 8929504
info@smkp.de, www.smkp.de

Romantik am Mittelrhein Romanticism on the Middle Rhine

Rhein-Touristik Tal der Loreley
Loreley-Besucherzentrum
D-56346 St. Goarshausen
Phone +49 6771 599093
Fax +49 6771 599094
info@tal-der-loreley.de
www.welterbe-atlas.de

Rüdesheim Tourist AG
Rheinstraße 29 A
D-65385 Rüdesheim am Rhein
Phone +49 6722 906150
Fax +49 6722 9061599
touristinfo@ruedesheim.de
www.ruedesheim.de

Tourist-Information Koblenz
Bahnhofplatz 17, D- 56068 Koblenz
Phone +49 261 31304
Fax +49 261 1004388
info-hbf@koblenz-touristik.de
www.koblenz-touristik.de

Adressen

Rhein-Nahe Touristik Bacharach e.V.
Oberstraße 45, D-55422 Bacharach
Phone +49 6743 919303
Fax +49 6743 919304
info@rhein-nahe-touristik.de
www.rhein-nahe-touristik.de

Tourist-Information Bingen
Rheinkai 21, D-55411 Bingen am Rhein
Phone +49 6721 184200
Fax +49 6721 184214
www.bingen.de

Schaufelradschiff GOETHE
KD Verkaufsservice
Phone +49 221 2088318
Fax +49 221 2088345
info@k-d.com, www.k-d.de

Schloss Stolzenfels
Kulturelles Erbe Rheinland-Pfalz
Schlossstraße, D-56075 Koblenz
Phone +49 261 51656
www.schloss-stolzenfels.de

Tourist-Information St. Goarshausen
Bahnhofstraße 8
D-56346 St. Goarshausen
Phone +49 6771 9100
Fax +49 6771 91015
info@loreley-touristik.de
www.loreley-touristik.de

Auf den Spuren der Römer entlang der Mosel
In the footsteps of the Romans along the river Mosel

Tourist-Info Rhein-Mosel-Gebiet
Rhein-Mosel-Str. 45
D-56281 Emmelshausen
Phone +49 6747 93220
Fax +49 6747 932222
info@das-zap.de
www.rhein-mosel-dreieck.de

Mosellandtouristik GmbH
Kordelweg 1, D-54470 Bernkastel-Kues
Phone +49 6531 97330
Fax +49 6531 973333
info@mosellandtouristik.de
www.mosellandtouristik.de

Tourist-Information Trier Stadt und Land e. V.
An der Porta Nigra, D-54290 Trier
Phone +49 651 978080
Fax +49 651 9780876
info@trier-info.de
www.trier-info.de

Tourist-Information Roemische Weinstrasse
Brückenstr. 46, D-54338 Schweich
Phone +49 6502 93380
Fax +49 6502 933815
mosel@touristinfo-schweich.de
www.roemische-weinstrasse.de

Villa Urbana in Longuich
Weinstraße 1, D-54338 Schweich
Phone +49 6502 5795
www.strassen-der-roemer.de

Tourist-Information Neumagen-Dhron
Phone +49 6507 6555
Fax +49 6507 6550
info@neumagen-dhron.de
www.neumagen-dhron.de

Tourist-Information Mehring
Bachstraße 47, D-54346 Mehring
Phone +49 6502 1413
Fax +49 6502 1253
www.mehring-mosel.de
info@mehring-mosel.de

Archäologiepark Römische Villa Borg
Im Meeswald 1, D-66706 Perl-Borg
Phone +49 6865 91170
Fax +49 6865 911717
info@villa-borg.de
www.villa-borg.de

Kaiserpalast in Konz
Saar-Obermosel-Touristik e.V.
Granastraße 22, D-54329 Konz
Phone +49 6501 6018040
Fax +49 6501 4718

Tourist-Information Bernkastel-Kues
Gestade 6, D-54470 Bernkastel-Kues
Phone +49 6531 500190
Fax +49 6531 5001919
info@bernkastel.de, www.bernkastel.de

Tourist-Information Traben-Trarbach
Am Bahnhof 5, D-56841 Traben-Trarbach
Phone +49 6541 83980
Fax +49 6541 839839
info@traben-trarbach.de
www.traben-trarbach.de

Klöster und Ihre Güter
Monasteries and their properties

Tourist-Information Amorbach
Altes Rathaus
Marktplatz 1
63916 Amorbach
Phone +49 9373 20940
Fax +49 9373 20933
touristinfo@amorbach.de
www.amorbach.de

Fürstlich Leiningensche Verwaltung
(Führung Abteikirche Amorbach mit Stumm-Orgel, Grüner Saal und Bibliothek)
Marktplatz 12, 63916 Amorbach
Phone +49 9373 87 15 45
abtei@fuerst-leiningen.de
www.fuerst-leiningen.de

Region Mainfranken GmbH
Geschäftsstelle
Ludwigstraße 10 1/2, D-97070 Würzburg
Phone +49 931 4526520
Fax +49 931 45265220
info@mainfranken.org
www.mainfranken.org

Südwestpfalz-Touristik e.V.
Unterer Sommerwaldweg 40-42
66953 Pirmasens
Phone +49 6331 809126
Fax +49 6331 809202
info@suedwestpfalz-touristik.de
www.suedwestpfalz-touristik.de

Stadt Hornbach
Nicoletta Semmet
Denkmalstr. 1
66500 Hornbach
Phone +49 6338 809153
semmet@stadt-hornbach.de
www.klosterstadt-hornbach.de

Schwarzwald – eine deutsche Idylle mit kulturellen Edelsteinen The Black Forest German idyll with cultural gems

Schwarzwald Tourismus GmbH
Ludwigstr. 23, D-79104 Freiburg
Phone +49 761 896460
Fax +49 761 8964670
mail@schwarzwald-tourismus.info
www.schwarzwald-tourismus.info

Hochschwarzwald Tourismus GmbH
Freiburger Str. 1, D-79856 Hinterzarten
Phone +49 7652 12060
Fax +49 7652 120689219
info@hochschwarzwald.de
www.hochschwarzwald.de

Ferien Südschwarzwald
Tourist-Information Höchenschwand
D-79862 Höchenschwand
Phone +49 7672 48180
Fax +49 7672 488010
info@ferien-suedschwarzwald.de
www.ferien-suedschwarzwald.de

Schwarzwälder Freilichtmuseum
Vogtsbauernhof
D-77793 Gutach (Schwarzwaldbahn)
Phone +49 7831 93560
Fax +49 7831 935629
info@vogtsbauernhof.org
www.vogtsbauernhof.org

Schwarzwaldmuseum Triberg
Wallfahrtstraße 4, D-78098 Triberg
Phone +49 7722 4434
Fax +49 7722 920110
info@schwarzwaldmuseum.de
www.schwarzwaldmuseum.de

Deutsches Uhrenmuseum Furtwangen
Robert-Gerwig-Platz, D-78120 Furtwangen
Phone +49 7723 9202800
Fax +49 7723 9202120
email@deutsches-uhrenmuseum.de
www.deutsches-uhrenmuseum.de

Deutsches Phono Museum
Bärenplatz 1, D-78112 St.Georgen
Phone +49 7724 8599138
deutsches_phonomuseum@st-georgen.de
www.st-georgen.de

Deutsches Trachtenmuseum
Klosterstraße 7
D-77716 Haslach im Kinzigtal
Phone +49 7832 706
www.trachtenmuseum-haslach.de

Tourist-Information St. Blasien
Am Kurgarten 1-3, D-79837 St. Blasien
Phone +49 7652 1206 8550
st.blasien@hochschwarzwald.de
www.stblasien.de

Tourist-Information Baden-Baden
Schwarzwaldstraße 52 und Kaiserallee 3
(Trinkhalle)
D-76530 Baden-Baden
Phone +49 7221 2752001
Fax +49 7221 275202
info@baden-baden.com
www.baden-baden.de

Kunstmuseum Basel
St. Alban-Graben 16
CH-4010 Basel
Phone +41 61 2066262
Fax +41 61 2066252
www.kunstmuseumbasel.ch

Adressen

Der Chiemgau und das Bayerische Meer
Chiemgau and the "Bavarian Sea"

Chiemgau Tourismus e.V.
Leonrodstraße 7, D-83278 Traunstein
Phone +49 861 9095900
Fax +49 861 90959020
info@chiemgau-tourismus.de
www.chiemgau-tourismus.de

Schloss- und Gartenverwaltung Herrenchiemsee
D-83209 Herrenchiemsee
Phone +49 8051 68870
Fax +49 8051 688799
sgvherrenchiemsee@bsv.bayern.de
www.herrenchiemsee.de

Tourist-Information Frauenchiemsee
Am Uferweg (Ostseite)
D-83256 Frauenchiemsee
Phone +49 8054 322 oder
+49 8054 9089504
info@fraueninsel-fuehrungen.de
www.fraueninsel-fuehrungen.de

Kur- und Tourismusbüro Prien
Alte Rathausstraße 11
D-83209 Prien am Chiemsee
Phone +49 8051 69050
Fax +49 8051 690540
info@tourismus.prien.de
www.tourismus.prien.de

Gäste-Information Wasserburg
Marienplatz 2 (im Rathaus Eingang Salzsenderzeile)
D-83512 Wasserburg am Inn
Phone +49 8071 10522
Fax +49 8071 10521

Tourist-Information Rosenheim
Kufsteiner Str. 4, D-83022 Rosenheim
Phone +49 8031 3659061
Fax +49 8031 3659060
www.touristinfo-rosenheim.de

Tourist-Information Chieming
Hauptstraße 20b, D-83339 Chieming
Phone +49 8664 988647
Fax +49 8664 988619

Tourist-Information Bernau
Aschauer Str. 10
D-83233 Bernau am Chiemsee
Phone +49 8051 98680
Fax +49 8051 986850
info@bernau-am-chiemsee.de
www.bernau-am-chiemsee.de

Place index

Ortsindex

Place index

Ortsindex

Place index

Bildnachweis

Axel Thünker DGPh 89
Bildnachweis: Schloßruine Hertefeld | Katharina Jaeger 68, 69, 70
Brennerei Ziegler 174, 176
Burg Boetzelaer 74, 75, 76, 77
Burghotel auf Schönburg 12, 108 (oben rechts und Mitte rechts)
Burghotel Schnellenberg | Jablosnki 98, 101
Chiemgau Tourismus e.V. 216, 217, 221
F. Foltz 113
Fotografische Werkstatt | Katharina Jaeger | www.fotografischewerkstatt.de 82, 83, 84, 85
Freilichtmuseum Vogtsbauernhof (Karl Schlessmann) 193,2
Grandhotel Römerbad 190, 191, 192
Guido Werner 16, 17,18, 21, 22, 23, 235 (links), 60, 61, 62 (links oben und links unten), 99, 100, 106, 107, 108 (oben links und Mitte links), 160 (Mitte rechts), 235 links, U 4 unten
Haus Brückhausen | Münsterland e.V. | www.muensterland.com; B&S Werbeagentur | www.werbeagentur.ms 6 (rechts oben), 102, 103, 104, 234 (oben links)
Henkell & Co. Sektkellerei KG | Alfred Gratien S.A.S.186, 187, 188, 189
Herrenhaus Barthélemy | Rosemarie Eifler-Bollen 2, 6 (unten), 146, 147, 148, 234 (unten links)
Höerhof 142, 143, 144, 145
Hotel Palmenwald Schwarzwaldhof 178, 179, 180
Iko Freese | drama-berlin.de 59
Ji-Elle | 157
Kalkarer Mühle am Hanselaerer Tor e.V. | Walter Schwaya 67
Kandertalbahn 197
Kleve Marketing GmbH & Co. KG 71
Kloster Hornbach 150, 151, 152, 153, 166, 167, 168, 169, 170, 171, U 4 Mitte
Kloster Marienhöh 11
Koblenz Touristik 140
Kröller-Müller-Museum | Marjon Gemmeke 87
Landhaus Bärenmühle 3, 7, 15 (oben links) 48, 49, 50, U 4 oben
Landhaus "LÖSCH" für Freunde 154, 155, 156
Märchenhotel 15 Mitte links, 120, 121, 122
Markus Braun 124
Medienzentrum Rheinland / LVR | Stefan Arendt 94
Mosellandtouristik GmbH 136, 137
P. Friesenhahn 125
Pfaffenkeller 15 Mitte rechts, 194, 195, 196
Romantikhotel Rittergut Bömitz 15, 28, 30
Rudolf Matthias von Frieling 31
Schloss Amerang |Reinhard Kirchner 8, 212, 213, 214, 215, 234 (unten rechts)
Schloss Anholt | Fürst zu Salm Salm 97
Schloss Bürgeln | Kluckert 203, 205
Schloss Hertefeld | Katharina Jaeger 232
Schloss Leyenburg 4, 9, 15 (oben rechts), 233 (oben rechts)
Schloss Ludwigseck | Bernd Seeger (www.seegerpress.de) 56, 57, 58, 234 (oben rechts)
Schloss Moyland 88
Schloss Ossenberg (Herzog Wilhelm Albert von Urach) 78, 79, 80
Schloss Waldeck 10, 52, 53, 54, Titel
Schloss Wissen 65, 66, 233 (unten rechts)
Staatsbad Bad Wildungen GmbH | R. Pfeil 55
Stadt Laufenburg 208, 209
Stadt Rheinberg 81
Stadtmuseum Münster | Tomasz Samek 105
Theater Chawwerusch 149
Stiftung Zollverein | Thomas Willemsen 92
Tobias Arnst 91
Tourist-Information Trier | 126, 127, 128, 129, 130
Usedom Palace 24, 25, 26
Uwe Köppen | Referat für Kommunikation der Stadt Duisburg 90
Uwe Riedel 95
Kunstsammlung NRW | Walter Klein 86
www.photone.fotograf.de 133

Bildnachweis

Bild-, Quellennachweis

Das Copyright für die abgebildeten Werke liegt, sofern nachfolgend nichts anderes aufgeführt ist, bei den jeweiligen Fotografen, Touristik-Informationen und Hotels. Die Fotos der einzelnen Hotels wurden uns von diesen zur Verfügung gestellt.
Trotz intensiver Recherche ist nicht auszuschließen, dass in jedem Fall die Urheberrechte ermittelt wurden. Wir bitten ggf. um Mitteilung an den Verlag.

Alle in diesem Buch enthaltenen Angaben wurden von den Autoren nach bestem Wissen erstellt und von ihnen und dem Verlag mit größtmöglicher Sorgfalt überprüft. Gleichwohl sind inhaltliche Fehler nicht vollständig auszuschließen. Daher erfolgen die Angaben im Sinne der Produkthaftung ohne jegliche Verpflichtung oder Garantie des Verlages oder der Autoren. Beide übernehmen keinerlei Verantwortung und Haftung für etwaige inhaltliche Unstimmigkeiten. Wir bitten dafür um Verständnis und werden Korrekturhinweise gerne aufgreifen. info@verlag-weimar.de

Picture Credits and References

The copyright for the reproduced work is, if nothing different is subsequently specified, owned by the respective photographers, tourist information offices and hotels. The photographs of the individual hotels were made available to us by these sources.
Despite having done intensive research, it is not to be ruled out that in each case the copyrights were in fact acquired. We ask if this is found to be the case that it be reported to the publishing house.

All the data quoted in this book was supplied by the authors to the best of their knowledge and the greatest possible care was taken by them and the publishing house to verify the accuracy of the data. Nevertheless the possible occurrence of errors in the content is not to be completely dismissed. Therefore the data in the sense of product liability is provided without any obligation or guarantee from the publishing house or the authors. Neither take any responsibility and liability for any discrepancies in the content. We therefore ask for understanding and will gladly look into queries regarding possible corrections to be made. info@verlag-weimar.de.de

AUSTRIA
Schlosshotels & Herrenhäuser
info@schlosshotels.co.at
www.schlosshotels.co.at

BELGIUM, NETHERLANDS & LUXEMBURG
Hampshire Classic Hotels
info@hampshire-hotels.com
www.hampshire-hotels.com/historic

DENMARK
Historic Hotels Denmark
info@historichotels.dk
www.historichotels.dk

FRANCE
Châteaux & Hôtels Collection
sales@chateauxhotels.com
www.chateauxhotels.com

GERMANY
Culture & Castles | Histohotels
Historic Hotels of Germany
info@histohotels.de
www.histohotels.de

GREECE
Yades Greek Historic Hotels
welcome@yadeshotels.gr
www.yadeshotels.gr

HUNGARY
Hungarian Castle
Hotels Association
www.hungariancastlehotels.com
info@hungariancastlehotels.com

IRELAND
Ireland's Blue Book
mail@irelandsbluebook.com
www.irelandsbluebook.com

ITALY
Abitare la Storia
mailbox@abitarelastoria.it
www.abitarelastoria.it

NORWAY
De Historiske
info@dehistoriske.no
www.dehistoriske.com

POLAND
Historic Hotels Poland
info@hhpoland.com
www.hhpoland.com

PORTUGAL
Hoteis Heritage Lisboa
heritage.hotels@heritage.pt
www.heritage.pt

PORTUGAL
Pousadas de Portugal
guest@pousadas.pt
www.pousadas.pt

SLOVAKIA
Historic Hotels of Slovakia
info@historichotelsofslovakia.com
www.historichotelsofslovakia.com

SPAIN
Hoteles Históricos de España
info@hoteleshistoricos.com
www.hoteleshistoricos.com

SWEDEN
Countryside Hotels
info@countrysidehotels.se
www.countrysidehotels.se

SWITZERLAND
Swiss Historic Hotels
info@swiss-historic-hotels.com
www.swiss-historic-hotels.com

UNITED KINGDOM
The Great Inns of Britain
enquiries@greatinns.co.uk
www.greatinns.co.uk

WALES
Welsh Rarebits
info@rarebits.co.uk
www.rarebits.co.uk

HISTORIC HOTELS OF EUROPE
info@historichotelsofeurope.com
www.historichotelsofeurope.com

pip / photocase.com
jagd1
www.jagd1.de
ERSTE ADRESSE FÜR JAGD
UND JAGDGELEGENHEITEN